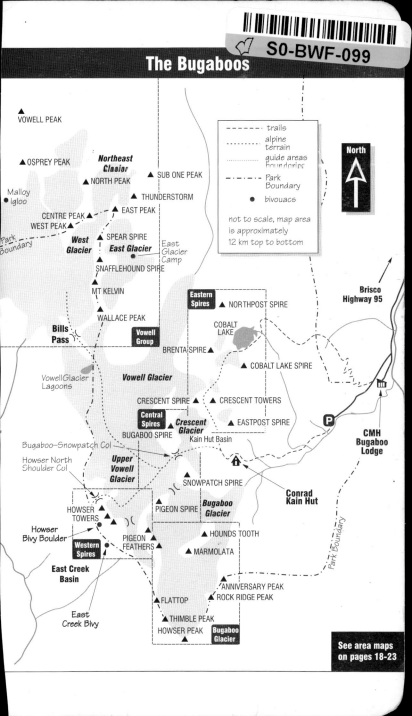

The
Bugaboos

Chris Atkinson
Marc Piché

One of the World's Great Alpine Rockclimbing Centres

Elaho Publishing

Squamish, B.C.

The Bugaboos

One of the World's Great Alpine Rockclimbing Centres.

© Chris Atkinson and Marc Piché 2003

Elaho Publishing Corporation, Squamish BC.

Printed in Canada by Kromar Printing Ltd, Manitoba.

Uncredited photos © Chris Atkinson, all other photographs © as credited.

Design, editing, topo assembly, photo editing, production: Kevin McLane.

Front cover:	The South Howser Tower and the Minaret.	*Chris Atkinson.*
Back cover:	Upper: Pigeon Spire and the Howser Towers.	*Chris Atkinson.*
	Lower: Bugaboo Spire and Snowpatch Spire.	*Chris Atkinson.*
	Inset: *Corto Zonal* on Snafflehound Spire.	*Chris Atkinson.*

Canadian Cataloguing in Publication Data

Atkinson, Chris and Piché, Marc

The Bugaboos.

ISBN 0-9733035-1-4

1. Rock climbing–British Columbia–Bugaboos, The–Guidebooks.

2. Mountaineering–British Columbia–Bugaboos, The–Guidebooks.

3. Bugaboos (B.C.), The–Guidebooks. I. Title.

GV199.44.C22B83 2003   796.52'23'0971165   C2003-910902-X

Disclaimer

Mountaineering is a hazardous activity carrying a significant risk of personal injury or death and should only be undertaken with a full understanding of all inherent risks. This publication is only a guide to the climbs, a composite of opinion from many sources, some of which may not be accurate, and the information contained may not reflect the circumstances of a particular climb on a given day. Use of this guide must always be conducted with the required experience and good judgement necessary for safety.

Elaho™ is a trademark of Elaho Publishing Corporation

NAVIGATING THE GUIDEBOOK

Acknowledgements ------------------------------------- 6
Dedication --- 7
Introduction --------------------------------------- 8-9
How to Use This Guide ------------------------------- 10
International Travel ------------------------------ 11-13
Local Resources ---------------------------------- 14-15
Driving the Bugaboo Approach Road --- 16-17
Maps of the Bugaboo Region -------------- 18-23
Trail Approaches: Kain Hut, Cobalt Lake ----- 24
The Conrad Kain Hut -------------------------------- 25
Camping and Bivouacing -------------------------- 26
BC Parks and Land Stewardship --------------- 27
Conservation and Courtesy ---------------------- 28
Natural History ------------------------------- 29-31
Bugaboos Terrain ------------------------------- 32-33
The Weather --------------------------------------- 34
Things To Do When The Weather is Bad ----- 35
Rockclimbing Near The Bugaboos ------------- 36
Winter --- 37
Reporting New Climbs ------------------------------ 38
History -------------------------------------- 39-40
Bugaboo Lodge ---------------------------------- 41-43
The Grading System --------------------------- 44-45
The Alpine Grades -------------------------------- 46-47
Recommended Climbs ----------------------- 48-49
About The Authors ---------------------------------- 50
The Bugaboo Style ---------------------------------- 51
Photo Gallery One ---------------------------- 52-87
Bugaboo Glacier Peaks ------------------------- 88
Eastern Spires ------------------------------- 112
Central Spires -------------------------------- 158
 Bugaboo Spire ---------------------------------- 160
 Snowpatch Spire ------------------------------- 178
 Pigeon Spire ------------------------------------ 220
Western Spires -------------------------------- 238
 The Howser Towers ----------------------------- 240
 Pigeon Feathers -------------------------------- 284
 Crossed Fish ------------------------------------ 296
 Little Snowpatch -------------------------------- 297
Photo Gallery Two ----------------------- 300-319
The Vowell Group ----------------------------- 320
The Conrad Group ------------------------------ 355
Index of Climbs and Peaks --------------------- 357
About Elaho Publishing ----------------------- 360

Sponsors (pages 54-87)

Alpine Club of Canada

Arcteryx

Assoc. of Canadian Mt Guides

Canadian Mountain Holidays

Bennett Surveys

Gripped Magazine

Metolius

Mountain Equipment Coop

Sierra Guides

Valhalla Pure

6 ACKNOWLEDGEMENTS

A book of this size is the result of a great deal of input from a wide variety of people ranging from full time climbers and mountain guides to weekend enthusiasts and park rangers. Without their information, opinions and encouragement, this book would lack much of its depth. We must first acknowledge all who have documented information in the past in the guidebooks, magazines and Kain Hut journal. Without them the history would be lost.

Primarily, we would like to thank Kevin McLane who first approached us with the idea of a Canadian guidebook to the Bugaboos, and whose experience and support was instrumental to the completion of this guide. Thank you also to Sean Isaac for his far-reaching contacts, vast knowledge of recent climbing history and keen enthusiasm. Their input had a major impact on development of this guide. And to Hans Gmoser, we all owe a debt of gratitude for his vision in the development of Bugaboo Glacier Provincial Park.

A special thank you goes out to Dave Cochrane and Lianne Marquis and the staff at the Canadian Mountain Holidays Bugaboo Lodge whose generous support and hospitality will not be forgotten. Deanna Andersen, Topher Donahue, Brad Harrison, Mark Klassen, Garth Lemke, Todd Offenbacher, Peter Oxtoby and Grant Statham all shared with us a huge amount of information and knowledge.

We wish to thank everyone below for providing much appreciated feedback, opinion, photos, route information, topo development and patiently answering a mountain of emails and phone calls.

Lars Andrews, Mark Austin, Sergio Ballivan, Joe Benson, Jia Condon, Jonny Copp, Eric Dumerac, Sean Easton, Guy Edwards, Scott Flavelle, Chris Geisler, Randall Green, JP Grenon, Leo Grillmair, Tim Haggarty, Kennan Harvey, Kai Hirvonen, Jeff Hollenbaugh, Bruce Howatt, Roko Koell, Josée Larochelle, Jake Larson, Paul Lasarski, Aaron Martin, Connie Macdonald, Rich Marshall, Kirk Mauthner, Alex McAfee, Barry McLane, Kelly McLeod, Paul McSorley, Rob Orvig, Mike Pennings, Nick Rapaich, Louis-Julien Roy, Dave Scott, Lizzy Scully, Kirt Sellers, Scott Semple, Brad Shilling, Cyril Shokoples, Mark Synnot, Carl Trescher, John Turk, John Walsh, Brian Webster, Richard Wheater, Heidi Wirtz, Kobi Wyss, Colin Zacharias, the East Creek Social Club and, with apologies, anyone else whom we may have forgotten.

We would also like to acknowledge the contributions of Jack Paterson, Wayne Sobool, Becky Bates, Hugh Ackroyd, Andrew Simpson, Garth Lemke, Jeff Haack, Julie Rohn, Susan Shaw and many other rangers and staff, both past and present at BC Parks. We are grateful for the assistance and information provided by Nancy Hansen, Ann Vanier and Dan Verral at the Alpine Club of Canada.

Last but certainly not the least we are ever grateful to Lydia Marmont and Lilla Molnar for their patience, hard work, kind support and company in the mountains.

Dedication

This guidebook is dedicated to all those who have brought their spirit of adventure and love of the mountains into the Bugaboos, and in particular to the late Guy Edwards whose carefree high spirits and cheerfulness was the essence of the Spires and an inspiration to all those whose lives he touched.

Long live Fast Eddy.

Guy Edwards
1972–2003

The Bugaboos is a magical alpine playground of wild weather, pristine wilderness and towering granite spires that are the home of alpine rock climbs as good as the best in the world. Beyond the four major summits of Bugaboo, Snowpatch, Pigeon and the Howser Towers are fine moderate mountaineering objectives, superb scrambles and rarely visited technical peaks that offer a superb experience for all climbers who travel beyond the crags.

It is, however, the long, classic alpine rock climbs that have given the Bugaboos its near-mythical reputation. Routes such as the *Beckey–Chouinard* on South Howser Tower, with nearly 800m of mostly 5.8-5.9 climbing, and legendary classics such as *West Ridge* of Pigeon Spire, *Northeast Ridge* of Bugaboo Spire and the *Snowpatch* and *Surfs Up* routes on Snowpatch Spire are reasons why the Bugaboos are a draw to climbers the world over. Climbs such as these, and the many sheltered multi-pitch cragging routes, serious bigwall ED2 odysseys, long ridge scrambles and little-known mixed ice routes, as well as the surreal feeling of just being there, create the Bugaboo Experience. This is truly an inspiring place. But be aware, the Bugaboos are a heavily glaciated, intricate alpine environment that requires experience and mountain savvy to travel safely through.

Geographically, the Bugaboos are a cluster of high granite spires within Bugaboo Glacier Provincial Park in the southeast region of the Province of British Columbia. They are centred on approximately West 116°48' by North 50°44' in the Purcell Mountain Range, which runs southeast to northwest from near the Canada-USA border at the Crowsnest Pass Highway (Hwy 3), north to Rogers Pass and the Trans Canada Highway (Hwy 1). The Purcells parallel the Rocky Mountains, which lie just to the east on the British Columbia and Alberta provincial border.

The main purpose of this guide is to provide the most complete and comprehensive collection of information that would guide climbers from around the world to this amazing area and help them experience all the different aspects of Bugaboo climbing.

The guide covers all the peaks, routes, approaches and descents encompassed within Bugaboo Glacier Provincial Park. The area is divided into two main Groups; the Bugaboos, and the Vowells, and includes an overview of the Conrad Group.

The Bugaboo Group: The main and most popular spires centered around the Conrad Kain Hut Basin, including Bugaboo,

Crescent, Pigeon and Snowpatch Spires and the Howser Towers. Subdivided into four sections.

The Bugaboo Glacier Peaks: These encompass the heavily glaciated summits and moderate climbs at the head of the Bugaboo Glacier.

The Eastern Spires: They are the drier, lower, less austere peaks that lie to the east of the main spires, offering superb short rockclimbs, and many magnificent scrambles.

The Central Spires: Consist of Bugaboo, Snowpatch and Pigeon Spires, which make up the heart of the Bugaboo Group and offer the majority of the most easily accessed alpine rock routes.

The Western Spires: The Howser Towers and the Pigeon Feathers in the East Creek Basin and home of the longest and wildest routes in the range.

The Vowell Group: The dramatic spires to the north of the main Bugaboo Group, across the flat expanse of the Vowell Glacier. The climbs are similar in nature to those in the main Bugaboo Spires but the peaks are generally more compact, with more technical glacial approaches and convoluted descents. The Vowells see far fewer climbers and offer a wilder experience, all within striking distance of the Kain Hut.

The Conrad Group: Comprised of the sprawling and heavily glaciated peaks to the west and northwest of the main Bugaboo and Vowell Groups,. The climbs in this region are characterized by very long glacial approaches and technically easier mountaineering objectives, providing an almost mini-expedition experience.

There is something for every climber in the Bugaboos, whether you're planning your first or hundredth trip, looking for short scrambles, mountaineering objectives, long free routes, or remote big walls. Come and immerse yourself in the climbing, the weather, the people and the spirit of the Spires, it is a very special place. We hope that you experince the same excited, childlike giggles that we get everytime we head up the trail. Cheers.

Chris Atkinson, Squamish.

Marc Piché, Canmore.

June 2003.

A few minutes spent reading this page will help clarify many of the conventions used in this guide.

♦   route heights are given either as an estimate of pitches to climb, or, for climbs that are not easily assessed in pitches, by metres of vertical gain. **In such cases, the actual climbing distance will be 25–50% greater than the vertical gain.**

♦   an overview map of the guidebook area is on page 1.

♦   in addition to technical grades for rock and ice, Alpine Engagement Grades are used (pages 44-47).

♦   photo-topos of a particular section are grouped after the section's text descriptions, with page references back and forth.

♦   the page number of the main photo-topo for a particular route, underlined, can be found at the right side of its route-line.

♦   at the foot of photo-topo pages, the page containing the text description is noted for each climb displayed.

♦   'left' and 'right' are applied as a climber views the terrain.

♦   abbreviations of source references are as CAJ; Canadian Alpine Journal and AAJ; American Alpine Journal.

♦   NAD27 grid references are shown [GR345822].

♦   some approximate elevations are shown [~2950m].

♦   read all of the prologue; it contains vital information on hazards, weather, and all manner of necessary resources and tricks.

♦   read the introductions to the peaks as well as the climbs, they contain vital information about approaches and descents.

♦   the descriptions for routes on each peak usually start with the most popular, most easily approached, or the first ascent route, and then flow in geographic order.

♦   use the page cross-references noted at the top and bottoms of the pages for the peak's approach and descent, and the area map.

♦   about the route-line: grades are explained on pages 44-47. Estimated times are given as round-trip from the Kain Hut Basin, ie, (6-8h), (1-2 biv), or exceptionally, from a noted base area, and **apply to the return trip camp-to-camp.** Times are relative to a party of two competent at that grade. The black diamond ♦ indicates climbs which are rarely-climbed and about which little is known.

There are three major international airports that serve as destinations into Canada and the Northwest USA, and are convenient for onward travel to the Bugaboos.

Calgary, Alberta

Calgary is generally the best choice for climbers flying in from afar, with the shortest road approach and greatest opportunity for a wide range of climbing in the Rockies. Calgary is 340 kilometres (210 miles) to the east of the Bugaboos, and has direct and connector flights to Europe, the USA and Asia. It is about a five-hour drive from Calgary westward to the Bugaboo trailhead, either via Highway 1 (the Trans Canada) and Highway 93 through Radium Hotsprings; or via Highway 1 and Highway 95 through Golden, BC. Access from Calgary passes by the Kannanskis Country Parks of Western Alberta and through Banff and Kootenay National Parks.

The towns of Canmore and Banff are approximately two hours drive west of Calgary in Alberta. The spectacular national and provincial Parks around Canmore and Banff provide opportunities for every aspect of the climbing pursuit, from short sport climbs to big, nasty alpine routes on high peaks, and everything in between. When the weather is bad in the Bugaboos, there can often be a very climbable environment around Banff. Within a couple hours drive of Banff are four of the climbs in Roper & Steck's *Fifty Classic Climbs of North America* (on Mounts Robson, Edith Cavell, Alberta and Temple), although consensus has it that the selection is outdated. Rocky Mountain Books of Calgary www.rmbooks.com publishes an excellent series of climbing guides for the Rockies, and many other mountain-related books. Banff and Canmore also offer much in the way of hiking, dining, drinking and general soft-adventure tourism.

Vancouver, British Columbia

For those climbers flying in from afar, the Vancouver approach offers many good options for a memorable climbing trip. Vancouver BC is approximately 850 kilometres (590 miles) west of the Bugaboos, and has direct and connector flights to Europe, the USA and Asia. It is about a twelve-hour drive eastward to the Bugaboo trailhead, via either Highway 1 (the Trans Canada) and Highway 95 south of Golden BC; or via the Crowsnest Highway 3 and Highway 95 north of Cranbrook, British Columbia.

Some stellar climbing opportunities exist near Vancouver. About an hour north is Squamish, a mecca of superb granite rockcimbs, with over 2000 routes, everything from bouldering to bigwall aid and freeclimbing on the Squamish Chief, all listed in *The Climbers*

Guide to Squamish by Kevin McLane www.elaho.ca.

The Coast Range Mountains of Canada and the Cascade Range of the northwest USA offer hundreds of long alpine rock and mixed alpine routes, seven of the climbs in Roper & Steck's *Fifty Classic Climbs of North America.* Just south across the American Border are Mounts Rainier, Forbidden Peak, Shuksan, Stuart and Liberty Bell and close to Vancouver are Mount Slesse, and via charter aircraft the legendary Mount Waddington, one of the world's great alpine ranges. Elaho Publishing of Squamish, BC publishes an excellent climbing guide to the Waddington range, as well as alpine and rock climbing guides to the Coast, Interior and Selkirk Mountains, most of which are on the way to the Bugaboos.

There are two especially attractive alpine climbs on the drive from Vancouver to the Bugaboos, offering short access and quality climbing. Yak Peak lies between Hope and Kamloops on the Coquihala Highway 5, and *Yak Check* (5.10, 14p, 10-12 hours car to car) is the route to do. It is fully described in *Alpine Select* by Kevin McLane (Elaho). Further along the Trans Canada, about eight or nine hours drive east of Vancouver is Rogers Pass, in the Selkirk Mountain Range where the imposing bulk of Mount Sir Donald dominates the view. The *Northwest Ridge* of Mount Sir Donald is fully described in Dave Jones' *Selkirks South* Alpine Guide (Elaho), and is included in the *Fifty Classic Climbs* book. The *Northwest Ridge* is well worth considering for an ascent enroute (1–1½ days), and is a useful yardstick for climbers to judge themselves by for the Bugaboos. An epic on Sir Donald usually translates into more epics in the Bugaboos.

Skaha Bluffs near Penticton is 4 hours east of Vancouver and is the outstanding sun-and-stone, mostly-sport, rockclimbing centre in western Canada. See *Skaha Rockclimbs*, by Howie Richardson (Elaho).

Spokane, Washington, U.S.A is approximately 320 miles (520 km) south of the Bugaboos and is the closest major American airport to the Bugaboos, although Seattle, Washington, 280 miles (450km) west of Spokane (5 hours south of Squamish), is a consideration too. From Spokane it is about a seven hour drive north to the Bugaboos on Highway 2, first north to Sandpoint, Idaho and then north on Highway 95 through Cranbrook, BC and Invermere.

Access north on Highway 93 from Missoula, Montana, through Whitefish, Montana and on into Canada through Cranbrook and Invermere is also possible. It is about 370 miles (600km) or a seven to eight hour drive from Missoula to the Bugaboos.

From Calgary, Alberta, via Highway 1 and Highway 13:

Calgary, Alberta	0 km	Hwy 1 West
Canmore, Alberta	103 km	Hwy 1 West
Banff, Alberta	129 km	Hwy 1 West
Castle Junction	158 km	Hwy 93 South
Radium Hotsprings, B.C.	262 km	Hwy 95 North
Turnoff: Brisco, B.C.	290 km	gravel road west
Trailhead: Bugaboos	336 km	parking lot

— if travelling via Highway 1 through Golden, BC:

Castle Junction	158 km	Hwy 1 West
Lake Louise, Alberta	185 km	Hwy 1 West
Golden, B.C.	264 km	Hwy 95 South
Turnoff: Brisco, B.C.	342 km	gravel road west
Trailhead: Bugaboos	389 km	parking lot

From Vancouver, B.C., via Highay 1 through Golden, BC:

Vancouver, B.C.	0 km	Hwy 1 East
Hope, B.C.	152 km	Hwy 5 North
Kamloops, B.C.	363 km	Hwy 1 East
Revelstoke, B.C.	571 km	Hwy 1 East
Rogers Pass	640 km	Hwy 1 East
Golden, B.C.	719 km	Hwy 95 South
Turnoff: Brisco, B.C.	797 km	gravel road west
Trailhead: Bugaboos	843 km	parking lot

From Vancouver, B.C., via Highay 3 through Cranbrook, BC:

Vancouver, B.C.	0 km	Hwy 1 East
Hope, B.C.	152 km	Hwy 3 East
Osoyoos, B.C.	396 km	Hwy 3 East
Castlegar, B.C.	621 km	Hwy 3 East
Cranbrook, B.C.	849 km	Hwy 95 North
Radium Hotsprings, B.C.	993 km	Hwy 95 North
Turnoff: Brisco, B.C.	1021 km	gravel road west
Trailhead: Bugaboos	1067 km	parking lot

From the USA:

From Seattle, Washington: to Spokane, Washington, 280 miles, 450 km

Spokane, Washington	0 miles	0 km	Hwy 2 North
Sandpoint, Idaho	78 miles	125 km	Hwy 95 North
Border Crossing, Kingsgate	142 miles	229 km	Hwy 95 North
Cranbrook, BC.	191 miles	308 km	Hwy 95 / 93North
Radium Hotsprings, BC.	280 miles	452 km	Hwy 95 North
Turnoff—Brisco, BC.	298 miles	480 km	gravel road west
Trailhead—Bugaboos	326 miles	526 km	parking lot

From Missoula, Montana, via Highway 93:

Missoula, Montana	0 miles	0 km	Hwy 93 North
Whitefish, Montana	125 miles	202 km	Hwy 93 North
Border Crossing-Roosville	185 miles	298 km	Hwy 93 North
Junction Hwy 93/95	246 miles	396 km	Hwy 93 / 95 North
Radium Hotsprings, B.C.	329 miles	530 km	Hwy 95 north
Turnoff—Brisco, B.C.	346 miles	558 km	gravel road west
Trailhead—Bugaboos	374 miles	604 km	parking lot

The Bugaboos are a remote area far away from big cities. Plan carefully as it becomes increasingly difficult to get necessary supplies as you near the Bugaboos. The following list should help.

Vancouver, British Columbia.
A very large city with all services and amenities. For more information visit: www.tourismvancouver.com

Golden, British Columbia.   Golden is a small town of about five thousand residents that has most amenities.   There are two major food stores, many gas stations, some good restaurants and coffee shops and many places to stay. There is a limited supply of climbing equipment. This is the last chance for supplies for those travelling from the west. See www.goldenbritishcolumbia.com

Calgary, Alberta.   A very large city with all the services and amenities. For more information visit: www.discovercalgary.com

Banff and Canmore, Alberta.   Banff and Canmore are popular mountain towns full of tourist attractions.   There are many places to stay such as the Alpine Club of Canada Clubhouse in Canmore and countless restaurants, food stores, gas stations. This is also the closest place to find a wide variety of climbing gear. See www.canmorealberta.com and www.banfflakelouise.com

Radium, British Columbia.   Home to the famous Radium Hot Springs. This is the last chance for supplies for those travelling from the east or south. There is a small grocery store and a few restaurants, gas stations and hotels. Some last minute items can be found here although most places close early. Invermere, 20 kilometres south, has a larger selection. For more information visit: www.rhs.bc.ca

Invermere, British Columbia. Similar to Golden in size, Invermere also has most of what you might need short of specialized climbing equipment.   There is a major food store, gas stations, some good restaurants and coffee shops and many great places to stay. Invermere has more choice then Radium and is a good final stop for those travelling from the south. For more information visit: www.invermere.com

Brisco, British Columbia.   Last but not least, approximately 200m north of the Bugaboo turn off on highway 95, is the Brisco General Store and gas station, the last civilization before the Bugaboos. They are open until 9:00 pm in the summer and carry a small variety of food items, hardware, alcohol and other unexpected items.

Maps. Enough information is provided within this guidebook so that climbers generally don't need to carry topographical maps when climbing in the main spires. If visiting the Vowells or the Conrad Groups maps are a good resource of reference and recommended. The Geological Survey of Canada produces 1:50,000 scale topographical maps. 82K/10 Howser Creek and 82K/15 Bugaboo Creek cover all the spires. A good source for maps is International Travel Maps and Books, www.itmb.com

Other Useful Contacts:

BC Parks. www.gov.bc.ca/bcparks/explore/parkpgs/bugaboo.htm
Telephone: (250)422-4200

Alpine Club of Canada.
www.alpineclubofcanada.ca Tel(403)678-3200

Mountain Magic Equipment (Banff).
Lots of climbing gear and a good source of information on climbs and conditions. www.mountainmagic.com

Mountain Equipment Coop.
Calgary and Vancouver locations www.mec.ca

Guides and Guiding Companies.
www.acmg.ca; www.acmgguides.com

Weather. www.accuweather.com Good satellite images.
www.weatheroffice.ec.gc.ca Environment Canada forecasts.
Look for Columbia South and East Kootenay forecasts.

Rescue. The Bugaboo Spires are a remote area with no organized rescue readily available. Parties must have the gear and knowledge necessary to successfully carry out a self-rescue. If additional, outside help is needed, contact the Radium–Invermere Royal Canadian Mounted Police (RCMP) who will then organize rescue volunteers from the Provincial Emergency Program (PEP). Contact with the outside world can be very difficult and time consuming from the Park. The Kain Hut custodians may have a satellite telephone, which can be used to call for help in emergencies, but custodians can be difficult to find as they have duties outside of the hut. The nearest cell phone coverage is at kilometre 23 on the road (almost two hours travel from the hut) and is marginal at best. In an emergency, the staff at the CMH Bugaboo Lodge can make the necessary phone calls to initiate a rescue.

Radium—Invermere RCMP (250) 342-9292
Golden RCMP (250) 344-2221

Access into the Bugaboos begins at the turn-off on Highway 95 at the small settlement of Brisco, 78 kilometres (48 miles) south of Golden, and 28 kilometres (17 miles) north of Radium Hotsprings. The access route follows a series of dirt logging and mining roads for 46 kilometres to the Bugaboos parking lot. Because of active logging and other industrial activity that occurs in the area, and the prevailing weather conditions, it is hard to predict exactly what shape the road will be in at any given time. That being said, the parking lot is nearly always accessible to higher clearance vehicles during the summer months. Four wheel drive vehicles are usually only required for a few muddy sections when the snow is just melting from the road, typically around late May to early June. Access before then is generally not possible because of the winter snowpack. Because the Park Rangers and Hut Custodians generally don't go into the area until mid-June, reliable sources of road information are not available until that time (B.C. Parks 250 422-4200). The road is normally drivable until late October.

When driving into the Bugaboos, be aware that at any time, **fast-moving, logging, fuel and pick up trucks may be encountered**. Be alert, drive with caution, and give working trucks the right of way.

Once at the parking lot, the first wildlife issues will be encountered. Porcupines, groundsquirels and other critters will abuse your vehicle, if left unprotected, by chewing on the rubber bits such as brake and fuel lines. Build a chickenwire fence around the lower half of your vehicle to keep them out: about 15 minutes of work. Enough chickenwire exists at the parking lot for its present capacity but it is a good idea to bring your own supply, especially for high-clearance vehicles. Wrap the vehicle entirely, securing the wire to the ground and the vehicle so the beasts cannot crawl underneath or overtop the wire. Rocks will keep the wire on the ground and sticks propping the wire against the vehicle will keep the critters from pulling the wire down and crawling overtop of it.

The only facilities at the parking lot are a single outhouse toilet and a B.C. Parks notice board. Theft from vehicles is very rare but it has happened. A small creek 100m up the trail usually runs all summer and is a filterable water source. Pack all garbage out with you from the parking lot to the nearest trash facilities in civilization.

HEADING INTO THE BUGABOOS — THE BUGABOO FOREST SERVICE ROAD

From Brisco:
South to Radium Hotsprings: 28 km, 17 miles.
North to Golden: 78km, 48 miles.

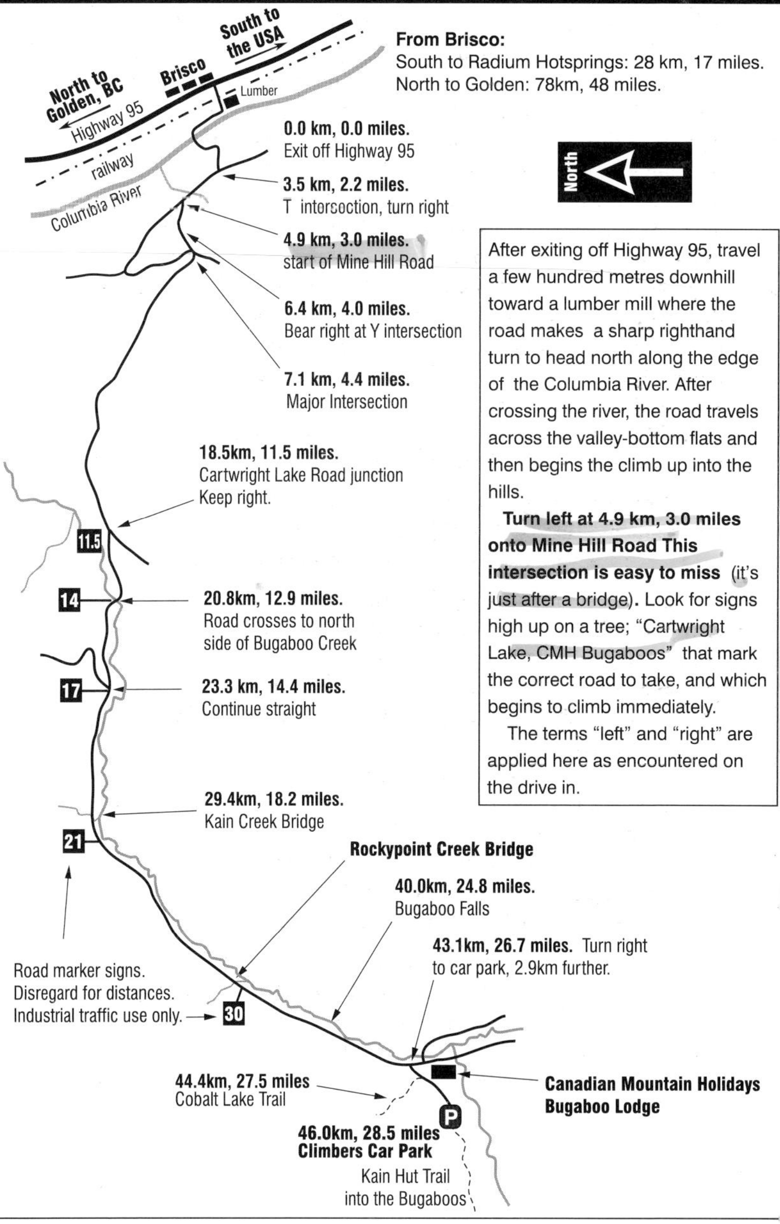

South to the USA
North to Golden, BC
Brisco
Lumber
Highway 95
railway
Columbia River
North
0.0 km, 0.0 miles. Exit off Highway 95
3.5 km, 2.2 miles. T intersection, turn right
4.9 km, 3.0 miles. start of Mine Hill Road
6.4 km, 4.0 miles. Bear right at Y intersection
7.1 km, 4.4 miles. Major Intersection
18.5km, 11.5 miles. Cartwright Lake Road junction Keep right.
11.5
14
20.8km, 12.9 miles. Road crosses to north side of Bugaboo Creek
17
23.3 km, 14.4 miles. Continue straight
29.4km, 18.2 miles. Kain Creek Bridge
21
Rockypoint Creek Bridge
40.0km, 24.8 miles. Bugaboo Falls
43.1km, 26.7 miles. Turn right to car park, 2.9km further.
Road marker signs. Disregard for distances. Industrial traffic use only.
30
Canadian Mountain Holidays Bugaboo Lodge
44.4km, 27.5 miles Cobalt Lake Trail
P
46.0km, 28.5 miles Climbers Car Park
Kain Hut Trail into the Bugaboos

After exiting off Highway 95, travel a few hundred metres downhill toward a lumber mill where the road makes a sharp righthand turn to head north along the edge of the Columbia River. After crossing the river, the road travels across the valley-bottom flats and then begins the climb up into the hills.

Turn left at 4.9 km, 3.0 miles onto Mine Hill Road This intersection is easy to miss (it's just after a bridge). Look for signs high up on a tree; "Cartwright Lake, CMH Bugaboos" that mark the correct road to take, and which begins to climb immediately.

The terms "left" and "right" are applied here as encountered on the drive in.

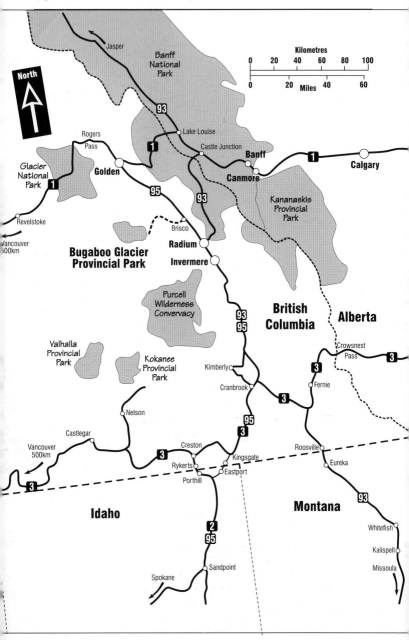

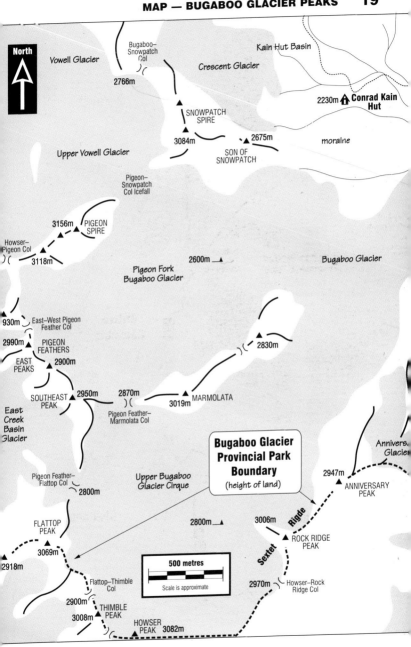

North

Vowell Glacier

Bugaboo–
Snowpatch
Col
2766m

Kain Hut Basin

Crescent Glacier

2230m Conrad Kain
Hut

SNOWPATCH
SPIRE

3084m

2675m

SON OF
SNOWPATCH

moraine

Upper Vowell Glacier

Pigeon–
Snowpatch
Col Icefall

3156m

PIGEON
SPIRE

Howser–
Pigeon Col

3118m

Pigeon Fork
Bugaboo Glacier

2600m

Bugaboo Glacier

930m

East–West Pigeon
Feather Col

2990m

PIGEON
FEATHERS

EAST
PEAKS

2900m

2830m

SOUTHEAST
PEAK

2950m

2870m

MARMOLATA

3019m

East
Creek
Basin
Glacier

Pigeon Feather–
Marmolata Col

**Bugaboo Glacier
Provincial Park
Boundary**
(height of land)

Annivers.
Glacier

2947m

ANNIVERSARY
PEAK

Pigeon Feather–
Flattop Col

2800m

Upper Bugaboo
Glacier Cirque

2800m

3006m

Ridge

FLATTOP
PEAK

2918m

3069m

Flattop–Thimble
Col

2900m

THIMBLE
PEAK

3008m

HOWSER
PEAK

3082m

ROCK RIDGE
PEAK

Sextet

2970m

Howser–Rock
Ridge Col

500 metres

Scale is approximate

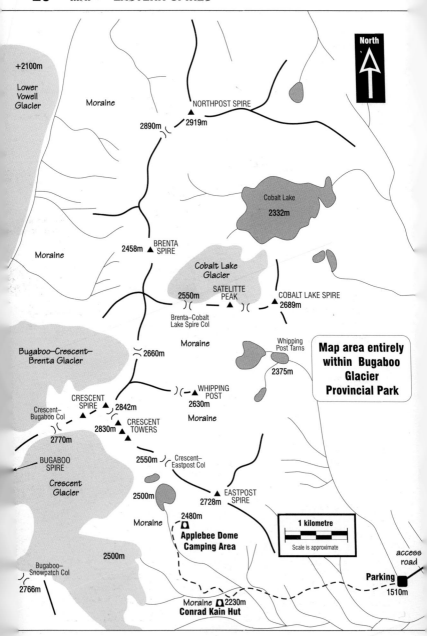

North

+2100m
Lower
Vowell
Glacier

Moraine

NORTHPOST SPIRE
▲ 2919m
2890m

Cobalt Lake
2332m

Moraine

2458m ▲ BRENTA
SPIRE

Cobalt Lake
Glacier

SATELITTE
PEAK
2550m ▲   ▲ COBALT LAKE SPIRE
2689m
Brenta–Cobalt
Lake Spire Col

Bugaboo–Crescent–
Brenta Glacier

2660m

Moraine

Whipping
Post Tarns
2375m

**Map area entirely
within Bugaboo
Glacier
Provincial Park**

CRESCENT
SPIRE ▲ 2842m
Crescent–
Bugaboo Col
2830m ▲▲ CRESCENT
TOWERS
2770m

▲ WHIPPING
POST
2630m

Moraine

BUGABOO
SPIRE

Crescent
Glacier

2550m
Crescent–
Eastpost Col

2500m

▲ EASTPOST
SPIRE
2728m

Moraine

2480m
⌂
**Applebee Dome
Camping Area**

1 kilometre

Scale is approximate

2500m

Bugaboo–
Snowpatch Col
2766m

access
road

Parking
1510m

Moraine ⌂ 2230m
Conrad Kain Hut

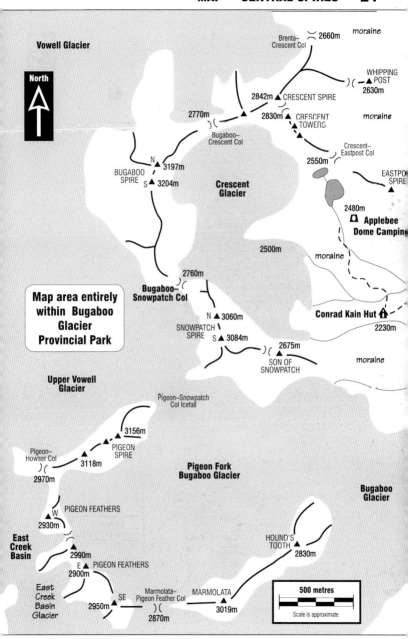

Vowell Glacier

North

Brenta–
Crescent Col ~ 2660m   moraine

WHIPPING
POST
▲
2630m

2842m ▲ CRESCENT SPIRE

2770m   2830m ▲ CRESCENT
                         TOWERS   moraine
                       ▲
Bugaboo–   ▼
Crescent Col   Crescent–
                        Eastpost Col
                     2550m   EASTPO
N ▲ 3197m   SPIRE
                                      ▲
BUGABOO
SPIRE   Crescent
S ▲ 3204m   Glacier
                             2480m
                        ⌂ Applebee
                          Dome Camping

                2500m   moraine

2760m

Bugaboo–   Conrad Kain Hut ⌂
Snowpatch Col   2230m

Map area entirely
within Bugaboo   N ▲ 3060m
    Glacier
Provincial Park   SNOWPATCH
                  SPIRE
                  S ▲ 3084m
                         ▲ 2675m
)(
                     SON OF
                     SNOWPATCH   moraine

Upper Vowell
Glacier

Pigeon–Snowpatch
Col Icefall

            ▲ 3156m
Pigeon–   ▲   PIGEON
Howser Col 3118m SPIRE   Pigeon Fork
)(Bugaboo Glacier
2970m
                                              Bugaboo
                                              Glacier

       W ▲ PIGEON FEATHERS
East   2930m
Creek
Basin   HOUND'S
        ▲ 2990m   TOOTH ▲
        E ▲ PIGEON FEATHERS   2830m
East   2900m
Creek
Basin   SE   Marmolata–   MARMOLATA
Glacier ▲   Pigeon Feather Col   ▲
         2950m   )(3019m
                  2870m

500 metres

Scale is approximate

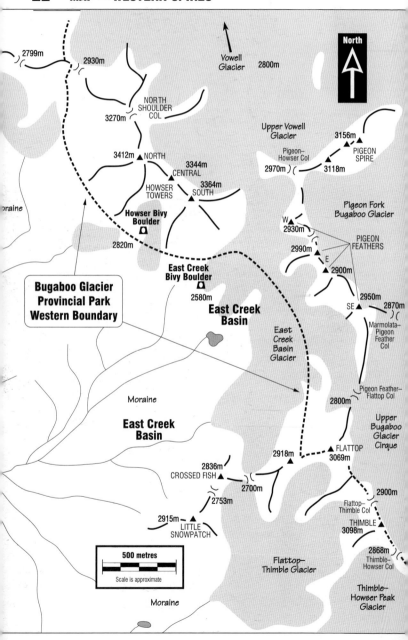

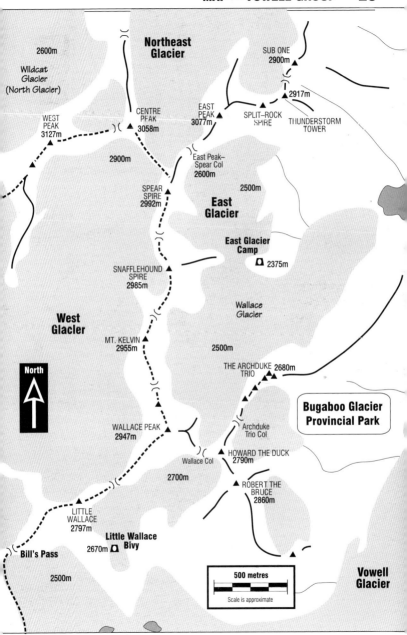

Northeast Glacier

2600m

Wildcat Glacier (North Glacier)

SUB ONE 2900m

2917m

WEST PEAK 3127m

CENTRE PEAK 3058m

EAST PEAK 3077m

SPLIT–ROCK SPIRE

THUNDERSTORM TOWER

2900m

East Peak–Spear Col 2600m

2500m

SPEAR SPIRE 2992m

East Glacier

East Glacier Camp 2375m

SNAFFLEHOUND SPIRE 2985m

Wallace Glacier

West Glacier

MT. KELVIN 2955m

2500m

North

THE ARCHDUKE TRIO 2680m

Bugaboo Glacier Provincial Park

WALLACE PEAK 2947m

Archduke Trio Col

Wallace Col

HOWARD THE DUCK 2790m

2700m

ROBERT THE BRUCE 2860m

LITTLE WALLACE 2797m

Little Wallace Bivy 2670m

Bill's Pass

2500m

500 metres

Scale is approximate

Vowell Glacier

Conrad Kain Hut and Applebee Camp Approach Trail

The Conrad Kain Hut can be seen from the parking lot, perched atop the bluffs looking south over the Bugaboo Glacier. From the car park, the trail leads through the forest, then up along the northern lateral moraines and begins to climb up through rock bluffs. In spots the trail has been carved and blasted out of the rocks. Cables, rock stairs and even an aluminum ladder make the going easier. The trail eventually breaks out into the basin below Eastpost Spire and Applebee Dome, crosses a creek and makes the final climb up to the hut. The trail is steep and ascends 700m over 4.6 kilometres. Water is not readily available once leaving the forest. Climbers burdened with the usual climbing gear generally take two to three hours to reach the hut and another hour to the Applebee Camping Area.

0.0 km	1510m	Bugaboo Parking lot
1.6 km	1525m	trail leaves forest, crosses boulder field
1.7 km	1560m	trail re-enters forest
3.5 km	1920m	aluminum ladder
4.6 km	2230m	Conrad Kain Hut (2170m Boulder Camp)
5.6 km	2480m	Applebee Camping Area.

Cobalt Lake Trail

Although climbers don't generally access the Bugaboos via the Cobalt Lake Trail it is useful for access into the Eastern Spires, as a foul weather loop circuit, or for the beautiful hike it is.

From the Bugaboo Parking lot backtrack along the access road for 1.6 kilometres to the trailhead opposite the Bugaboo Lodge. The trail switchbacks up through the forest into a basin and eventually gains a ridge with grand views into the main spires. From the pass follow the ridge right for a few hundred metres until able to gradually descend to the base of the broad *East Ridge* of Northpost Spire, right of Cobalt Lake. From here descend to beneath the outlet of the lake and follow a ramp left of the waterfall to gain the lake. To gain the Cobalt Lake Spire–Brenta Col and access to the main spires (page 130, 140) follow the height of land on the lefthand shore to gain snow slopes, on the flank of Cobalt Lake Spire, leading to the col. Ice-axes and self-arrest knowledge are needed.

0.0 km	1510m	Bugaboo parking lot
1.6 km	1510m	trailhead (backtrack along road)
5.3 km	2110m	Walter Lake junction
6.6 km	2385m	alpine pass
8.5 km	2330m	Cobalt Lake

During the 1960s the number of climbers visiting the Bugaboos skyrocketed. The small meadows around Cooper's Boulder near the site of the present day Kain Hut began to deteriorate rapidly. Around the same time the park was formed in 1969 it was decided to try and curb the impact the climbers were having on the area by building a shelter. Two small six-person fiberglass igloos were flown to the site and erected. It became immediately obvious that these shelters were inadequate and unappreciated by the climbers so the Alpine Club of Canada set out to build a better structure that would be more useful and fit into the area better.

In 1972 after many stumbling blocks the Conrad Kain Hut was finally flown to the site by helicopter and assembled. The hut was a tin roofed, gothic-arch wooden structure, able to house fifty climbers. It contained a kitchen and common room on the main floor and two floors of sleeping areas and sported big bay windows looking out onto the Bugaboo Glacier. The two fiberglass igloos were to be flown to various locations around the area for use as bivouac shelters but after a helicopter slinging issue only one usable shelter remained. It now sits below the west face of Osprey Peak in the Vowell Range.

Upon the completion of the Kain Hut, the Alpine Club of Canada turned the hut over to B.C. Parks for care, maintenance and operation. Two rangers were traditionally stationed at the Kain Hut but now a combination of Alpine Club Hut Custodians and Park Rangers oversee the hut.

The hut has changed little since 1972. The roofing and windows have been replaced and the cooking area upgraded. The greatest change has come to the back of the structure were it has been hit by avalanches at least three times during it's history.

At times the hut may seem crowded and noisy and perhaps a little decadent with its running water, stoves, lights and mattresses but sitting inside, warm and dry, while a wild Bugaboo storm rages outside it is easy to appreciate the luxury of the Conrad Kain Hut.

When staying at the Kain Hut please be considerate of the other occupants. The hut is not very soundproof and many climbers are in bed early for an alpine start.

Camping and bivouacs are restricted within the Kain Hut Basin and the Central Spires of Bugaboo Glacier Provincial Park. With the large numbers of users it is important to adhere to the regulations to maintain an unpolluted water source and to minimize impact on the fragile environment.

Camping in the Kain Hut Basin is restricted to the Conrad Kain Hut or Boulder Campsite, which is located five minutes below the hut and to Applebee Campsite, which sits above the hut on a knoll beneath Eastpost Spire, about a one hour hike from the hut with full packs. Camping fees exist (at present $5 per person per night) and climbers should check in at the Conrad Kain Hut for registration and payment. When tenting, avoid sensitive areas and the fragile vegetation. The Hut can hold forty people and provides sleeping mats, propane stoves and lights, running water, pots, pans and eating utensils. The Alpine Club of Canada runs the hut and charges about $20 per person per night, payable at the hut. The hut is often full at the height of the season and it is conceivable that climbers may not find space. Contact the Alpine Club at www.alpineclubofcanada.ca or phone 403 678-3200 in Camore, Alberta, for possible reservations. Please be considerate and courteous to the others in the hut and observe all the posted rules.

Bivouacs and camping are not permitted by B.C. Parks, at the Bugaboo–Snowpatch Col, the Pigeon–Howser Col, or nearby on the *West Ridge* of Pigeon Spire. The Pigeon–Howser Col was traditionally used by climbers intent on the *Beckey–Chouinard* on South Howser Tower. Now, climbers must descend into the East Creek Basin (about 20 minutes), outside of the park in order to bivy or camp (page 264).

Climbers who may have to bivy on the routes should keep in mind those who will follow, and act accordingly. Human waste should be disposed of in a responsible fashion and may need to be carried off the route.

The Vowells: The Vowell and Conrad Groups are within Bugaboo Glacier Park and all rules and regulations apply. Traditional bivouac and camping areas are discussed on pages 321-325 in the Vowell introduction. The Malloy Igloo near Osprey Peak is a small fiberglass dome with no amenities and sleeps six people.

In 1969, 358 hectares based around the Bugaboo Glacier were preserved as a park, while 24,624 hectares encompassing the main spires and the Vowells were set aside as an alpine recreation area. In 1995 these two were amalgamated into the 13,646 hectare Bugaboo Glacier Provincial Park. The park includes the main Bugaboo Spires, the Vowell Group and much of Vowell Creek. The wild and undeveloped East Creek valley is not protected within the park.

Nearly all of the climbing activity in the Bugaboos occurs within Bugaboo Glacier Provincial Park, with the surrounding area being crown land, both of which are administrated by the provincial government. In essence the Bugaboos belongs to the people, with climbers being the defacto guardians of the area. B.C. Parks oversees the park, but the rangers have neither the time nor resources to police climbers and clean up after them. So the preservation or degradation of this beautiful and unique area lies in the hands of the climbers. Treat it as your own.

A few basic B.C. Park rules apply:

♦ Fires are not permitted.

♦ Dogs and other domestic animals are not permitted.

♦ Damage to, collection or removal of any natural resources is prohibited, including flowers, plants and rocks.

♦ All garbage and refuse must be packed out and disposed of responsibly, especially from high use areas such as the Applebee Camping Area.

♦ Protect the water sources. Do all washing at least 30m from all water sources.

♦ Helicopter access inside the park is not allowed except under special permit from B.C. Parks.

♦ Bolting. In theory mechanized bolting is not permitted in the park although hand drilling and anchor replacement is generally seen as acceptable.

♦ All commercial activity within the park including guiding requires a park use permit, obtainable through B.C.Parks.

♦ Rules and regulations change over time, check the web site for updated information www.gov.bc.ca/bcparks

Despite the harsh and unyielding appearance of the Bugaboos the area is actually very fragile, and with the rising numbers of climbers visiting the area, heavy impact and the potential for conflict is increasing. For these reasons it is important to be responsible and accepting of others. We are all in this together and issues that are not resolved within the climbing community will be resolved for us by governing bodies. The general guidelines below must be considered.

♦   **Human waste** is becoming an increasing issue, both from a water contamination and an aesthetic point of view. Drainage from the peaks has far reaching effects on the watersheds. If climbers do not take a more responsible approach, more restrictions and regulations will appear to deal with it. Avoid high use and sensitive areas.

♦   **Overcrowding**. During good weather the more popular routes can often see six or more parties on a single climb. Respect other climbers right to be there, even if they are slower and less experienced, and treat them with respect. Consider alternatives and other options.

♦   **Huts and Camping.** Climbers schedules often conflict, with some groups arriving back from their climbs late, while others are planning on an early alpine start. Be considerate of others and plan accordingly.

♦   **Climbing litter**. Slings left on rappel stations weather quickly in the Bugaboos and pack rats often shred the webbing, making an unsightly mess. When backing up anchors remove the old tattered webbing and pack it out with you. Leaving it behind or throwing it off the climb is irresponsible.

♦   **Bolting and fixed gear.** Mechanized bolting, in theory, is not allowed within the park. When leaving gear behind or replacing fixed gear consider the impact it may have on the area and the climbing experience of others.

The intrusive rock of the granitic spires is approximately 135 million years old while the 'country' rock of the surrounding area dates back to more than 600 million to 1 billion years. Approximately 135 million years ago hot molten magma began to work its way toward the surface of the earth's crust. Stopped from reaching the surface by nearly 8 kilometres of earth above, the magma cooled slowly over the next 68 million years. Slow cooling resulted in large crystals being formed within the mass. The resulting rock, when cooled, became granite (quartz crystals, feldspar & mica flakes). If the lava of the Bugaboo batholith had broken the earth's crust and cooled much more rapidly, the resulting lava flow would have resembled hexagonal basalt. After an additional 67 million years of erosion, in which the covering country rock was worn away the spires became exposed. The shape of the spires today has changed very little from the original shape of the magma intrusion. For this reason, the granite near the edges of the Bugaboo group where it joins the country rock tends to be more broken and frail but very interesting from a geological point of view.

All of the glaciers of the Bugaboos are retreating at an alarming rate. Archival photos made by Byron Harmon in 1910 show much more extensive glaciation. The Bugaboo Glacier has receded approximately 1,000 metres since that time with the greatest measured retreat since 1933. Glaciers have receded during the last 100 years an equivalent distance that they advanced over the previous 2,000 years.

Plant Life

Few people visit the Bugaboos for the flowers although at times, it is impossible to miss them. From the highway to the Kain hut and beyond, many different flowers, trees and berries offer themselves for viewing. The forest in Bugaboo creek generally consists of relatively small spruce, lodge pole and ponderosa pine, balsam fir and a few dense stands of poplar, aspen and birch trees.

Once on the trail from the parking area, the trees are noticeably larger and there is lush undergrowth, consisting of blueberries, huckleberries, black currents, goose berries, raspberries, ferns, willows and many other marshy type plants.

Further along, the trail becomes a tunnel through the slide alder and is lined with berry patches (popular with the bears!), fireweed, arnica, buttercup, fleabane, anemone, and false hellebore.

Around and above the hut there is still an abundance of plant life scattered amongst the rocks such as heather, indian paintbrush and purple monkey flower. The Hut is the perfect elevation for the relatively rare western larch (tamarack) whose needles turn a fiery orange in the fall, and nestled on the rocky ridges and gravel moraines are fragile and slow growing moss campion with its tiny pink flowers and purple saxifrage (Latin for rock breaker) growing out of the cracks in the wildest places. Last but not least are the many different types of lichens (Goat food) growing at all elevations, which, when wet, renders sticky rubber useless.

Wildlife

Like the plants, most of the animal habitats in the area are elevation dependent. Once past the cows and famous waterfowl and raptor populations of the Columbia Valley, chances are good that the drive to the parking area will be somewhat safari-like, especially if driven at dusk or dawn. It is not uncommon to see black bear, white tail and mule deer, moose, hare, ground squirrels, grouse and the infamous, very hungry, tire- and brakeline-eating Bugaboo Porcupines! Less common yet still seen on or near the road are cougars, wolves, lynx, marten, elk and grizzly bear.

At and above treeline, the chance of seeing large animals is significantly less, but this does not mean that they are not there. Grizzly bears, although uncommon around the hut, have been seen traversing many of the glaciers, while travelling from one valley to the next. Marmots are often seen sun bathing on the boulders and Pikas can be heard squeaking away under the rocks as they gather incredible amounts of grass to be dried and stored for the winter. The mischievous Bushy Tailed Wood Rat (AKA packrat, snafflehound, Timmy) is seldom seen but often cursed after waking from a restless bivy to a pair of boots without shoelaces, and a rope which has been chewed into 50 separate metres! Wolverines have been spotted crossing the Vowell Glacier but a human encounter is rare. Mountain Goats are probably the most commonly seen of the large animals and are often found grazing on lichens on and around Eastpost and Crescent Spires or at the toe of the Vowell Glacier where they have found a rich mineral deposit which they lick in order to supplement their diet! Birds are also abundant in the Bugaboos but are far less restricted by ecological zones or altitudes. Spring time brings the migration of the bald and golden eagles, while most of them move on to the north, there are a number of them who nest in the valley and spend their summer soaring around the spires in search of kid goats, ground squirrels and whatever else suits their appetite. Ravens are also common in the area and are fun to watch on hot days while they play in the rising thermals. Ptarmigans are often difficult to see until they are almost underfoot as their plumage changes colour with the seasons and they are incredibly well camouflaged. With a keen eye and a little luck, a few varieties of hummingbirds, jays, grosbeaks, larks and falcons may also be spotted.

Please treat all wildlife with respect and do not approach animals for photographs or to satisfy your curiosity. In the event they approach you, initially stand still and then slowly back away.

This is only a small piece of the Natural History of the Bugaboos. In these days of increased traffic, if you find a 'neat rock' or anything else that would look good on your fireplace mantel, please remember that the people who saw it before you have left it there for your pleasure! Within the park it is unlawful to collect plants or rocks or to disturb wildlife, this is the reason dogs are not allowed in the park. Take only pictures and leave only footprints.

On the Bugaboos.

A part of the Purcell Range, the peaks are the western most of truly alpine character and contain several summits of an altitude well over ten thousand feet. The rock is largely granite, firm and weatherproof, lending itself to a mountain architecture truly startling. Some of the pinnacles seem quite inaccessible, and will succumb only to a formal siege, if at all. The best efforts of our finest rock climbing specialists would not be wasted here.

Eaton Cromwell, American Alpine Journal, 1933-36.

The Bugaboos is a wild alpine area that posses a unique and challenging combination of steep granite, unstable moraines, broken glaciers, long, committing routes, and harsh, unpredictable weather. There are few places which can pose such great challenge for both novices and veterans alike: one of the enduring appeals of the area. It is important to respect the seriousness of travelling in the Bugaboos: climbers have died from lightning strikes, rockfall, crevasse falls and shifting boulders. Every year, parties overestimate their level of experience and underestimate the nature and commitment of their climbs, resulting in many epics, unplanned bivouacs and the occasional tragedy. Nearly all could have been avoided with more knowledge, foresight and preparation.

Glaciers. The glaciers of the Bugaboos are very dynamic and change quickly throughout the season. Crevasses and bergshrunds can be unnoticeable one day and wide open the next. Roped travel is prudent on all the glaciers within the Bugaboos even though many climbers are seen unroped on the popular approaches. The bergshrunds in the area are much larger and more extensive than would normally be expected and rappels are often needed to descend over them. Use extra caution, stay roped up, and carry crampons and ice axes.

Scree and talus. Extensive glaciation and the rapid retreat of the ice has left Bugaboo talus extremely unstable and dangerous, a prime example is the approach gully to the west face of North Howser Tower. Use caution and avoid the moraines and talus slopes as much as possible. Huge boulders can shift and whole slopes can settle. Do not get above or below other climbers.

Rockfall. Rockfall in the Bugaboos tends to be of two types. Small, predictable, climber-generated rockfall and unpredictable releases of large flakes and blocks. Climber-generated rockfall can easily be avoided by not climbing beneath other parties and natural rockfall danger can be minimized by observing your surroundings and avoiding areas with rock scars, debris and other signs of rockfall activity. Remember, vertical erosion never sleeps. In the last six years large blocks and flakes have fallen from every one of the major spires.

The Elements. Bugaboo weather can be extreme and fast moving. Afternoon snow and lightning storms are common and alpine starts are needed to help avoid them. Fresh snow and high winds are associated with most storms and even during clear weather it is cold on the spires often requiring extra clothing and gloves for the belays. Most summers see a large snowfall to the valley, which makes even the trail hazardous for a day or two. These are high alpine peaks and the weather can be deadly. Knowledge is safety. Seek out weather forecasts both short term and long range and plan accordingly.

Approaches. Most of the approaches entail glacier travel, bergshrund crossings, loose terrain and fourth class climbing; all of this is usually done by headlamp during a pre dawn approach. The safest approach to this is to be familiar with the terrain. Do a reconnaissance day before the actual climb. This will make the approach faster, safer and less stressful and will allow for more time on the climb and descent. But do not stash gear at the base of the climb as packrats may destroy it.

Climbs. Many of the climbs in the Bugaboos are long and entail descent down a different route, making retreat from the climbs problematic. A lot of the spires also present narrow, convoluted, low-fifth class ridge sections near their summits. Climbing fast and safe can be a big challenge for many climbers in the Bugaboos. Being efficient with gear and belays and having clear communication are the best time savers. Being knowledgeable and experienced in moving over broken, convoluted terrain can also shave valuable time off a climb.

Going as light as possible is also a key to success here. Light single ropes or twin or double ropes help. Lightweight biners and hex's can lighten the rack without making it smaller. If encountering snow and ice on the descent, lightweight aluminum crampons, small or modular ice axes that fit inside the pack, and light mountain boots such as La Sportiva Trangos keep the weight reasonable. Knowledge is speed. The more you know about the approach, the climb and the descent, the faster you will be.

Descents. Nearly all of the technical climbs in the Bugaboos require a rappel descent down a different route, which means climbers are often going in blind to the descent. Scoping out the rappel lines and knowing the descent from its base back to camp can mean the difference between a daylight descent or an epic, unplanned bivy. If planning climbs on Snowpatch or Bugaboo Spires an effective strategy is to first climb the *West Ridge* of Pigeon Spire, which is a classic route itself. This will give intimate knowledge of the Bugaboo–Snowpatch Col and allow the descent routes on Bugaboo and Snowpatch Spire to be scoped out. Temper your enthusiasm, start small and build up to the big routes.

Volatile weather is a famous hallmark of the Bugaboos. Many epics in the spires began with " We started out under the star filled sky." Then at midday "We peeked over the ridge to get a look to the west, there were some small clouds in the distance but nothing serious…" Then less than an hour later "We heard a rumble in the distance and within minutes the sky was black and the Howsers were covered in cloud… We hadn't descended more than 100m before the hail started and the whole sky let loose, my ice axe was humming, I could see sparks flashing between my carabiners. We decided to wait it out…We spent a cold sleepless night admiring the wildest light show ever, we finished the descent at the crack of dawn under the same fading, starry sky we had started with 24 hours ago!"

The Summer Alpine Season. This generally starts late June and can last until the end of September. This being said, it can and usually will snow to the valley floor at least one day every month of the summer. The road to the trailhead is often covered by avalanche debris until early June and the trail to the Kain Hut will likely still have snowy sections near the end of June. July usually offers easier glacier travel, but lingering snow on the higher spires, while august offers drier and warmer climbing but more problematic approaches. September is cooler and the shorter daylight becomes noticable. There is no 'magic time' for weather but statistically mid-late august holds the warmest and driest weather.

General Weather Patterns. Most weather in western Canada comes from the Pacific. Weather from the southwest is generally warm and wet while a northwest flow is commonly associated with a cooler, more stable airmass.

Lightning. Climbers have been killed by lightning in the Bugaboos. Intense electrical storms are common throughout the season but tend to be more severe in July and early August. This is most often caused by warm air from the valleys to the west rising and condensing. As it meets cooler air and travels east towards the spires, the effect is compounded by the lifting of the airmass over the tall peaks of the Howser Towers, quickly pushing it to its threshold. The cumulative effect is a very serious and quick moving storm with intense lightning often accompanied by snow or hail. These storms usually start mid-afternoon and can last until late evening at which time they are no longer being fuelled by warm valley air. This, combined with the fact that it is difficult to see approaching weather from most of the routes in the spires, make it important to get a very early start. It is important to note that lightning storms associated with frontal weather can be expected at any time of the day. Read the forecast!

Rarely do trips to the Bugaboos consists of only sunshine. There are many things to do in and around the spires as well as down in the valley to keep busy during bad weather. Nowadays, the hut custodians get regular weather forecasts via satellite phones, which can help somewhat with strategy and planning.

The following list describes things to do around the Spires. It is important to note that many of the scrambles in the Bugaboo Glacier Peaks and the Eastern Spires can be great mediocre-weather day objectives, but be careful of lightning and slippery lichen.

◆ Rest, write, read, play cards, sort gear, share stories, read the hut log and share route information with other climbers.

◆ Boulder or top-rope around the hut and Applebee Camp.

◆ Climb any of the general mountaineering routes in the Bugaboo Glacier Peaks (page 89) or the *Pigeon Feathers Traverse* (page 99)

◆ Circumnavigate Bugaboo Spire by climbing up the Bugaboo–Snowpatch Col then down the Vowell and back over the Bugaboo–Crescent Col. The view of the north face is inspiring.

◆ Circumnavigate Pigeon and Snowpatch Spire via the Bugaboo and upper Vowell glaciers. (Good visibility helps for this one)

◆ Hike to Cobalt Lake (page 140) then onto Black Forest Ridge and down the Cobalt Lake Trail (page 24) to the road. From here, hike back to the hut via the climbers trail. A map is helpful. This trip can also be done in reverse.

◆ Practice rock rescue on the big boulder outside the hut, or crevasse rescue on the Bugaboo Glacier.

◆ Hike out and drive to Radium Hot Springs for a soak and a shower at the hot-pools and for pizza and beer or to get more food supplies for climbing.

◆ There is a lot of good mountain biking on the many established trails in and around Golden and Invermere.

◆ Go rockclimbing elsewhere. It is often drier around the Banff/Canmore area (page 36).

◆ Go check out Banff for a couple of days.

Often, when the weather is too wet to climb in the Bugaboos, it is favourable enough at some of the nearby crags to kill a few hours before returning to the spires. However, there are several great rockclimbing areas in western Canada, most of which have their own guidebooks for easy reference. Many are conveniently situated on route to the Bugs and make for a nice stop over along the way.

If driving **from the Calgary area** there are several great limestone and quartzite sport and multi-pitch climbing centres. The three crags listed below are described in *Bow Valley Rock* by Chris Perry and Joe Josephson and *Bow Valley Sportclimbs*, by John Martin and Jon Jones both published by Rocky Mountain Books. www.rmbooks.com. There is also a lot of classic alpine climbing in the Rockies, information on which can be found in *Selected Alpine Climbs of the Canadian Rockies* by Sean Dougherty (Rocky Mountain).

Yamnuska. Close to Calgary and about a four-hour drive from the Spires is the limestone face of Yamnuska. 'Yam' is home to over 70 routes between 3 and 12 pitches long.

Banff and Canmore. A four-hour drive from the Bugaboos, there is an abundance of limestone sportclimbing in Cougar Canyon and Grassi Lakes and long multi-pitch climbing on the East End Of Rundle and Ha-Ling Peak.

Lake Louise. A four-hour drive from the Bugaboos, the Back of the Lake crag has awesome quartzite cragging in a spectacular setting.

If driving **from the Vancouver area**, there are two significant climbing destinations along the way. Neither one is located on the direct route to the Bugaboos but both can be reached with minor detours.

Squamish. Famous for its perfect granite and long multi-pitch climbs, Squamish is a great place to warm up before heading to the Spires. Located one hour north of Vancouver and twelve hours from the Bugaboos. See *The Climbers Guide to Squamish* by Kevin McLane, from Elaho Publishing www.elaho.ca.

Skaha. Located south of the Trans-Canada Highway near the city of Penticton in the Okanagan Valley and a seven-hour drive from the Spires. Skaha is a sport climbing area famous for its warm dry conditions and is a great place to wait out foul weather on the way to the Bugaboos. *Skaha Rockclimbs* by Howie Richardson is the guidebook, available through Elaho Publishing www.elaho.ca.

Winter generally brings a whole new crowd to the Bugaboos. The world famous sport of heli-skiing started here in 1965 and has been going strong ever since. Ski touring is slowly gaining popularity in the Spires as they are commonly used as the starting point for the well-known Bugaboos to Rogers Pass ski traverse. Most parties take ten to fourteen days to complete this tour, which is described in Chic Scott's book *Summits and Icefields* published by Rocky Mountain Books. www.rmbooks.com

Winter access is difficult as the road does not get ploughed and either snowmobiles or helicopters are required. For these reasons, winter climbing in the area has never really caught on. Most, but not all of the peaks have had winter ascents over the years but difficulty and cost of access in the winter has discouraged most potential traffic. Of particular note are the first winter ascents of the *Beckey–Chouinard* on the South Howser Tower in 1982 by Scott Flavelle and Phil Hein, the first winter ascent of the *Northeast Ridge* of Bugaboo Spire in 1985 by Joe Buszowski and Bernard Ehmann, and the first winter ascent of Snowpatch Spire via the *Snowpatch Route* in 1975 by Heiri Perk and Walter Renner, and via the *Kraus–McCarthy* in 1999 by Kirk Mauthner and Brad Shilling. Very little ice forms in the Spires and that which does is often the result of strong melt-freeze cycles on the sunny aspects, which often fall off a few days after they form. The most consistent ice and mixed climbing in the range is on the high, shady faces like the east face of the South Howser Tower and can often be found year-round.

The Conrad Kain Hut, although unlocked, is officially closed during the winter months due to the fact that it has been hit at least three times in its history by avalanches.

During the first ascent of the West Face of Bugaboo Spire on
August 5th 1959 Ed Cooper and Elfrida Pigou discovered old
leather climbing boots and a few human bones. They were thought
to be the remains of the sole missing person from a lightning strike
accident just below the summit in 1948.

Guidebooks are only as good as the information provided by climbers, and one of the the hardest parts of guidebook writing is trying to decipher ambiguous route information. Climbers are often frustrated by guidebooks that lead them astray or confuse them, so for the sake of future Bugaboo climbers, here is a guide for submitting new route, or revised route information, that hopefully will help avoid confusion in the future.

Traditionally, climbers have recorded new route information in the Kain Hut scrapbook, but on more than one occasion it has gone missing, so in addition to writing it up in the scrapbook, please e-mail information to thebugaboos@yahoo.com and/or mail photos and information to Chris Atkinson P.O.Box 1115, Squamish, British Columbia Canada V0N 3G0. Updated information to the Bugaboos will be displayed on the Bugaboo link at www.elaho.ca.

♦   First ascent information including full names of the climbers, date, complete grade and route name.

♦   Written overview to the climb listing the peak, geographic location, relationship to other climbs and a general description of the type of climb it is as well as times for the approach, the climb and descent and the number and location of any bivouacs.

♦   Pitch by pitch description including grade and length.

♦   A line drawing of the route including pitch grade, length and belays, the relationship to other climbs and the position of any bivouacs.

♦   A photo with the route marked on it including bivouacs, belays and pitch grade and length. A good scan or photocopy of the relevant photos in the guidebook works well.

♦   Contact information for the first ascent party.

♦   Reference to any publications that will contain relevant information on the route.

Once a climb has been put up it is part of the climbing community and climbing history and sharing that information is a good service to fellow climbers. So in advance we thank all the future contributors for their generosity and effort.

Aboriginal peoples known as the Ta-Na-Ha, were the first to come to the Bugaboo area. They were part of the Kootenai Nation and would have used the surrounding area during their seasonal food gathering and spiritual ceremonies.

The Miners. The first non-native people to enter the Bugaboo area were the gold prospectors in the late 1800s. The first claim was in Bugaboo Pass, immediately south of the main spires, in 1891 and sparked a short two year gold rush. No gold was ever found and most claims were abandoned after only a few years. Limited prospecting occurred in the area through the 1930s with additional activity in the 1940-50s, mostly for copper. The last activity was in the early 1970s with test drilling in Bugaboo Pass.

The spires were originally known as the Nunatuks or the Spillimacheen Spires. It is thought that the Bugaboo name stems from the old mining term Bugaboo that describes a promising but elusive motherload that never panned out.

The Loggers. Along with the miners came the first loggers into the area in the 1930s. Their roads were pushed far up into Bugaboo creek quite early on and were instrumental in allowing climbers relatively easy access into the spires. Logging continues today in most of the valleys surrounding the Bugaboos.

The Climbers. Although glimpsed from the Rockies and from Rogers Pass in the Selkirks, the climbing potential of the Bugaboos wasn't uncovered until 1910 when Conrad Kain, a young Austrian immigrant, entered the area while working as the mountain guide for the Wheeler–Longstaff–Harmon survey expedition. This was the start of Conrad's legacy in the Bugaboos. 1911 saw Kain solo many of the Septet peaks to the south, and after his ascent of Mount Robson, the highest peak in the Canadian Rockies, in 1913 he returned to the Bugaboos for his 1916 tour de force. Kain, accompanied by Albert and Bess MacCarthy, Henry Frind and the Vincents made first ascents of many of the Bugaboo Glacier Peaks, North Howser Tower, the highest peak in the area, and Bugaboo Spire, which he considered his greatest achievement. Kain was to make three more trips into the area before his death in 1935, with Peter Kaufman and J. Monroe Thorington, doing first ascents of Marmolata, Crescent Spire and peaks as far away as the Conrad Group. The style in which Conrad guided these climbs was impeccable, fast, light and bold.

The 1960s. The next major wave of climbers came during the explosion of Yosemite climbing around 1960 and included Fred Beckey, Yvon Chouinard, Layton Kor, Ed Cooper and Brian Greenwood. This era saw first ascents of most of the major walls and was the turning point for the Bugaboos, with hard free climbing and bigwall techniques brought to the alpine, epitomised by Fred Beckey and Yvon Chouinard's ascent of the southwest buttress on South Howser Tower, as with Kain's ascents, in the best and boldest of style.

The 1970s. Next to come were the likes of Chris Jones, Galen Rowell, Hugh Burton and Steve Sutton who pushed the edge further with their huge routes on the west face of North Howser Tower. This was the start of the age of the longest and hardest routes in the most remote areas. As the 1970s wore on, free climbing standards were pushed way up by climbers such as Art Higbee, David Breashers, Eric Weinstein, Alex Lowe and Hugh Herr, with routes like *McTech Arete* and *Sunshine Crack*. And Yosemite-like routes such as Darrel Hatten's *Tom Egan Memorial* were put up. The 1970s also saw the start of the first recreational climbers coming to climb the standard and classic routes on the main spires. At the same time a resurgence of traditional guiding began in the Bugaboos with Canadian Mountain Holidays' (CMH) Boulder Camp Climbing Schools as well as independent guides bringing clients into the area.

The 1980s. More and more strong climbers began to filter in and fill in the gaps on the faces. The first winter ascents began to happen, as well, with Joe Buszowski and Bernhard Ehmann's ascent of Bugaboo Spire's *Northeast Ridge* and Scott Flavelle and Phil Hein's ascent of the *Beckey–Chouinard* on South Howser Tower.

The 1990s. The late 1990s saw renewed enthusiasm and another wave of hard first ascents taking place. The east faces of Bugaboo and Snowpatch Spires and more notably the west faces of the Howser Towers and the Pigeon Feathers saw great activity. Long, technical and bold new routes and first free ascents were put up by climbers such as Kennan Harvey, Topher Donahue and Patience Gribble, Todd Offenbacher, Mark Synott, Jerry Gore, Warren Hollinger, Cameron Tague, Eric Greene, Jonny Copp, Mike Pennings, Craig Luebben, Nils Davis and Guy Edwards. Most notable were Guy Edwards and Micah Jessup's free ascent of the complete south face of Snowpatch Spire and Topher Donahue and Kennan Harvey's free ascent of *All Along the Watchtower* on the west face of North Howser Tower. As well, Sean Isaac, Brian Webster and Scott Semple were not only putting up wall routes but produced two long and sustained mixed lines on the Howser Towers. Meanwhile the Minaret on South Howser Tower saw it's first free ascent by Heidi Wirtz and Lizzy Scully in 2002 and the south face of Snowpatch saw a bold winter attempt by Kirk Mauthner and Brad Shilling.

by Hans Gmoser

The first time I saw the Bugaboos was from the summit of Mount Verendrye in July 1952. Seven years later I started spending 4 weeks there each summer, climbing with clients, and I often wondered what the place would look like in the winter. Although glaciation was heavy, I didn't think the skiing would be that great.

My curiosity got the better of me in the spring of 1964 and I organized a one-week ski touring trip to the Bugaboos. We pushed and cajoled my VW station wagon up the road and when things got really bad we proceeded by ski doo. The night was spent on the road, and the next day we made it to the Stone&Gillis Lumber Camp which Jim Stone had kindly invited us to use. After another night we drove the ski doo a little further up the valley towards the glacier, shouldered our packs and began to ski up the tongue of the Bugaboo Glacier. It was a beautiful day, so we dropped our packs and headed towards the peak of Anniversary. As we climbed higher I was spell bound not just by the incredible scenery but also by the many places one could ski. By the time we reached the summit, I was convinced that this would be the place to try skiing with a helicopter.

A year later on April 4th 1965, having made arrangements with Jim to use his camp again, I returned with a group of 6 skiers for one week of Heli-Skiing followed by another group of 12 from Boston. We had a 3-seater Bell B-1 helicopter. The pilot, Jim Davies, and two passengers sat on the same bench, a huge bubble gave an unobstructed view of the mountains, and the slow rate of climb (but for us it seemed spectacularly fast) gave plenty of time to drink it all in and pick a route for the descent.

Hans Gmoser

Every morning Jim and I would consult the 1:50,000 maps to see where we might fly. Once in the air I would point to a peak and Jim would either nod his head or point to another peak. If we both nodded at the same peak he would land. Before landing I would ask him where he would pick us up. He'd bank the helicopter into a turn, survey the valley below and then point to a clearing. Once out of the helicopter and once he had brought up the rest of the party, we were on our own until we reached that clearing.

The two weeks were so impressive that 70 skiers came the next year and we used the lumber camp for 6 weeks. The year following we had a 10-week season with 150 skiers, and everyone urged me to build a lodge.

This would be a huge change from how I had operated for the last 12 years. I had no investments and no debt. If I had a place to sleep at night and wasn't hungry, then the world was in order as far as I was concerned. Now I was getting advice from all kinds of people and I knew I would have to borrow, what were for my partner Leo Grillmair and me, huge sums. To make a go now took more than not just being hungry when you went to bed!

Philippe Delesalle, an architect from Calgary, a long time friend and skiing and climbing companion, created the design for the lodge. We wanted it to be comfortable, but also simple and rustic. I thought that there should be showers inside and toilets outside. Fortunately there were enough people who thought differently and they convinced me that the toilets belonged inside.

For financing, I chose a strong proposal that imposed some fiscal discipline on us. This was a very important element for a financial illiterate. We started construction in June 1967 and the lodge opened in February 1968. In the finishing days of the construction we worked day and night to get the place finished on time.

Although very simple by today's standards, the lodge was a huge success. 260 skiers came as guests in the first winter, and we quickly realized that the lodge was too small and basic. There were just three double rooms and everyone else slept in dorm rooms. For the first year many couples thought this was a hoot. Nancy Greene spent her honeymoon in a 6-bed dorm! But before too long people wanted more privacy.

In the spring of 1969 we began construction on the first addition of Bugaboo Lodge. The addition doubled the size of the lodge. We put in some private rooms and moved the toilets and showers to the top floor so there was no longer any need to traipse down the stairs in the middle of the night.

Prior to constructing the lodge I had applied to lease 40 acres of Crown Land from the British Columbia Government. They finally gave us 10 acres with an option to purchase it as soon as the lodge was built. We exercised this option and applied for more land to allow us to build a staff house. Eventually we ended up with 30 acres.

When Heli-hiking started in the Cariboos in 1978 we immediately felt that this was something we should also do in the

Bugaboos, so in the summer of 1979 we started a third addition. We added a few rooms with private baths, got rid of the dormitories, and added a larger dining room and kitchen.

Around Bugaboo Lodge the grounds were constantly being improved. When we got the property in 1967 it was the site of an abandoned sawmill. It actually looked as though a war had been fought on it. Logs and sawdust piles everywhere! Bit by bit the logs were all cleaned up, the sawdust piles bulldozed down, grass and trees seeded everywhere, a pond created with walkways and stone borders.

In 1985 we added a new spa building and while the atmosphere of the lodge charmed everyone, people's expectations changed and before long there was far more demand for rooms with ensuite facilities than we could provide. 1987 saw the fourth addition to the Lodge. It was a huge undertaking, adding more rooms with private baths, even space for a few single rooms; a larger and very modern kitchen, spacious bar and dining room, and a new entrance all gave the lodge a totally new feel. Along with all these additions came improvements to the fuel storage facilities, to keep them abreast of ever more stringent regulations. The same goes for sewage and wastewater treatment. All these are of great concern in such an area.

For me personally it is very gratifying to see that those who have followed after me have been meticulous in their upkeep of the lodge and its surroundings and have continuously improved the place.

Leo Grillmair and his wife Lynn, in the mid 1970s at Bugaboo Lodge.

The grading system within this guide incorporates several levels of assessment included on the route-line for each climb.

Alpine Grade: This is based on the European alpine grading system, which rates the overall seriousness of the route, including all objective and subjective elements. It expresses an engagement level that takes into account psychological and physical commitment, magnitude, hazards and time required as well as technical difficulties (page 46-47).

Technical Grade: This utilizes the Yosemite Decimal System (YDS), the Water Ice Grade (Wi), and in a few cases the Mixed Grade (M). It rates the pure technical difficulties of the climb.

3rd Class. Scrambling, where a rope is not normally used. Exposure moderate with a low commitment factor.

4th Class: The tricky middle ground between scrambling unroped and fully-belayed low-5th technical climbing. Often with intimidating exposure, using short-roping technique or running belays.

5th Class: The standard Yosemite Decimal System grades (YDS), are used in this guide to rate the technical nature of the climb. Because of the subjective nature of climbing in the alpine and a common lack of well-travelled information, the ratings of 5.10 and above are divided into three groups only; 5.10-, 5.10, 5.10+.

A0-A4: Aid climbing using all means. A0 (fixed gear) to A4, and are 'old-style', ie., not modern New Wave ratings.

C1-C3: Clean aid (C1–C3), where no hammers are used to make placements. Climbs are usually done with only cams and wires. Fixed gear is often present.

Wi2-Wi4: Water Ice (Wi) grade. Wi3 is steep, straightforward climbing using two tools and is often the grade of the steep ice between bergshrunds and the rock. Wi4 is steep to vertical ice and is often the grade of the convoluted ice found in the gullies and chimneys in the Bugaboos.

Mixed: Mixed Climbing (M) grade. Used on only three routes. It effectively denotes dry tooling techniques were employed on the first and only ascent or, as with the *Big Hose*, are common practice. The following is a comparison of how strenuous an M grade may feel. M4=5.8, M5=5.9, M6=5.10, M7=5.11.

Time: This gives a relative time frame for each route. Times are usually round trip from the Kain Hut Basin or a logical camp and are given for the return trip camp to camp. For the Vowells, times are for the climb and descent only and do not include the approaches. They are relative to a party of two, competent at that grade. For day climbs it is stated in hours whereas for multi-day routes, it is described as the number of bivys usually required. This is a very relative means of measurement as some climbers experience unplanned bivys on routes commonly done in a day while others are doing one day ascents of multi-day wall routes.

Length: The length for technical, pitched out climbing is given as the number of pitches. This is a relative number as some parties may run out a 60m rope on every pitch and others may belay more often. The newer climbs tend to have longer pitches and there for fewer. For the less technical climbs the route length is given in metres which represents the vertical relief between the base of the climb and the summit. It doesn't include the approach or glacier travel, which in some cases can be more demanding than the actual climb.

Beware that many of the grades in this book are based on limited information and may not be exact. A number of climbs from the 1970s were traditionally under-graded and much of the old fourth class involves what we'd consider today to be low- and sometimes mid-fifth class climbing.

International Grading Systems Compared

Yosemite	French	German	British			Australian
5.9	5c	6	5a			18
5.10a	6a	6+		E1		19
5.10b	6a+	7-	5b		E2	20
5.10c	6b	7				20
5.10d	6b+	7	5c			21
5.11a	6c	7+		E3		21
5.11b			6a		E4	22
5.11c	6c+	8-				22
5.11d	7a	8		E5		23
5.12a	7a+	8+	6b			24
5.12b	7b	9-			E6	25
5.12c	7b+	9				26
5.12d	7c	9	6c	E7		27
5.13a	7c+	9+				27
5.13b	8a	10-	7a			28
5.13c	8a+	10		E8		29

F   **Easy**   *Facile*

Very easy climbs with minimal hazards, typically scrambles, steep walking or easy glacier travel. Commonly Third Class.

PD   **Not Very Difficult**   *Peu Difficile*

Can be considered an introductory level for novice climbers, with third and fourth class rockclimbing, reaching into low-fifth class and presenting relatively low hazard. Long climbs, or exposed snow routes generally not exceeding 45°.

AD   **Fairly Difficult**   *Assez Difficile*

This grade demands competence at all aspects of alpine terrain and technique. The main difficulties are often considerable amounts of fourth class and low-fifth class, but shorter climbs can commonly reach up to 5.7. The AD grade covers many ice climbs up to 50°, knife-edge ridges and mixed climbing.

D   **Difficult**   *Difficile*

Significant undertakings for experienced climbers, climbs at this grade demand at least the same terrain competence as AD routes, but also higher technical skills on rock and ice. From long, consistently fourth to mid-fifth climbs (*Snowpatch Route*), to shorter, non-committing climbs well into 5.10 (Snowpatch *Sunshine*), or largely fourth class but committing climbs. This tends to be the grade of the more difficult ice climbs, often involving complicated icefalls.

TD   **Very Difficult**   *Trés Difficile*

This is the defining grade of 'hard' climbs. Climbs in this grade are commonly long, with considerable amounts of mid-fifth climbing, routinely to 5.9 (*Beckey–Chouinard*), or shorter but technically much harder climbs. Short sections of aid are possible. More so than the lower grades, climbs can present significant objective danger. Some may hold considerable amounts of mixed climbing and steep ice with sections up to 70° or more. Escape opportunities can be few and descent is often 'over the top'.

ED   **Extremely Difficult**   *Extrêmement Difficile*

ED routes require an exceptionally high level of skill and experience on alpine rock and ice, including a tolerance for sustained objective danger in highly committing situations. Difficulty is commonly sustained fifth-class well into 5.10 with possible aid, or major mixed climbs encompassing ice and rock that can be vertical. Climbs where retreat may be very hazardous are commonplace. Climbs in this grade are physically punishing and routinely exceed 1000m in length. ED1, ED2, ED3, ED4, denote a range of difficulty from 'harder than TD' up to the most demanding climbs in the world.

The list below is presented to show how Alpine Grades in this guide compare with those of other well-known Canadian and American climbs. The grade definitions as detailed on pages 46, and in the 2002 Canadian Alpine Journal pp77-79, should be applicable in principle to all the climbs.

British Columbia

Mt. Combatant, *Belligerence*	ED3
Mt. Tiedemann, *South Buttress*	ED2
*Howser Towers, *Watchtower*	ED2
*Howser Towers, *Seventh Rifle*	ED2
Moby Dick, *Ohno Wall*	ED1
Mt. Combatant, *Skywalk*	ED1
Steinbok, *Edwards-Spagnut*	ED1
Mt. Waddington, *Wiessner-House*	TD+
*Howser Towers, *Beckey–Chouinard*	TD+
Moby Dick, *Boomerang*	TD+
Les Cornes, *Springbok Arete*	TD+
Slesse, *Northeast Buttress*	TD
*Bugaboo Spire, *Cooper–Gran*	TD
Mt. Clarke, *North Ridge*	TD-
Mt. Waddington, *Bravo Glacier Rt.*	TD-
Stiletto Needle, *Ice Chimneys*	TD-
Mt Combatant, *Kshatrya*	D+
Mt Grainger, *Southeast Pillar*	D+
*Snowpatch Spire, *Sunshine Crack*	D+
*Snowpatch Spire, *Surfs Up*	D
*Crescent Spire, *McTech Arete*	D-
*Snowpatch Spire, *Kraus–McCarthy*	D-
Joffre, *Central Couloir*	D-
Sir Donald, *Northwest Ridge*	D-
*Bugaboo Spire, *Northeast Ridge*	D-
Nesakwatch *Enchainment*	D-
Tantalus, *Southeast Spur*	AD+
Mt. Assiniboine, *North Ridge*	AD+
*Snowpatch Spire, *Snowpatch Rte*	AD+
Claw Peak, *West Ridge*	AD+
Alpha, *East Ridge*	AD
*Bugaboo Spire, *Kain Route*	AD
Sir Sandford, *Northwest Ridge*	AD-
*Brenta Spire, *South Ridge*	AD-
*Pigeon Spire, *West Ridge*	PD
Joffre Peak, *Southeast Face*	PD
Uto Peak, *Southwest Ridge*	PD
Wedge Mt, *Northeast Ridge*	PD

* indicates climbs in this guidebook

Canadian Rockies

Mt. Alberta, *North Face*	ED3
Mt. Robson, *Emperor Ridge*	ED2
Mt. Kitchener, *Grand Central Couloir*	ED2
Mt. Andromeda, *Andromeda Strain*	ED1
Mt. Temple, *Greenwood-Locke*	TD+
Mt. Deltaform, *Supercouloir*	TD
Mt. Edith Cavell *Nor. Face Chouinard*	TD
Mt. Robson, *North Face*	TD-
Mt. Columbia, *North Ridge*	TD-
Mt. Andromeda, *Shooting Gallery*	D+
Mt. Athabaska, *North Face*	D+
Mt. Temple, *East Ridge*	D
Mt. Alberta, *Japanese Route*	D
Mt. Robson, *Kain Route*	D-
Mt. Louis, *Kain Route*	D-
Mt. Edith Cavell, *East Ridge*	AD+
Mt. Andromeda, *Skyladder*	AD+
Mt. Athabasca, *North Ridge*	AD
Mt Lefroy, *West Face*	AD
Mt. Victoria, *Southeast Ridge*	PD+
Mt. Athabaska, *North Glacier*	PD

United States

Keeler Needle, *Harding Route*	TD+
Bear Mtn, *Northwest Buttress*	TD-
Grand Teton, *North Face*	D+
Pingora, *Northeast Face*	D+
Mt Stuart, *North Ridge Complete*	D+
Nooksack Tower, *Beckey-Schmidke*	D+
Grand Teton, *Complete Exum Ridge*	D
Mt. Rainier, *Liberty Ridge*	D
Grand Teton, *East Ridge*	D-
Mt. Redoubt, *Northeast Face*	AD+
Polemonium Peak, *V-Notch Couloir*	AD+
Mt. Baker, *North Ridge*	AD
Mt Whitney, *East Face*	AD
Forbidden Peak, *West Ridge*	AD
Pingora, *South Buttress*	AD
Mt. Rainier, *Disappointment Cleaver*	PD+
Mt. Shuksan, *Fisher Chimneys*	PD+

48 RECOMMENDED CLIMBS *page*

	#	Route	Feature				page
	1	Anniversary Glacier	Anniversary Peak	PD-	3rd	750m	92
	9	North Face-Centre	Howser Peak	PD	4th	220m	95
	13	SE Ridge	Flattop Peak	PD	4th	180m	97
20	East Ridge	Marmolata	AD-	5.6	280m	101
	26	NE Ridge	Eastpost	F	4th	180m	115
	34	Direct SE Ridge	Eastpost	PD	5.6	550m	117
	56	Lion's Way	Crescent Tower	PD+	5.6	6p	127
	62	Ears Between	Crescent Tower	AD	5.7	6p	129
	60	Thatcher Cracker	Crescent Tower	D-	5.10	7p	128
	44	Energy Crisis	Crescent Spire		5.11+	2p	122
	39	Paddle Flake Direct	Crescent Spire	D-	5.10	6p	120
	45	McTech Arete	Crescent Spire	D-	5.10-	6p	123
	67	South Ridge	Brenta Spire	AD-	4th	450m	132
	70	SE Spur	Brenta Spire	AD	5.6	410m	134
	71	Another Fine Day...	Brenta Spire	AD	5.7	9p	134
	76	Free Heeling	Northpost	D+	5.10++	5p	138
	84	Kain Route	Bugaboo	AD	5.6	450m	163
	95	Northeast Ridge	Bugaboo	D-	5.8	12p	166
	87	Cooper-Gran	Bugaboo	TD	5.11	12p	164
	89	Midnight Route	Bugaboo	TD	5.9 A3	12p	164
	121	Buckingham Route	Snowpatch	AD+	5.8	8p	200
	100	Snowpatch Route	Snowpatch	D-	5.8	17p	182
	133	Kraus-McCarthy	Snowpatch	D-	5.9	8p	204
	125	Flamingo Fling	Snowpatch	D	5.10-	10p	201
	128	Super Direct	Snowpatch	D	5.10	8p	202
	132	Wild Flowers	Snowpatch	D	5.9	8p	204
	135	Furry Pink	Snowpatch	D	5.10+	8p	205
	141	Surfs Up	Snowpatch	D	5.9	9p	207
	117	Bugaboo Corner	Snowpatch	D+	5.10-	5p	197
	118	Banshee	Snowpatch	D+	5.10	9p	197
	119	Sunshine Crack	Snowpatch	D+	5.11-	9p	198
	126	North Summit Direct	Snowpatch	D+	5.11+	8p	201
	127	Tower Arete	Snowpatch	D+	5.12-	8p	202
	113	Tom Egan Memorial	Snowpatch	TD	5.9 A3	13p	186
	115	Power of Lard	Snowpatch	TD	5.12+	10p	187
	112	Sweet Sylvia	Snowpatch	TD+	5.12	11p	186
	107	Les Bruixes Es Pen...	Snowpatch	TD+	5.10+ A3	12p	184
	144	ASTA	Snowpatch	TD+	5.9 A3	17p	215
	149	West Ridge	Pigeon	PD	5.4	500m	223
	154	Wingtip	Pigeon	D-	5.10-	8p	225
	159	Cleopatra's Alley	Pigeon	TD	5.10 A2	13p	227
	158	Cooper-Kor	Pigeon	TD-	5.10	18p	226
	198	Beckey-Chouinard	South Howser	TD+	5.10	20-22p	272
	208	Cameron's Pillar	South Howser	TD+	5.11+	8p	282
	200	Catalonian Route	South Howser	ED1	5.10 A2	20p	273

202	Bad Hair Day	South Howser	ED1	5.12-	18-24p	278
203	Italian Pilar	South Howser	ED1	5.10+ A4	14-20p	278
205	Doubting the Mill...	South Howser	ED1	5.10 A3	12-18p	279
206	Southwest Pillar	South Howser	ED1	5.10+ A3	12-18p	279
195	Fear And Desire	Central Howser	TD+	5.10 A3+	9p	269
196	Chocolate Fudge...	Central Howser	TD+	5.9 A2	10p	269
178	East Face–South Rdg	North Howser	AD	5.6	200m	245
182	Northeast Face	North Howser	AD+	5.6 Wi3	12p	248
183	North Ridge Integral	North Howser	AD+	5.4	500m	248
194	Southwest Face	North Howser	TD+	5.10 A1	16-20p	268
186	Watchtower	North Howser	ED 2	5.12-	30-34p	254
187	Armageddon	North Howser	ED 2	5.11+ (A2)	30-34p	254
188	Warrior	North Howser	ED 2	5.9 A3	30-34p	255
189	Spicy Red Beans...	North Howser	ED 2	5.12- (A1)	30-32p	255
190	Mescalito	North Howser	ED 2	5.9 A3	30-34p	255
191	Seventh Rifle	North Howser	ED 2	5.11 (A1)	30-34p	256
192	Young Men on Fire	North Howser	ED 2	5.11- A4	30-34p	256
193	Shooting Gallery	North Howser	ED 2	5.10 A2+	30-34p	257
209	Gar Wall	Pigeon Feather	D+	5.10 A2	7p	285
210	Fingerberry Jam	Pigeon Feather	D+	5.12-	5p	285
212	Lost Feather	Pigeon Feather	TD-	5.10 A3	9p	286
214	Wide Awake	Pigeon Feather	TD-	5.10+ A2	8p	287
218	Archduke Traverse	Archduke Trio	AD+	5.7	200m	334
225	South Face	Wallace	AD	5.7	7p	337
234	Southeast Ridge	Snafflehound	TD	5.10+	480m	339
235	Cuento Corto	Snafflehound		5.10	2p	339
251	Southeast Ridge	Centre Peak	AD	5.6		344
253	Count Chocula	Centre Peak	AD	5.7	7p	344
254	Love at First Bite	Centre Peak	AD+	5.9	6p	344
255	Reflections	Centre Peak	AD+	5.10-	4p	344
259	High Anxiety	West Peak	AD+	5.10-	4p	345
261	West Face	West Peak	TD+	5.8 A2	13p	345
	North Ridge	Conrad	PD-	3rd		355

Traverses

Pigeon Feathers Traverse	Pigeon Feathers	PD	4th		99
Sextet Ridge Traverse	Anniversary-Howser	PD+	4th		90
Vowells Classic Traverse	Spear to Wallace	AD	5.4		332
Petit Rochefort Traverse	Marmolata-Pigeon	AD	5.6		90
Brenta-Northpost Traverse	Brenta-Northpost	AD+	5.7		135
Howser Traverse	Howser Towers	TD+	5.10 A2		241

Mixed Routes

170	Perma Grin	South Howser	D+	M5 Wi4	7p	243
172	Big Hose	South Howser	D+	5.9 Wi4 M5	7p	243
197	Spinstone Gully	Central Howser	TD+	M7	8p	243

Chris Atkinson and Marc Piché are both Professional Mountain Guides, members of the Association of Canadian Mountain Guides (ACMG), and the International Federation of Mountain Guiding Associations (IFMGA). Over many years, they have guided extensively throughout the Bugaboos as well as internationally. Between them they spent over one thousand days in the Bugaboos and the Vowells, and have established numerous new climbs.

Chris Atkinson did his first trip into the area in 1981 when he climbed the *Northeast Ridge* of Bugaboo Spire, and spent the late 1980s stationed at the Kain Hut as the Park Ranger, gathering much of the information that was to become this guidebook. Since then he has climbed over sixty different routes in the Bugaboos and has been back many, many times climbing, photographing, and putting up new climbs.

Marc Piché first climbed in the Bugaboos in 1993 and has acquired an exhaustive knowledge of the region through several years of guiding clients on alpine rock and as a heli-ski guide from CMH's Bugaboo Lodge. Beyond his professional activities, Marc has climbed and skied extensively throughout the Vowells and Bugaboos and has explored many of the remote corners that are now detailed in this guide.

Marc Piché

Chris Atkinson

The Ten Essentials: A Bugaboo Approach.

1. Fitness.
2. A positive attitude.
3. A pocket full of power bars, gels and water.
4. Headlamps, and an early start.
5. Super lightweight mountain boots, crampons and ice axe.
6. Lightweight ropes and hardware; extra webbing for rappels.
7. Comfortable rock shoes.
8. Lightweight, slim fitting raingear; a lightweight bivy tarp.
9. Camera (for making your friends jealous).
10. This Guidebook.

One-Day Enchainments.

In the late 1980s, Peter Croft soloed the Beckey–Chouinard, the Kraus–McCarthy, the McTech Arete and the Northeast Ridge on Bugaboo before returning to the hut. Hamish Fraser was with him on the Beckey–Chouinard, but went off-route and climbed well up the then-unclimbed Lost in the Towers before he heard Croft's distant voice over to the left, enquiring what was he doing over there. He reversed the cracks and continued up the Beckey–Chouinard and the Kraus–McCarthy.

One day in 2001, Aaron Martin soloed the Northeast Ridge of Bugaboo, the West Ridge of Pigeon, the Beckey–Chouinard, and the Kraus–McCarthy.

In 2002, Jeff Hollenbaugh and Jonny Copp simul-climbed the Northeast Ridge of Bugaboo, the Beckey–Chouinard, the West Ridge of Pigeon, and the Kraus–McCarthy.

Enchainments are fun, where technical challenge takes second place to the joy of travel and climbing, and climbers of even modest ability can, with careful planning, accomplish two or three climbs in a single day. Go try.

Guide Tom Raudaschl and clients at the top of the Gendarme, *Kain Route*, Bugaboo Spire.
photo: Marc Piché

Dennis Herman, initial pitches,
Buckingham Route, Snowpatch Spire.

Dan Redford on pitch 1 of *Paddle Flake Direct*, first ascent, Crescent Spire.

Yosemite Alf,
bouldering at the Kain Hut.

Ron Quilter, au cheval on the *West Ridge* of Pigeon Spire.

Big wall approach,
East Face of Snowpatch.

Experience the Bugaboos with Canadian Mountain Holidays

Heli-Hiking and Mountaineering Adventures

Enjoy helicopter access to spectacular high alpine terrain and relax at the end of the day in our private lodge, featuring casual gourmet dining and spa amenities. Our multi-day hiking and mountaineering trips are led by professional ACMG and IFMGA guides, and tailored to accommodate all abilities and interests.

CMH HELI-HIKING

Extraordinary in Nature

1.800.661.0252

www.CanadianMountainHolidays.com

Lizzy Scully heading down to the Hut after the first ascent of *Bad Hair Day* on the Minaret of the South Howser Tower.

Cathy Dunlop, Weissner Overhang pitch of *Snowpatch Route* on Snowpatch Spire.

Technical
Leadership

*Anatomic Harness
Designs*

*Innovative Softshell
Technology*

*Thermoform Pack
Suspensions*

*Advanced Hardshell
Engineering*

ARC'TERYX
EVOLUTION IN ACTION

-www.arcteryx.com-

Climber: Scott Milton
Photo: Sandra Studer

Scott Milton in Arapiles

Kevin McLane on the second ascent of *Westside Story* on Crescent Spire. *Paddle Flake* route in background (page 79).

Kevin McLane starting the traverse from the North to the South summit of Bugaboo Spire

John Bird above *Surf's Up Ledge*, Snowpatch Spire.

Joe Benson approaching *Tail Feather Pinnacle*, first ascent, Pigeon Spire.

Gripped

The Climbing Magazine

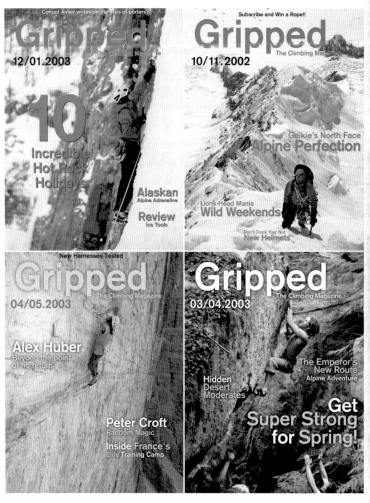

Bring the world of climbing to your door.

www.gripped.com

Marc Piché on the Kain Hut Trail

Dean Hart and Randy Atkinson
on the 2nd pitch of *Sunshine Crack*,
Snowpatch Spire North Face.

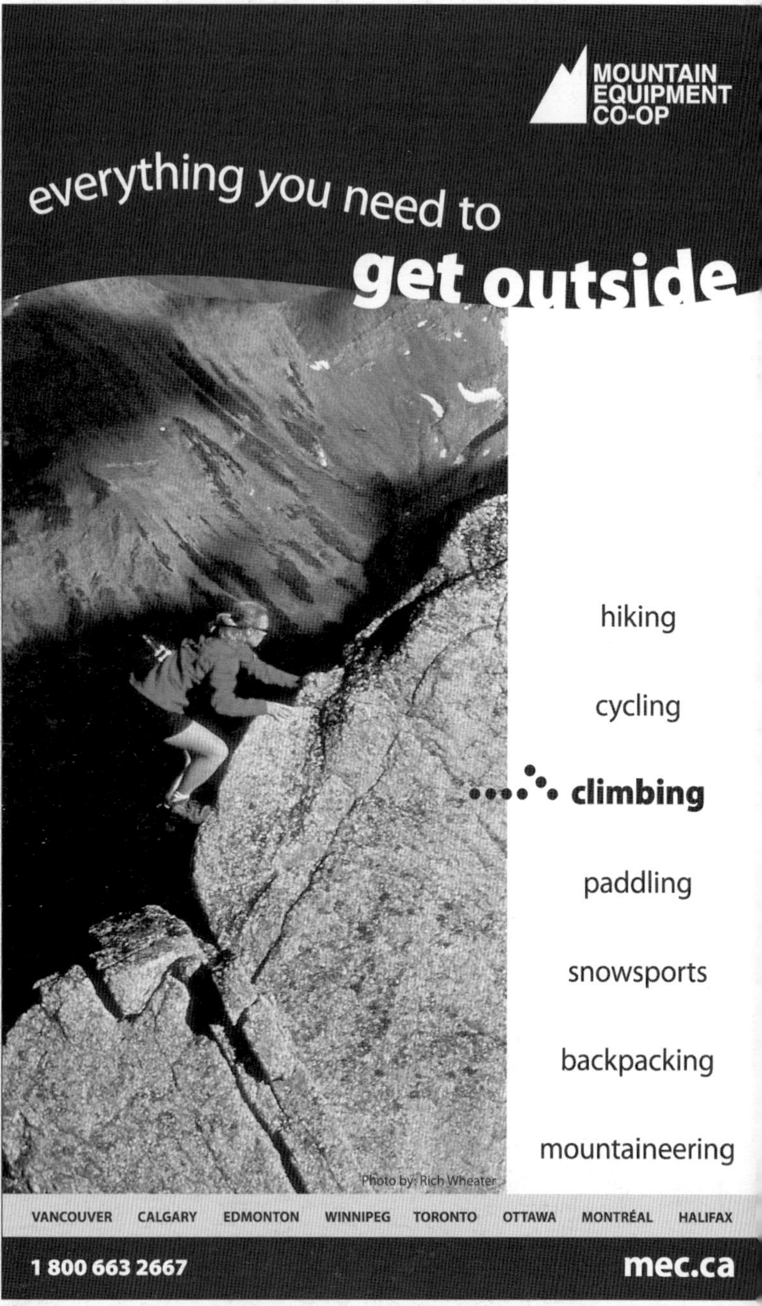

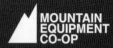

MOUNTAIN
EQUIPMENT
CO-OP
everything you need to
get outside
hiking
cycling
climbing
paddling
snowsports
backpacking
mountaineering
Photo by: Rich Wheater
VANCOUVER CALGARY EDMONTON WINNIPEG TORONTO OTTAWA MONTRÉAL HALIFAX
1 800 663 2667
mec.ca

Kevin McLane on the first pitch of *Surf's Up*, Snowpatch Spire, heading up right to the belay near the big corner.

Kain Hut

On the Kain Hut Trail.
Snowpatch Spire ahead.

The first rappel off Snowpatch
Spire down the *Krause–McCarthy*.

Approaching the crux of the Gendarme, *Kain Route*, Bugaboo Spire.

METOLIUS
metoliusclimbing.com

The Conrad Kain Hut,
Bugaboo Glacier beyond.

Applebee campsite
Bugaboo–Snowpatch col beyond.

Bennett Surveys Ltd

Legal, Land, and Engineering Surveyors

www.bennettsurveys.com

Southwest British Columbia

Bennett Surveys is a provider of survey and related services to clients ranging from individual landowners to developers of some of the most complex projects in southwestern British Columbia.

Neil Bennett

Bennett Surveys Ltd

Professional Surveyors

201 - 275 Fell Avenue

North Vancouver, BC

Canada   V7P 3R5

ph 604-980-4868

fx 604-980-5856

email neil@bennettsurveys.com

website www.bennettsurveys.com

North Vancouver, Surrey, and Squamish, BC.

Climbers on *Paddle Flake*, pitch 4, Crescent Spire. See page 63.

Upper pitches, *Sunshine Crack*,
Snowpatch Spire North Face.
climber: Derek Flett
photo: John Walsh photography.

Bergfuhrers Rudi Gertsch and Sid
Feuz (80 years of age),
West Ridge of Pigeon Spire.
photo: Marc Piché

Applebee campsite
Bugaboo Glacier
peaks beyond.

Igloos and tents at the site of the
Kain Hut, circa 1970.

The Conrad Kain Hut, overlooking the approach up Bugaboo Creek.

A rare empty moment at the Kain Hut.

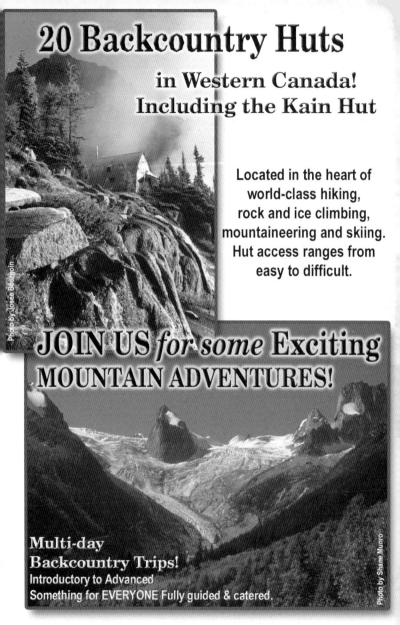

Sierra Climbing Guides

Guiding the Bugaboos, Canada, and the world.

Sean Easton
A.C.M.G. Alpine Guide

www.sierraclimb.com
Sean@sierraclimb.com
(604) 319-4657

Photo: Pat Morrow

Heidi Wirtz (l) and Lizzy Scully (r) hiking out of East Creek Basin after the first ascent of *Bad Hair Day* on the Minaret of South Howser Tower.

Chickenwire Brigade, Bugaboo car park.

Kevin McLane on pitch 3 of the
Northeast Ridge of Bugaboo Spire.

On the summit of Marmolata,
Snowpatch Spire south face beyond.

BUGABOO GLACIER PEAKS

The Bugaboo Glacier Peaks rise above the heavily glaciated and crevassed terrain that dominates the view from the Conrad Kain Hut, where the Bugaboo Glacier splits to flow around Hound's Tooth and Marmolata Peaks. The upper reaches of the glacier are bounded by Anniversary, Rock Ridge, Howser, Thimble and Flattop Peaks and by the multiple summits of the Pigeon Feathers, which in turn connect to Pigeon Spire. The south and east faces of Pigeon Spire and the south face of Snowpatch Spire descend onto the Pigeon Fork of the Bugaboo Glacier. Crossed Fish and Little Snowpatch extend west off Flattop Peak into the drainages of East Creek. The steeper western walls of the Pigeon Feathers are on the opposite side to the Bugaboo Glacier and are approached through the Bugaboo–Snowpatch Col to the Pigeon–Howser Col and down into the East Creek Basin. The small satellite bluff extending from the southeast ridge of Snowpatch Spire is known as Son of Snowpatch and separates the Bugaboo Glacier from the Kain Hut Basin.

Anniversary Peak	2947m	**Flattop Peak**	3069m
Rock Ridge Peak	3006m	**Pigeon Feathers**	2990m
Howser Peak	3082m	**Hounds Tooth**	2830m
Thimble Peak	3008m	**Marmolata**	3019m

Climbs: The climbs described in this section include all those on the peaks within the Bugaboo Glacier cirque except for the climbs on the south and east faces of Pigeon Spire and the south face of Snowpatch Spire which are described within the Central Spires section of this guidebook (page 159).

Although the peaks are of substantial elevation, the Bugaboo Glacier sits high within its cirque, hence the vertical relief of the climbs is less than the surrounding spires. Snow and ice run high on most of the faces and all the approaches involve extensive glacier travel. For these reasons most of the climbs are of the mountaineering variety, with the technical rock sections being short and stepped. The rock of the central and western part of the cirque is of good quality but deteriorates drastically along Rock Ridge and Anniversary Peaks. Early in the season the glacier travel is easy and straight-forward but by August the bergshrunds that ring the Marmolata–Pigeon Basin become challenging to cross.

Traditionally the Bugaboo Glacier Peaks were visited when poor weather kept climbers from the main spires, encouraged by the lower commitment and easier technical grades. The mountaineering style of climbing on these peaks makes a nice addition to the Bugaboo climbing experience, especially in good weather.

Approaches and Descents. The approaches and descents for the Bugaboo Glacier Peaks are decribed in the intro to each peak.

Anniversary Peak ... page opposite		**Flattop Peak** .... page 97
Rock Ridge Peak ... page opposite		**Pigeon Feathers** .. page 98
Howser Peak .... page 94		**Hounds Tooth** ...... page 100
Thimble Peak .... page 96		**Marmolata** .... page 101

Note that the time given on the route-line for the climb; ie. (5-7h), indicate **the required time for a round trip ascent from the Kain Hut**. For those based at Applebee Dome, add about one hour.

Grand Traverses and Enchainments: The Bugaboo Glacier peaks, because of their interconnecting ridge–lines and high cols lend themselves well to enchainments and grand traverses. Most of the first ascents were done in this manner. It is conceivable that a very strong party could link all of the Bugaboo Glacier summits in a single day. Many variations are possible but two traditional combinations exist.

Sextet Ridge Traverse: Conrad Kain guided this traverse on all of the first ascents of the peaks. It ascends the *Anniversary Glacier Route* of Anniversary Peak and then follows the ridge over Rock Ridge Peak down its *Southwest Ridge* and up the *East Ridge* of Howser Peak. The *Northwest Ridge* is descended to complete the traverse. It is mostly third class travel.

Petit Rochefort Traverse: This is a wonderful outing, an enchainment that links the summits of Hound's Tooth, Marmolata, the Southeast and East Pigeon Feathers and Pigeon Spire. It offers varied, aesthetic climbing on both rock and ice at a moderate, technical level.

Start with the *Northwest Ridge* of Hound's Tooth and continue to the summit of Marmolata via the *East Ridge*. Descend the *West Ridge* to gain the Pigeon Feathers. Traverse the Southeast and East Pigeon Feathers and gain the *West Ridge* of Pigeon Spire. Climb and descend Pigeon's *West Ridge*. To complete the loop, descend the upper Vowell Glacier to gain the rappel route down the Snowpatch–Pigeon Col Icefall. This leads back to the flats of the Pigeon Fork of Bugaboo Glacier where the route began.

Anniversary and Rock Ridge Peaks   2947m; 3006m

These are the glaciated, red and black rock summits easily viewed through the front windows of the Conrad Kain Hut. They make up the southern retaining wall of the Bugaboo Glacier as it descends out of its high cirque down to the terminus. Anniversary Peak is connected to Rock Ridge and Howser Peaks to the west via a long continuous ridge line that is the dividing height of land between the north and south forks of Bugaboo Creek.

Approach: There are two approaches to these peaks.

(1) **The Anniversary Glacier approach** involves descending from the Conrad Kain Hut to the flats of the Bugaboo Glacier and then gaining the hanging glacier on the northeast side of the peak, which is easily viewed from the hut. This is the traditional approach to start the Grand Traverse of the Bugaboo Glacier Peaks.

(2) **The second approach is via The Pigeon Fork** of Bugaboo Glacier and through the Marmolata–Pigeon Feathers Col to the upper Bugaboo Glacier Cirque. From the Conrad Kain Hut follow faint and discontinuous trails from behind the largest boulder beside the hut up towards the toe of Son of Snowpatch. From there, follow the base of the rock slabs down around the toe to pick up snow and ice. Ascend the right side of the glacier to avoid icefalls and gain the flat glaciated basin below the impressive south face of Snowpatch and the east face of Pigeon. From here the route to the Marmolata–Pigeon Feathers Col can be seen. A large continuous bergshrund lies below the col, usually easiest to cross at its far left side where it runs into the rock wall of Marmolata Peak. From the Marmolata–Pigeon Feathers Col, easy glacier walking leads across the upper Bugaboo Glacier Cirque.

Descent: The standard descent from Anniversary Peak is along and up the intervening ridge that connects to Rock Ridge Peak and down the *Southwest Ridge* to the Rock Ridge–Howser Col and the upper Bugaboo Glacier Cirque. The bergshrund below the col is easily crossed throughout the season on normal years. From the upper Bugaboo Glacier Cirque, the Marmolata–Pigeon Feathers Col is crossed to access the Pigeon Fork of the Bugaboo Glacier. The descent continues under the south face of Snowpatch Spire and down around the toe of Son of Snowpatch to the Kain Hut cirque. The bergshrund on the Pigeon Fork side of the Marmolata–Pigeon Feathers Col can often be large and continuous and is usually most easily crossed on the Marmolata side up against the rocks. The Anniversary Glacier Route can also be reversed and is often used as the ski touring descent.

1 Anniversary Glacier Route PD- 3rd   (7-8h) 750m *106*

*Conrad Kain, Henry Frind, Albert MacCarthy, Bess MacCarthy, Mrs George Vincent, John
Vincent, August 1916*   *CAJ 8:17*

The Anniversary Glacier is the hanging glacier seen directly south from the
Conrad Kain Hut and above the flats of the Bugaboo Glacier. It sits in its own
basin left of the summit of Anniversary Peak and although it no longer runs
into the Bugaboo Glacier, early season snows still link the two. This is a
popular ski touring route.

    To reach the Anniversary Glacier follow the trail from the Conrad Kain
Hut down to Boulder Campsite. Cross the moraine ridges, rock slabs and
early season snow–slopes to gain the Bugaboo Glacier beneath the bulk of
the main icefall. Descend down to the flatter section of the Bugaboo Glacier,
which is crossed to beneath the Anniversary Glacier. Snow–slopes, scree and
moraine walls are ascended to gain the actual glacier. The easiest line varies
with the snow cover but generally runs from below the right side of the glacier
to gain the ice on the far left side. Climb the glacier and exit where the
bergshrund allows. A straightforward ridge can be followed to the summit.
Rock becomes exposed on the upper ridge later in the season.

    To descend, either reverse the *Anniversary Glacier Route* or traverse
over Rock Ridge Peak and down the *Southwest Ridge* to gain the Rock
Ridge–Howser Col and the upper Bugaboo Glacier Cirque.

2 Anniversary Chute   PD 3rd   (7-8h) 650m *106*

Ed Cooper, Art Gran, Roman Sadowy, August 1959   *CAJ 43:75*

The Anniversary Chute is the hanging snowfield immediately right of the
Anniversary Glacier and leads directly to the summit. First climbed by Cooper,
Gran and Sadowy in August of 1959, today it sees more ski descents than
ascents.

    Approach as per the Anniversary Glacier Route. From the flats of the
Bugaboo Glacier climb directly up to the Anniversary Chute which is more
of a crescent shaped snow–slope than a conventional chute. In early season
the climb is snow from bottom to top and is straightforward, reaching 45°
near the top. The slope can be exited left to gain the upper ridge of the
Anniversary Glacier Route or a steeper gully can be followed directly to the
summit. Later in the season the bottom and top of the slope melts out to
become poor quality, third class rock.

    To descend reverse the route, descend the *Anniversary Glacier Route*
or traverse over Rock Ridge Peak to the Rock Ridge–Howser Col and the
upper Bugaboo Glacier Cirque.

*Anniversary and Rock Ridge peaks were first traversed in August 1916
by the Kain–Frind–MacCarthy-Vincent party during a trip that
included their first ascents of North Howser Tower and Bugaboo Spire.*

ANNIVERSARY PEAK // ROCK RIDGE PEAK

Rock Ridge Peak

3 Southwest Ridge   PD- 3rd   (6-8h) 150m *108*

Conrad Kain, Henry Frind, Albert MacCarthy, Bess MacCarthy, Mr. & Mrs George Vincent, August 1916

CAJ 8:23

The *Southwest Ridge* runs from the Rock Ridge–Howser Col to the summit of Rock Ridge Peak. This ridge continues down from the summit northeastward to connect to a flat section of ridge with Anniversary peak.

The upper Bugaboo Glacier Cirque is reached via the Pigeon Fork of the Bugaboo Glacier and through the Marmolata–Pigeon Feathers Col. From the Conrad Kain Hut follow faint and discontinuous trails from behind the largest boulder beside the hut up towards the toe of Son of Snowpatch. From its base of Son of Snowpatch follow the base of the rock slabs down around the toe to pick up snow and ice. To avoid the icefalls ascend the right side of the glacier to the flat glaciated basin below the south face of Snowpatch Spire and the east face of Pigeon Spire. From here the route to the Marmolata–Pigeon Feathers Col can be seen. A large continuous bergshrund exists below the col and is usually easiest to cross on its far left side where it runs into the rock wall of Marmolata Peak. From the Marmolata–Pigeon Feathers Col, easy glacier walking leads across the upper Bugaboo Glacier Cirque to the Rock Ridge–Howser Col. From this col follow the ridge–crest to the summit of Rock Ridge Peak, then down the intervening ridge and across to the summit of Anniversary Peak 60m lower. This ridge is composed of poor quality rock and is best climbed in early season when snow covers much of the ridge.

To descend, reverse the route back to the upper Bugaboo Glacier Cirque. As an alternative, the *Anniversary Glacier Route* can be descended down to the flats of the Bugaboo Glacier and on up to the hut.

4 Northwest Ridge   PD 4th   (6-8h) 190m *110*

First ascent unknown

This is the rocky spur which runs from the upper Bugaboo Glacier Cirque to the summit. From the upper cirque, easily gain the toe of the ridge and follow it to summit.

5 North Face   PD 3rd   (6-8h) 200m *110*

First ascent unknown

The north face is the snow and ice face that is easily viewed from the Conrad Kain Hut. From the upper Bugaboo Glacier Cirque easily gain the base of the face. Cross, or end run, the bergshrund and climb snow or ice. A final short rock step can be climbed directly or bypassed on either the right or left on snow. Anniversary Peak may also be ascended via the left edge of the face to gain the ridge between the two summits.

The Beckey–Chouinard has been climbed in under 48 hours, from Squamish to Squamish, by Sean Easton and Andrew Wexler.

Howser Peak   3082m

Howser Peak is the highest summit of the Bugaboo Glacier Peaks, not to be confused with the Howser Towers of the Western Spires, which contain the *Beckey–Chouinard* and *All Along the Watchtower* routes. Howser Peak stands as a broad snowy and glaciated peak extending southwest off the Anniversary–Rock Ridge ridgeline. It shares a lower col with Thimble Peak to the northwest. Howser Peak cannot be seen from the Conrad Kain Hut. The peak was first climbed by the Kain–Frind–MacCarthy–Vincent party during a traverse of Anniversary and Rock Ridge in August of 1916.

Approach: Approach to all the routes on Howser Peak is via the Pigeon Fork of the Bugaboo Glacier and through the Marmolata–Pigeon Feathers Col to the upper Bugaboo Glacier Cirque. From the Conrad Kain Hut follow faint and discontinuous trails from behind the largest boulder beside the hut up towards the toe of Son of Snowpatch. From the toe follow the base of the rock slabs down around the toe to pick up snow and ice. To avoid the icefalls ascend the right side of the glacier to the flat glaciated basin below the south face of Snowpatch Spire and the east face of Pigeon Spire. From there the route to the Marmolata–Pigeon Feathers Col can be seen. A large continuous bergshrund exists below the col and is usually easiest to cross on its far left side where it runs into the rock wall of Marmolata Peak. From the Marmolata–Pigeon Feathers Col, easy glacier walking leads across the upper Bugaboo Glacier Cirque.

Descent: The standard descent is down the *Northeast Ridge* to the Rock Ridge–Howser Col. From the col the upper Bugaboo Glacier Cirque is accessed. The bergshrund below the col is easily crossed throughout the season in normal years. From the upper Bugaboo Glacier Cirque the Marmolata–Pigeon Feathers Col is crossed to access the Pigeon Fork of the Bugaboo Glacier. The descent continues under the south face of Snowpatch Spire and down around the toe of Son of Snowpatch to the Kain Hut basin. The bergshrund on the Pigeon Fork side of the Marmolata–Pigeon Feathers Col can often be large and continuous and is usually easiest to cross on the Marmolata side, up against the rocks. The *Anniversary Glacier Route* can also be reversed and is usually used as the ski touring descent.

6 East Ridge   PD- 3rd   (6-8h) 220m *108*
Conrad Kain, Henry Frind, Albert MacCarthy, Bess MacCarthy, Mr. & Mrs George Vincent,
August 1916   *CAJ 8:23*

The route is the low-angled ridge crest that runs from the Rock Ridge–
Marmolata Col. As viewed from the upper Bugaboo Glacier Cirque or the
main spires it is the lefthand skyline. This was the line of first ascent of the
peak.

From the upper Bugaboo Glacier Cirque gain the Rock Ridge–Howser
Col. The bergshrund is easily crossed throughout the season in normal years.
From the col follow easy snow up the ridge to a minor rock knoll which blocks
the ridge. Seasonal snow will dictate the route over the knoll. Beyond, an
easy snow ridge leads to the summit. The upper snow ridge can be gained
directly from the upper Bugaboo Glacier via snow and ice on the north side,
thereby avoiding the rock knoll.

7 Northwest Ridge   PD 4th   (6-8h) 220m *108*
Eaton Cromwell, Paul Kaufmann. August 1930   *AAJ 1:298*

This is the steep snow ridge which runs up from the Howser–Thimble Col.
As viewed from the upper Bugaboo Glacier or main spires, it is the righthand
skyline. First climbed in August 1930 by Cromwell and Kaufman it was used
as the descent by Conrad Kain's 1916 party.

From the upper Bugaboo Glacier, the base of the route is gained at the
Howser–Thimble Col. In early season steep snow can be climbed to gain
the ridge proper which is easily followed to the summit. Once the seasonal
snow has melted the ridge becomes mostly rock. It is of poorer quality but
difficulties should not exceed fourth class.

8 North Face Right   PD 4th   (6-8h) 220m *108*
William Buckingham, Arnold Guess, Robert Page, Earle Whipple, July 1958   *Harvard 1959:21*

To the immediate left of the *Northwest Ridge* is a remnant piece of hanging
glacier that still reaches up to the ridge. Although hard to distinguish early
season it becomes apparent later on. The route climbs this to gain the
Northwest Ridge. The bergshrund is usually passed on the right. The nature
of this face is changing drastically with glacial recession.

9 North Face Centre   PD 4th   (6-8h) 220m *108*
Eric Bjornstad, Ed Cooper, July 1960   *CAJ 44:74*

Directly below the summit is a rotten rock face, and to the left of this lies an
ice bulge. The route climbs up between the two. Conditions vary widely year
to year.

In September 1994, over the course of three days on the first ascent of
Young Men On Fire, Jerry Gore and Warren Hollinger survived
unscathed from numerous heavy storms, but were finally hit by lightning
near the summit, sustaining burns and being temporarily paralysed.

Thimble Peak 3008m

Thimble Peak sits between Howser Peak to the southeast and Flattop Peak to the northwest. It's snow cover feeds Bugaboo Glacier to the northwest, Rory Creek to the south and East Creek to the northwest. Thimble Peak is hidden from view from most areas within the main Bugaboo Group.

Approach: Approach via the upper Bugaboo Glacier Cirque as per Howser Peak (page 94).

Descent: Only two routes have been climbed and either can be descended.

10 North Ridge   PD- 4th   (5-7h) 110m *109*
Eaton Cromwell, Paul Kaufmann, August 1930   *AAJ 1:299*

This is a short and straightforward climb. From the Marmolata–Pigeon Feathers Col traverse around the east side of Flattop Peak to gain the Thimble–Flattop Col. Ascend steepening snow to the summit. In the later season fourth class rock becomes exposed near the summit. To descend reverse the route, or descend the southeast side.

11 Southeast Ridge   PD- 3rd   (5-7h) 140m *109*
En Descente: Eaton Cromwell, Paul Kaufmann, August 1930   *AAJ 1:299*

This route is very similar in nature to the *North Ridge*. From the upper Bugaboo Glacier Cirque gain the Howser–Thimble Col, and ascend steepening snow to the summit. Later in the season third class rock becomes exposed near the summit. To descend reverse the route or descend the *North Ridge*.

At eight o'clock we were again roped up and set off at high speed for the pass between No's 2 and 3 [Snowpatch and Bugaboo] and reached it at 8:45, catching the last rays of the afterglow from a most brilliant, crimson sunset.

A.H. MacCarthy, Canadian Alpine Journal, 1917.

Flattop Peak　　　　　　　　　　　　　　3069m

Flattop and Thimble Peaks sit between the prominent col with Howser Peak and the wide col with the Pigeon Feathers. Flattop Peak is conspicuous due to a large radio repeater that sits on the summit. Crossed Fish and Little Snowpatch Peaks run west from Flattop's western summit.

Approach: Flattop Peak is most often approached from the Marmolata–Pigeon Feathers Col as per the approach to Howser Peak (page 94). For climbers camped in the East Creek Basin, Flattop Peak is quickly approached through the Flattop–Pigeon Feathers Col.

Descent: Descent is down the *Northeast Ridge*. In early season it is straightforward snow. By late season rock is exposed on much of the face. Descent can also be made down the *Southeast Ridge* to where it flattens then down snow to the upper Bugaboo Glacier Cirque. No rappels are established on either route.

12　Northeast Ridge–Face　　PD　3rd　　　(5-7h)　170m　*109*
Eaton Cromwell, Paul Kaufmann, August 1930　　　　　　　　　　*AAJ 1:299*

This is the triangular face that rises from the Pigeon Feathers Col and faces into East Creek. Until recently the face was snow covered year round, making it an easy climb, however as the snow has melted rock has become exposed. The difficulty of the face is hard to predict but shouldn't exceed fourth class. Beware of loose and falling rock. From the Flattop—Pigeon Feathers Col gain the base of the ridge and follow it directly to summit.

13　Southeast Ridge　　　　PD　4th　　　(5-7h)　180m　*109*
En Descente: Eaton Cromwell, Paul Kaufmann, August 1930　　　*AAJ 1:299*

This is the ridge that runs up from the Thimble–Flattop Col. The ridge rises out of the col, flattens out in the middle section and steepens again to the summit. It can be climbed in its entirety or the middle section can be gained directly from the upper Bugaboo glacier Cirque. Rock is exposed on the lower and upper ridge in late season.

Some things don't change.
Camp was reached at 8 pm and the next day we reluctantly turned our backs on the many spires whose intimate acquaintance we had not made, but with resolve to return to them at the first good opportunity.

A.H. MacCarthy, Canadian Alpine Journal, 1917.

Pigeon Feathers   2930m—2990m

The Pigeon Feathers form the headwall of the Pigeon Fork of the Bugaboo Glacier. They run from the Marmolata Col right across to the base of the West Ridge of Pigeon Spire. Officially there are three summits of the Pigeon Feathers, but more minor summits exist. On the Bugaboo Glacier side, snow runs to very near the summits of all but the west, or northernmost peak. The most impressive aspect of the Pigeon Feathers are their west faces which drop steeply into the East Creek Basin, forming a multitude of impressive faces and towers. The climbs rising from East Creek Basin are covered in the Western Spires section of the guide (page 239).

Approach: To approach the Pigeon Feathers gain the toe of Son of Snowpatch from the Kain Hut Basin (page 91). Working around the toe to pick up snow and ice and the ascent up to the glacial flats below the south face of Snowpatch Spire and the east face of Pigeon Spire. The large continuous bergshrund below the Feathers requires that the bergshrund be crossed below either the Marmolata Col or below the col between the west and east peaks near the Pigeon Feed Wall on Pigeon Spire. Alternatively the Feathers can be gained from the start of Pigeon Spire's West Ridge via the Bugaboo–Snowpatch Col and the upper Vowell Glacier approach. From the start of the *West Ridge* of Pigeon Spire descend the easy glacier to the col between the west and east feathers.

Descent: Either end of the Pigeon Feathers ridge–line can be descended onto the Pigeon Fork of the Bugaboo Glacier and followed down past Snowpatch Spire, around the toe of Son of Snowpatch, and back to the Kain Hut Basin. Bergshrunds and crevasses will dictate the route and can often bar access to large parts of the glacier. The easiest line is traditionally closer to the Marmolata side. An alternative descent through the central spires can be used if traversing south to north. From the col between the West and East Feathers ascend easy glacier to gain the start of the *West Ridge* of Pigeon Spire. From there the upper Vowell Glacier can be descended to gain the Bugaboo–Snowpatch Col and access to the Kain Hut Basin. Another alternative would be to descend the upper Vowell Glacier to gain the Snowpatch Spire side of the Snowpatch–Pigeon Icefall. A rappel route exists here which leads down rock (via bolted anchors) to gain the glacial flats at the base of the south face of Snowpatch Spire. An in-depth description can be found in the Snowpatch Spire section (page 180).

14 & 15 Southeast, and East Pigeon Feathers Traverse **

PD 4th   (5-6h)   80m   *109*

W. Doub, R.Irvin, Geoge Whitmore, September 1953   *CAJ 37:404*

The Southeast and East Feathers are easily climbed via steep snow. The classic route is to traverse the two Feathers and their minor summits from either direction. Enjoyable, moderate and varied snow-climbing is encountered. The Marmolata Col approach is used if linking this traverse to climbs of Marmolata and the upper Bugaboo Glacier Peaks. The Bugaboo–Snowpatch Col and upper Vowell Glacier approach is often used to climb the West Ridge of Pigeon Spire and then traverse the Pigeon Feathers from north to south and descend back to the Kain Hut basin via the Pigeon Fork of the Bugaboo Glacier. This makes for a circumnavigation of Snowpatch and Pigeon Spires.

West Peak (Fingerberry Tower)

16 Northeast Ridge   PD 5.4   (5-7h)   60m

W.Briggs, Peter Robinson, August 1952   *CAJ 36:99*

The west or northernmost Feather [2930m] is known as Fingerberry Tower. It sits isolated near the end of the West Ridge of Pigeon Spire. To climb its *Northeast Ridge* exit the glacier above the col with the main Feathers, close to the beginning of the *West Ridge* of Pigeon Spire. A slight descent then a steepening fourth class ridge leads to the summit of the isolated tower. Some low fifth class climbing is encountered. The view into East Creek Basin is spectacular. Descent is by downclimbing the ridge.

First Ascent Bugaboo Spire.
Conrad Kain, Albert & Beth MacCarthy, John Vincent August 1916.

Left Valley	*4:30 am*
First Summit	*12:45 am*
Second Summit	*2:40 pm*
Descent	*3:20 pm*
Returned	*8:00 pm*
Total Time	*17½ hours valley to valley, both summits.*

Note: this was achieved with no trail, the party bushwacked from the valley floor to the alpine.

Hounds Tooth   2830m

Hound's Tooth is the lower, eastern sub-peak of Marmolata, and along with Marmolata, it separates the two forks of the Bugaboo Glacier. When viewed during the final few kilometres when driving up the Bugaboo access road, it appears as a lone peak surrounded by ice and looking much more prominent than, in fact, it is.

Approach: From the Conrad Kain Hut follow faint and discontinuous trails from behind the largest boulder beside the hut up towards the toe of Son of Snowpatch. From the base of Son of Snowpatch follow the base of the rock slabs down around the toe to reach snow and ice. To avoid the icefalls ascend the right side of the glacier to the flat glaciated basin below the south face of Snowpatch Spire and the east face of Pigeon Spire. From there the route to Hound's Tooth and Marmolata can be seen. Make an ascending traverse around crevasses to gain the snow slope between the two peaks.

Descent: Descent is down the *Northwest Face* although most parties link Hound's Tooth with the *East Ridge* of Marmolata.

17 Northwest Face   PD- 3rd   (4-5h)   100m *110*
Layton Kor, William Sanders, August 1960   *CAJ 44:83*
This short outing is the standard route on the peak and pretty much the only one climbed. Gain the base of the Hound's Tooth–Marmolata Col. Cross the bergshrund at the far left side and follow snow to near the col. Third class rock leads to the summit.

18 North Face Variation   PD 5.6   (4-6h)   140m *110*
G. Marinakis, H.Marinakis August 1982
From below the bergshrund, traverse in left to reach the rock in the shallow depression of the small north face. Follow wet, mossy rock to summit. The actual line is vague but the first ascentists encountered a 5.6 chimney. Mostly fourth class.

19 Gilcrest Raabe Route   PD 4th   (4-6h)   220m *110*
J.Gilcrest, P.Raabe, August 1971
This route gains and ascends the snowpatch on the top of the east face. From the glacial flats below the south face of Snowpatch Spire traverse across the basin to access the rock just above the main icefall. Climb fourth-class rock and ledges out left and up to reach the snow. Many variations exist for exiting the glacier and gaining the bottom of the snowfield. Four pitches of snow or ice lead to the summit.

A traverse is an ascent and descent over the top 'down the other side'.

A Grand Traverse is across many peaks, typically by their via normales.

Marmolata   3019m

Marmolata and its sub-peak Hound's Tooth, make up the peak that separates the two forks of the Bugaboo Glacier. It is easily viewed from the Conrad Kain Hut, sitting above the icefall of the Pigeon Fork of Bugaboo Glacier.

Approach: as for Hounds Tooth, page opposite.

Descent: Descent from Marmolata is down the *West Ridge* Three 25m rappels are followed by 25m of downclimbing and a scramble to the Marmolata–Pigeon Feathers Col. The rappel stations are fixed pitons with webbing.

20 East Ridge *   AD- 5.6   (6-8h) 280m *111*

Conrad Kain, Eaton Cromwell, Peter Kaufmann, August 1930   *AAJ 1:298*

This enjoyable climb is the most well-travelled route, and also the line of the first ascent of the peak.

Gain the base of the snow slope between Hound's Tooth and Marmolata. Cross the bergshrund on the far left side and climb snow to gain the small notch right of the actual col. Follow the exposed ridge crest to the summit. The rock is looser on the north side. A 5.6 boulder move is encountered on the initial ridge before it flattens and another similar move occurs near the summit. The rock is otherwise classic fourth-class terrain.

21 North Face   PD 5.6   (6-8h) 280m *111*

G.Bell, D.Michael, August 1962   *AAJ 3:292*

This shadowed face holds scattered snow throughout the season, presenting broken alpine terrain with many down-sloping ledges. From the Pigeon Fork basin of Bugaboo Glacier ascend the triangular snow face directly below the summit. The first ascent line climbed over mixed terrain to gain the *East Ridge* 50m below the summit. Many variations are possible. The route is mostly fourth class, but multiple short fifth class steps will likely be encountered.

22 West Ridge–North Face   PD 5.6   (6-7h) 140m *111*

E.Gale, Rex Gibson, B.Hampsen, I.Kay, J.McDonald, A.Styles, D.Wessel, July 1946 CAJ 30:158

This is the ridge running up from the Marmolata–Pigeon Feathers Col, most often used as the descent for the *East Ridge*. The original line of ascent traversed out on the north face at the first difficulties before ascending down-sloping ledges to the summit ridge. Modern day parties will find the most aesthetic line closest to the ridge crest but the final two steps will need to be passed on the north face ledges. Originally graded fourth class, short mid fifth class sections will be found near the ridge crest.

An enchainment is the climbing of two or more peaks by routes chosen only for their aesthetic qualities, commonly done as one-day adventures.

Note: Little is known about the following south face routes, as the first ascent parties described them in vague terms.

23 South Face–West End   PD+ 5.6   ♦   (6-9h) 160m
J.Brett & ACC Party, July 1959   *CAJ43:123, AAJ 12:135*
From the Marmolata–Pigeon Feathers Col, work diagonally up the south face to a point some 60m below the summit ridge, via a series of slabs and cracks of moderate difficulty. The final open chimney in the white cliff band is 5.6.

24 South Face   PD+ 5.6   ♦   (6-9h) 220m
Gilbert Fryklund, Robert Kruszyna, August 1960   *AAJ 12:386*
This route generally follows the most prominent rib in the centre of the face, halfway between the west ridge and the southeast buttress and finishes very near the true summit. The first ascent party described it as follows: "From the upper Bugaboo Glacier cirque ascend easy ledges to wide talus covered ramp halfway up. Above ramp are two parallel cracks. Climb left crack (5.6) to flake which projects just left of crack, then move to right crack and finish pitch. Stay right of rib and complete climb by two chimneys interspersed with scrambling". 2½hr from glacier

25 Southeast Buttress   AD- 5.4   ♦   (6-10h) 300m
John Turner, M.Ward, July 1959   *AAJ 12:135*
This route lies to the right of the steepest yellow portion of the buttress and is gained by a tongue of snow of unknown size and condition. Climb three pitches to below an overhang, traverse right into a narrow gully and ascend it for about 50m to where it widens. Climb a dihedral for 10m then over an overhang on the right. Traverse left and descend 3m, to avoid another overhang. Ascend a steep slab to gain the *East Ridge* which is followed to the summit. The first ascent party took 7 hrs on the face, graded it NCCS IV and recommended it.

The summer came to an end with a trip to the Howser and Bugaboo Spires and it was in this group that we made an ascent which I found as interesting and difficult as any I have encountered in the Alps. None of my subsequent ascents in the rockies (over fifty first ascents) provided such thrills as Bugaboo Spire.

Conrad Kain, American Alpine Journal 1929-32.

MARMOLATA

MARMOLATA — EAST RIDGE

ROUTE: 20 (101).

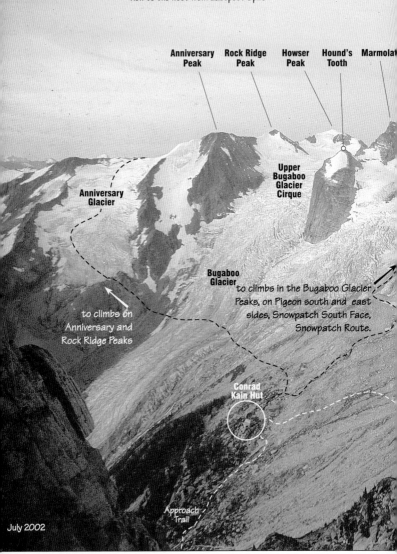

BUGABOO GLACIER PEAKS — EASTERN SIDES

view to the west from Eastpost Spire

Anniversary Peak

Rock Ridge Peak

Howser Peak

Hound's Tooth

Marmola

Upper Bugaboo Glacier Cirque

Anniversary Glacier

Bugaboo Glacier

to climbs in the Bugaboo Glacier Peaks, on Pigeon south and east sides, Snowpatch South Face, Snowpatch Route.

to climbs on Anniversary and Rock Ridge Peaks

Conrad Kain Hut

Approach Trail

July 2002

BUGABOO GLACIER PEAKS PANORMAMA

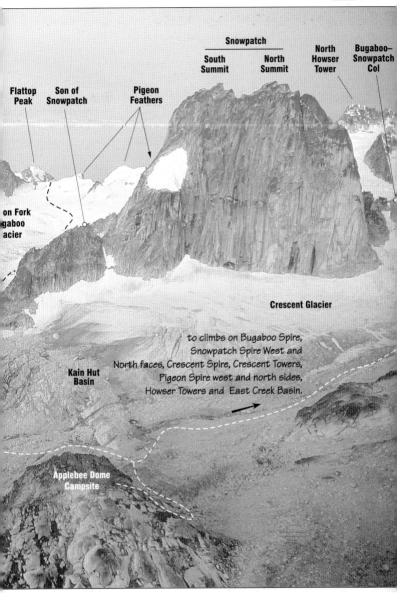

Snowpatch

South Summit **North Summit** **North Howser Tower** **Bugaboo–Snowpatch Col**

Flattop Peak **Son of Snowpatch** **Pigeon Feathers**

on Fork
gaboo
acier

Crescent Glacier

to climbs on Bugaboo Spire,
Snowpatch Spire West and
North faces, Crescent Spire, Crescent Towers,
Pigeon Spire west and north sides,
Howser Towers and East Creek Basin.

Kain Hut Basin

Applebee Dome Campsite

BUGABOO GLACIER PEAKS PANORMAMA

BUGABOO GLACIER FROM CONRAD KAIN HUT TRAIL

Frenchman
Anniversary Glacier
Anniversary Peak
Rock Ridge Peak
Upper Bugaboo Glacier Cirque
Hound's Tooth
Marmola
20
19
21
2
1
5
4
The Flats
Bugaboo Glacier
July 2002

SOUTHERN BUGABOO GLACIER PEAKS

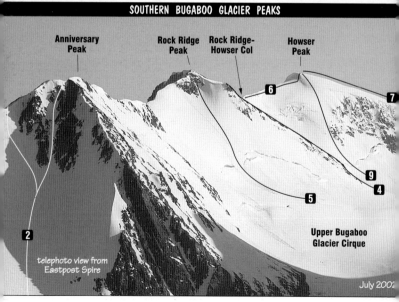

Anniversary Peak
Rock Ridge Peak
Rock Ridge-Howser Col
Howser Peak
6
7
5
9
4
2
Upper Bugaboo Glacier Cirque
telephoto view from Eastpost Spire
July 2002

ROUTES: 1 2 4 5 (92–93) 6 7 9 (95) 19 (100), 20 21 (101) 22 (101)

HOWSER PEAK — NORTH FACE

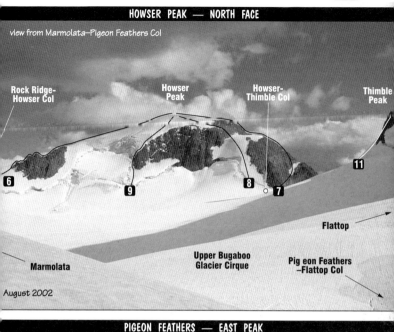

view from Marmolata–Pigeon Feathers Col

Rock Ridge-
Howser Col

Howser
Peak

Howser-
Thimble Col

Thimble
Peak

6

9

8

7

11

Flattop

Marmolata

Upper Bugaboo
Glacier Cirque

Pig eon Feathers
–Flattop Col

August 2002

PIGEON FEATHERS — EAST PEAK

view from the southeast peak of Pigeon Feathers

East Peak
Pigeon
Feathers

Pigeon–
Howser Col

Pigeon Feather Gully
East Creek Basin Approach

149

Pigeon Feed Wall–
Pigeon Spire

Pigeon Fork
Bugaboo Glacier

ROUTES: **6 7 8 9** (95)   **11** (96)   **149** (223)

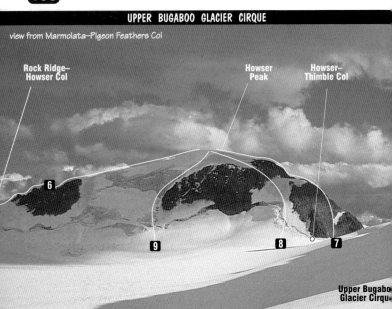

UPPER BUGABOO GLACIER CIRQUE

view from Marmolata–Pigeon Feathers Col

Rock Ridge–
Howser Col

Howser
Peak

Howser–
Thimble Col

6

9

8

7

Upper Bugaboo
Glacier Cirque

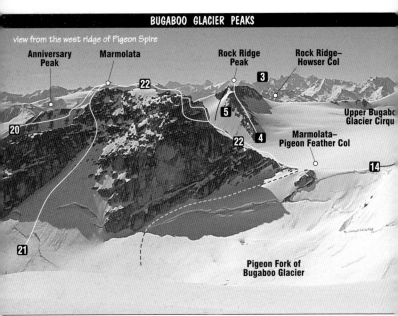

BUGABOO GLACIER PEAKS

view from the west ridge of Pigeon Spire

Anniversary
Peak

Marmolata

Rock Ridge
Peak

Rock Ridge–
Howser Col

22

3

5

20

Upper Bugaboo
Glacier Cirque

Marmolata–
Pigeon Feather Col

4

22

14

21

Pigeon Fork of
Bugaboo Glacier

ROUTES: **3** **4 5** (93) **6 7 8 9** (95) **14** (99) **20 21 22** (101).

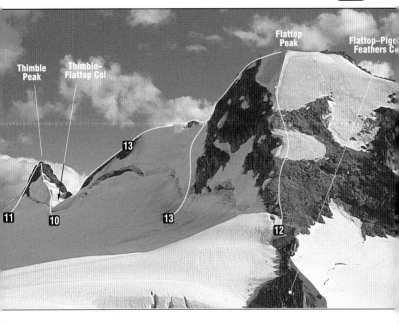

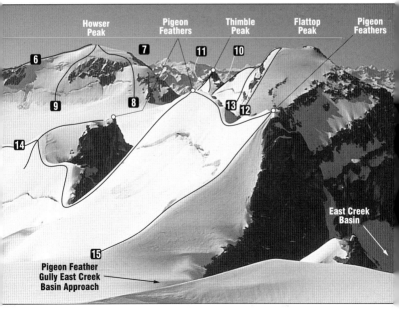

BUGABOO GLACIER PEAKS — EASTERN SIDES

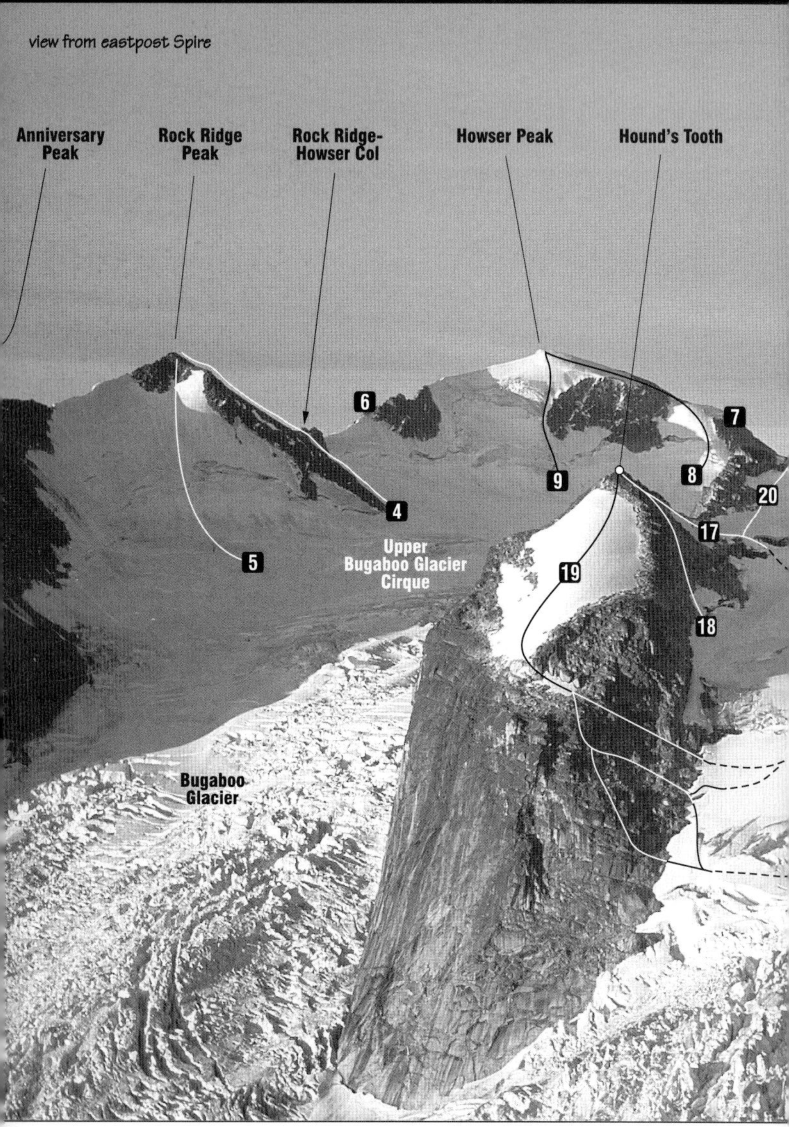

view from eastpost Spire
Anniversary Peak
Rock Ridge Peak
Rock Ridge-Howser Col
Howser Peak
Hound's Tooth
6
7
9
8
20
4
17
5
Upper Bugaboo Glacier Cirque
19
18
Bugaboo Glacier

ROUTES: **4 5** (93) **6 7 8 9** (95) **17 18 19** (100) **20** (101)

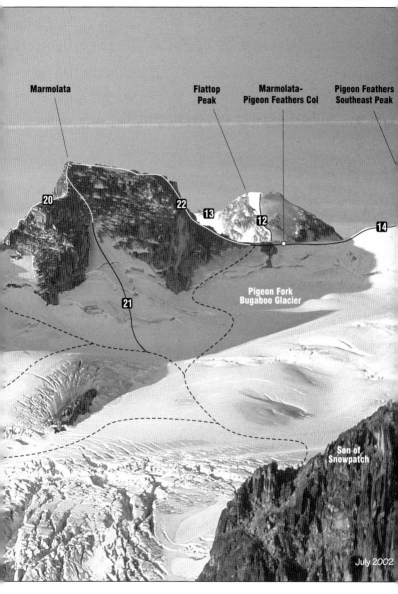

Marmolata

Flattop
Peak

Marmolata-
Pigeon Feathers Col

Pigeon Feathers
Southeast Peak

20

22

13

12

14

21

Pigeon Fork
Bugaboo Glacier

Son of
Snowpatch

July 2002

On pitch 2 of *McTech Arete*, Crescent Spire.

EASTERN SPIRES

The Eastern Spires consist of the peaks east and northeast of the Kain Hut Basin including those draining into Cobalt Lake. The area is bounded on the southwest by the Crescent Glacier and Applebee Dome and on the northwest by the lower Vowell Glacier and its outwash plain.

The eastern spires are lower than the central spires and are consequently somewhat sheltered from the main brunt of the weather. Eastpost Spire stands sentinel over Applebee Dome Camping Area and the Conrad Kain Hut. The rock on Crescent Spire is of excellent quality but deteriates on Eastpost and Cobalt Lake Spires. The Cobalt Lake Area is to the east of Crescent and Eastpost Spires and is characterized by lower, less technical routes on more broken rock with small pocket glaciers and seasonal snowfields. The steep talus slopes that dominate this area can be unstable and present a hazard.

Eastpost Spire	2728m	**Crescent Towers**	2830m
Crescent Spire	2842m	**Cobalt Lake Spire**	2689m
Brenta Spire	2958m	**Northpost Spire**	2919m

Climbs: All of the summits in the Eastern Spires area can be gained via third or fourth class routes, which makes the area a good choice to visit during inclement weather. The views back into the main spires are spectacular during good weather. The faces of Crescent Spire and Towers and Eastpost Spire that look down upon the Kain Hut Basin are well developed with multi–pitch cragging routes. Brenta and Northpost Spires, although not well developed, offer longer climbs. Many parties climb Eastpost Spire or *Lion's Way* on Crescent Tower as an introduction climb. The technical routes on Crescent Spire and the Crescent Towers don't require alpine starts and are of lower commitment making them a good choice for semi–rest days or during threatening weather.

Grand Traverses and Enchainments: As with the Bugaboo Glacier Peaks, the lower technical nature of the eastern summits and the long ridge–lines and high cols make the eastern spires well suited to enchainments and grand traverses. The most aesthetic linkage is to gain Crescent Spire from the Crescent Glacier via the *Southwest Gully–South Ridge*, and follow the entire ridgeline over Brenta Spire and Northpost Spire finishing at the outlet of Cobalt Lake. Very strong parties have added Cobalt Lake Spire and Eastpost Spire to the enchainment on the way back to the Kain Hut Basin.

EASTERN SPIRES: PHOTO–TOPOS 140 — 157

Eastpost Spire — 2728m

Eastpost Spire can be seen from the main Kain Hut Trail where it emerges from the final switchbacks into the basin below the hut. Its craggy southwest face stands above Applebee Camping Area and the Kain Hut. Eastpost Spire shares a col on its west side with the Donkeys Ears (South Tower) of Crescent Tower.

The climbs described in the Eastpost Spire area include the routes on and around Applebee Dome camping area. No glacier travel is required, and when winter snows have melted (mid to late July) no ice axes are needed. Approach shoes are usually adequate.

The cliffs immediately below the Applebee Campsite, as well as the cliffs on the lower slopes of Eastpost Spire, house much potential for cragging. This is an ideal low-commitment area for marginal-weather climbing and local guides and climbers have historically used this area for just that reason. The rock is generally very good, although moss and dirt will require new routes be cleaned. The more orange-coloured rock on Eastpost is friable in places, some liking it to 'English gritstone'. Many routes on the cliffs below and around the camping area have been repeatedly cleaned, climbed, overgrown, and cleaned again over the years. Most of the climbing in this area has gone unrecorded, so the feeling of exploration remains. When cleaning new climbs, keep in mind environmental considerations versus the significance and permanence of the climb.

Crescent Spire →
Crescent Towers →

EASTPOST SPIRE SOUTH FACE

View from near Applebee Campsi

Approach: The approach to most of the routes on Eastpost Spire is through the Applebee Camping Area. From the Conrad Kain Hut follow the trail above the outhouse boulders, up the moraine ridges, past the waterfall and onto the camping terraces. Primitive trails lead up to the *Northwest Ridge* and the Crescent Towers Col and scree slopes and ledges access the south face.

Descent: Descent from Eastpost Spire is via the *Northwest Ridge*. From the summit, downclimb clean rock right of the northeast ridge–crest to gain the *Northeast Ridge* lower down. Scree and ledges are traversed on the north face above the snow–slopes to regain the northwest ridge well beyond the summit block and the shoulder of the northwest ridge proper. Scramble down the lower ridge to gain an upper col and sandy trails down the south side to Applebee Campsite. Descent is third-class terrain with no established rappels.

---

26 **Northeast Ridge**   *   F   4th   (3-5h)   180m
Eaton Cromwell, F.North, August 1938   *AAJ 3:368, 4:82*
This climb is hidden from view from the Kain Hut Basin.

From Applebee Camping Area traverse vague trails above the tarns to gain the Crescent–Eastpost Col. Follow snow–slopes on the north flank to gain a col in the ridge between the northeast and main summits. Climb clean rock on the left side of the ridge to the summit. The northeast summit is gained from the col as well (Fourth class, G.Englehard, F.North, E.Feuz, August 1939). Later in the season the upper snow–slope melts out exposing loose and hazardous scree–covered slabs.

---

27 **Northwest Ridge**   F   4th   (3-5h)   180m   *144*
First ascent unknown
This is the left–hand skyline when viewed from Applebee Camping Area. The standard ascent line on Eastpost Spire is a combination of the northwest and northeast ridges.

From Applebee Dome follow vague trails up to a sandy gully which gains the col higher on the ridge from the Crescent–Eastpost Col. Scramble the ridge until a short, steep wall forces an exit onto ledges on the north side. Follow boulder–covered ledges across the upper north face, and pass beneath the final summit tower to gain the upper *Northeast Ridge*. Climb clean rock on the left side of ridge to the summit.

The northwest ridge can be followed all the way to the summit. From the short, steep wall work out right to gain slabs on the west side. The actual ridge crest can be followed but easier variations on the west side avoid the towers. Mostly fourth class but some short, mid–fifth class sections may be encountered.

---

28 **West Face**   .   AD- 5.8   (4-5h)   3p   *144*
Eatman, B.McKown, D.Perkins, August 1975
At the far left side of the south face, this short route climbs a groove system on a small left-facing wall to gain the *Northwest Ridge* near the first step.

29 Shelton Route   AD+   5.10+   (4-6h)   4p   *144*
J.Shelton, August 1974

Located on the left side of the south face, this route follows a shallow corner to gain a slab that exits onto the *Northwest Ridge* at the first step.

From Applebee Dome hike across scree slopes to reach the first grassy ledge system on the far left side of the west face. Traverse along the ledge for about 50m, then climb a groove for 6m to reach the shallow corner. Follow the corner for one or two 5.10 pitches to gain the slab. Climb the righthand corner in the slab to gain the *Northwest Ridge*.

30 **Flaming Hack Arête**   AD+   5.11+   (4-6h)   4p   *144*
Topher Donahue, Patience Gribble, August 2000   *AAJ 39:203*

This is a direct finish to *Shelton's Route*. It avoids the easy slabs and gains the ridge higher up. Follow the initial pitches of *Shelton's Route* to the start of the slab. Climb a steep wall on the right to gain a ledge and the right edge of the first arête. Follow the arête to the *Northwest Ridge*.

31 **South Face Left**   AD+   5.7 A3   (5-7h)   5p   *145*
Gay Campbell, Stan Fuka, Phil Nelson, Peter Zvengrowski, July 1967   *AAJ 16:176*

South Face Left starts directly below the summit and follows a prominent left–facing corner system that merges into a chimney/gully system.

From Applebee Dome traverse scree slopes to gain the mossy ledge system at the far left side of the south face. Follow the ledge past *Shelton's Route* and along the base of a weathered face until a point is reached directly below the summit. Follow a left–facing dihedral past a small overhang to a huge chimney system. The first ascent party used aid but the roof should go free at 5.10. Follow a chimney system up right to the summit.

32 **South Face**   AD+   5.6 A2   (5-7h)   5p   *145*
Layton Kor, W.Sanders, July 1960   *CAJ44:83*

The exact position of this climb is uncertain but it lies between *South Face Left* and *Classic Grit*. The first ascent was described as follows …

" From the very broken centre part of the face, climb a long aid pitch in steep cracks, traversing right then to a long open book. Ascend this corner (rotten) to exit just west of summit; some aid used near end ".

33 **Classic Grit**   AD+   5.10-   (5-7h)   6p   *145*
Andy Selters, Dave Turner, July 1989   *AAJ 32:185, 39:203*

This longer route ascends the leftfacing corner systems on the right side of the south face.

From Applebee Dome traverse scree slopes to below the summit and pick up a lower access ledge. Follow it to near its end then climb face cracks 5m left of a long shallow left–facing corner. Gain the corner on the second pitch and follow it for three pitches to a large sandy ledge. Bypass the corner on the left on the last pitch. Climb up and right to bypass a roof. *Mountain Fairytale* (Urban Golob, Slavko Rozic August 1996) variation follows an A3 corner straight up. The original route traverses out right to gain the next chute, which is followed to the *Southeast Ridge* in two 5.10 pitches.

34 Southeast Ridge *   PD 5.6   (4-6h) 550m *145*

Upper Ridge; M.Sherrick & Party, August 1955   *AAJ 13:242*
Complete Ridge; Hans Gmoser, Jack .McKenzie, Kim Mitchell, John Manry. July 1961

This route rises from the basin below Applebee Dome and the Conrad Kain Hut and forms the right skyline of Eastpost Spire.

From the Conrad Kain Hut, hike back down the trail toward the carpark to where it crosses the main creek and begins to descend into the rocky switchbacks. From there, head up the meadowed slopes where many options exist to access the ridge. The ridge can be followed directly the entire way, giving short mid–fifth class steps on both the upper and the lower section. Easier deviations can be made to the right. When linked with a descent of the *Northwest Ridge* it makes a good traverse of Eastpost Spire.

35 East Face   F 4th ♦   (4-7h) 450m

AAC Party, July 1946   *CAJ 30:154*

This climb sits hidden from view from all the Bugaboo Spires.

Several lines were climbed during the 1946 AAC Camp and described as of "only moderate difficulty". Approach was made from Bugaboo Creek up the drainage from Cobalt Lake (which is the waterfall encountered on the Bugaboo Trail). A more appropriate approach may be around the base of the *Southeast Ridge* or through the Crescent–Eastpost Col and down the drainage around the base of the Northeast Peak of Eastpost Spire.

Crossing the eastern glacier close along the cliffs of No. 2 peak [Snowpatch Spire east face], they presented a most forbidding aspect, as if trying to scare us from any search for a vulnerable spot that may possibly lie on the southwest side of the mountain.

A.H. MacCarthy, Canadian Alpine Journal, 1917

Crescent Spire	2842m

Crescent Spire is the first summit east of the base of the *Northeast Ridge* of Bugaboo Spire. It is separated from the Crescent Towers group by a broad sandy gully leading to the col between them. Both are easily viewed from the Crescent Glacier. Crescent Spire's title is misleading as it is dwarfed by the surrounding spires, and the vertical relief above its cols is minor. The south face, though, which looks onto the Crescent Glacier is important. The two prominent dihedrals directly below the summit are the McTech Area; a dozen multi–pitch 5.10's less than an hours approach from the Kain Hut and thirty minutes from Applebee Camping Area. The area is used for cragging and is popular during semi-rest days and in mediocre weather. Approach shoes are adequate for the approach and the walk-off descent. A chain anchor rappel route exists down *McTech Arête,* making for an easy descent from all but the first belay station.

Approach: The two approaches to Crescent Spire are relatively short and non–threatening. From the hut, there are two variations.

1. Follow the trail junction above the outhouse boulders up the approach trail towards Applebee Dome. When it comes level with the rock slabs on the left an unmarked and indistinct junction is encountered. The righthand trail climbs to above the waterfall and onto Applebee Dome, and the lefthand one climbs above the rock slabs towards the Bugaboo–Snowpatch Col. The first option is to follow the Applebee Dome Trail to the camping area slabs. From

CRESCENT SPIRE SOUTH FACE

Bugaboo Spire

Crescent Towers

early-season snow

view from Crescent Glacier

there, follow braided trails through the moraines on the left side of the tarns, eventually breaking out onto the remains of the Crescent Glacier below the Crescent Towers. Follow snow and ice to the base.

2. Alternatively, follow the left trail up towards Bugaboo–Snowpatch Col. It crosses a small outwash plain and climbs a small drainage. Follow the vague drainage up and right bypassing the Bugaboo–Snowpatch Col base. The route picks its way through boulders to gain the glacier below Bugaboo Spire. Follow the snow and ice to the south side of Crescent Spire and Towers.

Descent: There is both a walk-off and a rappel route.

(1) **To walk off all of the McTech area routes**, gain the ridge and scramble over boulders and broken terrain up right towards the summit (15min). From near the summit, scramble right down steppy terrain, trending left to reach the Crescent Spire–Towers Col. (10min). Follow trails and scree down the broad sandy gully and traverse back to the base of the climbs (10min). This option is suited to approach shoes but a little long and rough for rock shoes.

(2) **The rappel route starts near the** apex of the *McTech Arête* on a small wall overlooking *Westside Story*. The chains are on the face and not visible from above, but a small cairn should mark the spot. The route descends between *Westside Story* and *McTech Arête* but can be accessed from belay 4 and 5 on *McTech Arête*. The chain anchors are set up for seven rappels with a single 60m rope. If using double 60m ropes use the first station at 20m (*McTech Arête* belay 5) followed by three double rope rappels to the ground. Chain anchors on belays 2 and 3 on *McTech Arête* can also be used to reach the rappel station above *Roof McTech* there by avoiding the first belay on *McTech Arête*.

| 36 | **West Ridge** | F | 5.4 | (3-4h) | 180m | *146* |

Robert Brinton, Howard Fuller, Homer Gates, August 1938　　　　　*CAJ 26:18*

This is the ridge that runs up from the Bugaboo–Crescent Col. This col is guarded by steep slabs above the Crescent Glacier (the approach to the Northeast Ridge of Bugaboo Spire) that are most often soloed en route to Bugaboo Spire. The slabs below the col are steep, exposed, low fifth class but the ridge itself is a scramble.

From the base of the large corner systems of the McTech Area, follow the edge of the snow and ice uphill towards Bugaboo Spire. A few hundred metres along is a right–leaning slabby wall. The rock of the slab takes on an orange-green-gray colour. Climb fourth-class terrain, with low-fifth moves, up the left side of the slab to exit left off small ledges and steep blocks to the Bugaboo–Crescent Col. From the col scramble the blocky ridge to the summit. Good views of the *Northeast Ridge* of Bugaboo and Brenta.

Descend down the south ridge to the Crescent Spire–Towers Col and follow the broad sandy southwest gully back to the Crescent Glacier.

37 **WIMTA**   AD+   5.10-   (6-8h)   5p   *146*
John Moreland, David Vachon, August 1983

Who is McTech Anyway lies left of the McTech Area near the approach slabs to the Bugaboo–Crescent Col.

Start about 160m left of the *Left Dihedral* below, and left of a large slab capped by an arch. **1:** Climb the right–facing crack on the right side of an orange slab and then continue up the face crack to belay on a slab (5.10-). **2:** Climb the slab to a thin finger–crack, following it to a pod belay (5.10-). **3:** Continue up cracks trending right then left to a chimney belay (5.10). **4:** The original route climbs out right up a featured wall with multiple cracks. Follow cracks to belay between two roofs (5.8). A direct finish above the third belay is possible. **5:** Climb to ridge–crest.

Bring extra nuts and TCUs

38 **Clean and Dirty**   AD+   5.10-   (6-8h)   6p   *146*
Michel DuFresne, Kelly MacLeod, August1997

This route starts about halfway between *McTech Arête* and the approach slabs to the *West Ridge*. The route traverses right to climb clean then dirty rock left of the *Paddle Flake* pillar.

Follow the base of the wall left from *McTech Arête* for about 200m to where the base begins to turn up. Follow snow or scree up to access a ramp that cuts right into the face. Follow ramp to first belay. **1:** Climb the short right–facing corner to a ledge, traverse right to a short downclimb and continue right to the base of an arching crack. **2:** Climb a clean flake crack (5.6) to exit right below a fin (5.10-). Traverse right along the top of a chimney to a ledge at the base of a right–facing corner. **3:** Climb the corner to a second roof and move out onto a wall and up to a horn belay. **4:** Climb to a ledge, traverse right then up a dirty left-trending corner crack. Climb crack to belay in boulders. **5:** Climb a rightfacing corner, then follow cracks and weaknesses to the ridge (5.5).

39 **Paddle Flake Direct** **   D-   5.10   (6-8h)   6p   *147*
Chris Atkinson, Dan Redford, August 1989

This is a major variation of *Paddle Flake* that avoids the *Left Dihedral* via sharp finger–cracks to the left. It is sustained for its grade and has good, varied climbing.

1: Climb finger-cracks 3m left of the *Left Dihedral* bypassing the first overhang to the left and the second overhang to the right to a cramped belay (5.10). **2:** Follow face cracks and face climbing to a belay below the steeper upper wall (60m 5.10-). **3:** Continue to the base of the headwall and climb out right to gain the left side of a slender paddle-shaped flake. Climb the left side of the flake to an alcove belay (5.10-). *Paddle Flake* joins here. **4:** Step out right then up a hand-crack on the left edge of the bigger paddle flake curving out right and through a roof to a small belay above. Strenuous (5.10). **5:** Follow hand, fist and offwidth cracks in two leads to the ridge crest (5.10). Options exist.

Bring extra nuts and TCUs for the first two pitches and extra cams for hand and fist–cracks on the upper pitches.

---

40 **Paddle Flake** *   D- 5.10   (6-8h)   6p *147*

Joe Benson, Randall Green, August 1988

Paddle Flake follows *Left Dihedral* for three pitches before breaking out left to climb the long, slender flakes on the steeper left wall. The large flake that was the start of the original *Left Dihedral* route fell off in the 1990s making the corner harder.

1: Climb the main dihedral to belay above a small overhang (5.9). As an alternative, climb the first pitch of *Westside Story* bypassing its first belay along a footrail to belay near the corner (5.9). **2:** Follow the main dihedral to horizontal cracks in the right wall and belay, utilizing flakes and cracks on the right wall (5.7). **3:** Face climb (5.9) left out of the main corner to gain the right–hand side of the first smaller paddle flake. Follow the flake to an alcove belay at its top. *Paddle Flake Direct* joins here (5.10-). **4:** Climb a hand–crack arching right to a roof, which is climbed to a small belay (5.10). 5: Follow hand, fist and offwidth cracks in two leads to the ridge crest (5.10). Options exist.

Extra cams for hand and fist–cracks on the upper pitches are useful.

---

41 **Left Dihedral**   D- 5.11+   (6-8h)   6p *147*

Brian Greenwood, R.Lofthouse, August 1968   *AAJ 16:414*
FFA Andy Magness, Jason Magness, July 1997

This is the left–most of two obvious dihedrals that split the south face of Crescent Spire. The corner was one of the original cragging routes to be climbed in the Bugaboos then rated 5.8 A2. The climb acts as a funnel for rocks knocked from the upper pitches of *McTech Arête* and the rappel route. The large flake that was the start of the original *Left Dihedral* route fell off in the 1990s making the corner harder.

1: Climb the main dihedral to a belay above a small overhang (5.9). As an alternative climb the first pitch of *Westside Story* bypassing its first belay along a footrail to belay near the corner (5.9). **2:** Follow the main dihedral to horizontal cracks in the right wall and belay, using flakes and cracks on the right wall (5.7). **3:** Climb the corner to a sling belay (5.10-). **4:** Continue for about 15m of thin laybacking to belay on a small ledge to the right. Protect with # 00, 0 and 1 TCUs (5.11+). **5:** Climb via wild, full stemming with good protection to a sling belay under a roof (5.10+). **6:** Climb out right to gain cracks on the right face and follow them to the ridge. Some loose rock (5.8).

Bring extra TCUs for the crux pitch.

The full traverse of the Howser Towers has been completed once only, on the first ascent in 1965, north to south, by Yvon Chouinard, Eric Rayson, and Doug Tompkins.

42 Westside Story — D- 5.10- — (6-8h) — 6p *147*

Urban Golob, Slavko Rozic, August 1996 — AAJ 1997:203

Between *Left Dihedral* and *McTech Arete* lies a face with several crack lines running through it. This climb runs up the right-hand margin of this face in the lower half and follows the vague buttress that forms the wall's right-hand side higher up. The route is characterized by good and varied climbing.

Start up the first weakness 10m right of *Left Dihedral*. **1:** Follow flakes and small corners up and left to a small ramp. A few metres up the ramp pull over a block with a six inch crack on its right side to a flake belay at the righthand end of a gangway or continue 5m further to chain anchors on the rappel route (5.9, 35m). **2:** Climb directly up the wide crack above the belay. This wide crack turns to shallow corners and face climbing near its end (5.10a). Some moss still exists in the small cracks of the face climbing section. Belay in an alcove (5.10-, 55m). **3:** Climb up and left out of the belay on clean and positive face holds (little pro) until it is possible to step right to a small slabby amphitheatre. Follow a solitary crack up the lefthand edge of a slab to an overhanging headwall. Climbers off route on *McTech Arête* may end up here. Climb cracks and flakes up to exit left to a small stance and parallel wide 10 inch cracks. Follow right then left crack to pedestal belay (5.9, 55m). A direct line up the buttress is possible. **4:** Climb over a chockstone above the belay and follow a ramp up and left then head back right to steep jam cracks in a groove. Follow the crack as it widens to 18 inches. Easier climbing leads to ledge belay. *McTech Arête* joins here (5.9 30m). **5:** 20m of easier climbing leads to the top in 20m

43 Roof McTech * — 5.10+ — (4-8h) — 2p *147*

E.Doub, Alex Lowe, July 1979

Ten metres right of *Westside Story* a roof hangs 30m up with three cracks running through it. *Roof McTech* climbs through the roof via the right crack and joins *McTech Arête* at the second belay. Both the middle roof crack and the left crack have been climbed but grades are unknown.

Start 10m left of *McTech Arête* and 15m right of *Left Dihedral*. Climb shattered rock and flakes for 25m to reach a roof. Climb the right crack through the roof via stemming and jamming to a face-crack above which is followed to a belay at a small stance (5.10+, 50m). Follow a face-crack branching right to belay at the *McTech Arête* chains (5.9, 25m).

44 Energy Crisis ** — 5.11+ — (4-8h) — 2p *147*

Hugh Herr, Dan Peterson, August 1980

Between *Roof McTech* and the open book dihedral of *McTech Arête* lies a parallel rightfacing, arching corner. *Energy Crisis* follows this corner in two pitches to join *McTech Arête* at the second belay. This is a strenuous and aesthetic climb.

Start 5m left of *McTech Arête*. **1:** Climb sharp, clean rock to a sling belay level with the roof on *Roof McTech* (5.10, 30m). **2:** Continue up the steep, arching corner using fingertips, laybacking and stemming. Follow the corner to a face-crack and belay at the *McTech Arête* chains. This is a wild and sustained pitch (5.11+, 40m). Bring RPs and extra TCUs for the crux pitch.

45 **McTech Arête** ***   D- 5.10-   (6-8h)   6p   *147*
Doug Klewin, Pat McNurtney, August 1978
FFS Peter Croft

This is a bugaboo classic. Between the two main corner systems on the south face of Crescent Spire is a broad, indistinct arête. McTech Arête climbs corner and crack systems up the arête to gain the ridge–crest. This was the first free route up the wall and is by far the most popular.

1: From the top of the large boulder at the base, climb up flakes to the base of a small corner with a roof in it. Step left to gain another crack and climb a short squeeze chimney to the top of a pillar. Belay here or a few metres higher at the junction with a crack heading out left. Beware of the loose flake (5.9, 35m). **2:** Follow the hand and finger-crack heading up left from the corner to a small alcove. Climb out of the alcove and up a cloosed corner, utilizing a pedestal and cracks out left to gain a ledge. Belay at the chain anchors (5.10- 35m). **3:** Climb short corners and broken ground up and right for 15m to a chain anchor, belay here (5.4, 15m). A variation follows the ramp out left but the best climbing on the route is out right. **4:** From the anchors, step right behind a flake. Climb the first clean corner, then undercling right around a roof to another corner. Follow the second corner up and through a roof to gain a ledge on the left. This is a superb, clean continuous pitch. Chain anchors exist further along the ledge (5.9, 35m). **5:** Climb face cracks out right to gain the corner, which is followed to a small ledge and chain anchors (5.8 35m). A short pitch exists above here, but many parties rappel from this point. **6:** Scramble up and through a short steep corner. Scramble left around the arête and climb the face up and right to the ridge crest (5.7, 30m). To gain the rappel chain anchors, scramble down towards the *Left Dihedral* for about 5m to a small cairn. The chains are on the outside face. If rappelling from the top of pitch five three 60m rappels or six 30m rappels reach the base. The rappel route by-passes the chain anchors on belays two and three of the *McTech Arête* and descends near *Westside Story*.

Extra nuts for pitch 2, extra cams for hand and fist–cracks on pitch 4.

46 **McTech Direct**   D- 5.10   (6-8h)   6p   *147*
E.Doub, Alex Lowe, July 1979

This route is a one pitch variation of *McTech Arête*. On pitch 2 follow the sustained fist–to–offwidth crack in the corner through a bulge to gain broken ground above. Continue for 10m to the chain anchors at the top of pitch 3 on *McTech Arête*. Borrow all the wide gear you can.

The Kain Route has been climbed in one day from Canmore, Alberta.

47 Woza Moya   D- 5.10-   (6-8h)   6p *147*

D.Hoffman, A.Long, July 1973
FFA unrecorded

The climb follows the righthand of the two large corner systems on the south face of Crescent Spire. The lower half is a series of multiple small towers and cracks while the upper half is a series of bulges and roofs in the corner. Many minor variations are possible on this climb: originally rated 5.6 A2

1: Climb any one of several crack systems in the lower corner area to gain small belay ledges (5.10, 35m). **2:** Climb the corner to a belay in broken ground (5.9, 40m). It is possible to continue another 10m to the chain belay at the top of pitch 3 on *McTech Arête* and finish up that route. **3:** Follow a corner and cracks to a belay below the first roof (5.8, 30m). **4:** Climb cracks on the left wall and corner through and around bulges and roofs (5.9, 30m). It is possible to escape up the left wall in places. **5:** Follow the main corner through the final bulge or climb cracks out left to the ridge (5.8, 30m)

48 Dunlop's Dangle   D- 5.10-   (6-8h)   6p *147*

Chris Atkinson, Cathy Dunlop, August 1989

To the right of the right dihedral is a wall festooned with face cracks. Dunlop's Dangle climbs the middle crack on the lower face and trends right to climb the right edge of the upper face. A direct finish from pitch three would be a logical climb.

Start a few metres right of the *Woza Moya* Cracks. **1:** Climb a face crack, step right and up another face crack to belay at a horizontal crack 10m below a roof (5.8, 30m). **2:** Climb directly up through a small roof, continuing up face cracks to a sling belay at a horizontal break (5.10, 30m). **3:** Continue up face cracks trending right to a belay at a black lichen–covered ledge (5.10, 45m). **4:** Follow cracks out right to gain a belay at the top of a gray slab directly above the previous belay (5.8, 30m). **5:** Follow cracks up right to broken ground (5.9 30m). **6:** Continue up cracks and blocks to the top. (5.8, 30m).

Bring RPs, TCUs and extra nuts for finger–cracks on pitches 2 and 3, which are often bottoming.

49 Surprisingly Subsevere   D- 5.10-   (6-8h)   6p *147*

E.Doub, Alex Lowe, July 1979

This line is of very similar nature to *Dunlop's Dangle*. It steps out right at the top of the first pitch and parallels *Dunlop's Dangle* to the top.

1: Climb the first pitch of *Dunlop's Dangle* (above) (5.8, 30m). **2:** Traverse right along the horizontal crack to gain another face crack leading through a small roof.. Above the roof follow the crack to belay at small ledges (5.10-, 35m). **3:** Step right along a horizontal break to gain a hand-crack, which is followed to a sloping ledge. Belay at the right end of the ledge (5.9, 35m). **4:** Follow a chimney and cracks to broken ground (5.9, 30m). 5: Follow cracks and blocks straight up (5.9, 30m). Continue to the top (5.8, 30m).

50 Southwest Gully—South Ridge   F   3rd   (3-4h)   160m   *146*
First ascent unknown

Between Crescent Spire and the Crescent Towers lies a broad sandy gully
running up from the Crescent Glacier. Scramble up braided trails in the scree
to gain the Crescent Spire–Tower Col. Follow scree, boulders and short steps
up the left side of the ridge to gain the summit. This route is often used to
approach Brenta Spire by descending down Crescent Spire's *Northeast Ridge*
to the Crescent–Brenta Col.

51 Southeast Slopes   F 4Ul   (3-4h)   260m
Conrad Kain, J.Monroe Thorington, June 1933   *AAJ 2:189*

This was the original route on Crescent Spire; it now has little to recommend
it. From the Crescent–Eastpost Col follow snow slopes up underneath the
Crescent Towers to gain broken terrain leading to the Crescent Spire–Towers
Col. Follow the *South Ridge* to the summit.

52 Northeast Ridge   PD+   5.6   (4-5h)   300m   *150*
First ascent unknown

This is the ridge dropping from the summit of Crescent Spire to the col with
Brenta Spire. It is most often descended in order to climb the *South Ridge*
on Brenta Spire and is then climbed on the return. It can, however be climbed
from the Crescent–Brenta basin.

From the Crescent–Eastpost Col drop down the drainage to underneath
the small tower of the Whipping Post. Traverse around this and up the basin
to gain the wall leading up to the Crescent–Brenta col. From directly below
the col, gain ledges leading up and left. Follow these over third class terrain
to a steep wall. Climb up and right to a handrail leading down and right. Follow
this across to ledges. Climb fourth class terrain up and right to gain the col.
Follow the mostly fourth class ridge until forced along ledges on the right
side of the ridge. A five metre, mid-fifth class section is encountered.
Continue along ledges to regain the ridge at a sandy col. Follow snow to a
short, steep blocky section, then more snow and boulders to the summit.

*The lower reaches of No. 3 [Bugaboo Spire] above the saddle [Bugaboo
Snowpatch Col], for about 1200 feet, varied at angles from 30 to 60
degrees, with two thirty foot chimneys and one smooth slide, the whole
stretch affording every possible kind of interesting rock work.*

A.H. MacCarthy, Canadian Alpine Journal, 1917.

Crescent Towers	2830m

Crescent Towers are a collection of broken summits between Crescent Spire and Eastpost Spire, separated from the former by a broad sandy gully and a high col, and from Eastpost Spire by a low col (which gives access to the Cobalt Lake area). The two southern towers, also known as the Donkey's Ears, can be seen from Applebee Dome. The Central and North Towers are best viewed from the Crescent Glacier below Bugaboo Spire.

Approach: As with Crescent Spire, the Crescent Towers can be accessed from the Conrad Kain Hut either via Applebee Dome or the Crescent Glacier. See the Crescent Spire approach (page 118).

Descent: There are at least three descent routes, all requiring some downclimbing, a few short rappels and with loose rock.

(1) **Off Central Towers and *Lion's Way,*** head down between the Central and North Towers into the broad, sandy gully. Scramble down a worn path in the rubble to pick up rappel slings.

(2) **Off the Donkey's Ears, (southern towers),** two options exist. From the eastern ear, rappel east down a steep wall. Scramble north, then east, to gain the eastern slopes. Stay high to avoid the worst of the rubble, short rappels may be needed. Follow the eastern slopes down and right to snow and the Crescent–Eastpost Col.

(3) It is also possible to descend from the eastern ear down the ridge line directly to the Crescent–Eastpost Col. Downclimbing and several short rappels. Less loose than the eastern slopes.

North   Central   Donkeys Ears (South)

Crescent Spire

CRESCENT TOWERS SOUTH FACE

early-season snow

view from Crescent Glacier

North Tower

53 North Ridge   F   5.6   (4-5h)   40m   *148*
Eaton Cromwell, G.Englehard, August 1938   *AAJ 3:369*
Scramble from the Crescent Glacier up the broad, sandy southwest gully to
the Crescent Spire–Tower Col. Follow the ridge from the col to the summit
climbing mostly fourth class on the left side of the crest. To descend reverse
the route.

54 Northwest Side   F   5.4   (4-5h)   60m   *148*
A.Damp, C.Damp, August 1972   *CAJ 36:73*
Scramble from the Crescent Glacier up the broad, sandy southwest gully
towards the Crescent Spire–Tower Col. Just as the gully pinches climb out
right up broken terrain that is followed onto an indistinct buttress to gain a
chimney. Continue up the chimney and steep ground to gain the ridge–crest
and summit. Fourth class, with 90m of mid–fifth. To descend,, downclimb
the *North Ridge*.

Central Tower

55 Northwest Gully   F   4th   (4-5h)   80m   *148*
A.Damp, C.Damp, August 1972   *CAJ 36:73*
Halfway up the broad, sandy southwest gully and underneath the steep wall
of the North Tower is a series of loose gullies between the north and Central
Towers which are followed to the Central Towers. Many options exist. The
descent route from the Central Towers goes this way.

56 Lion's Way **   PD+ 5.6   (6-7h)   6p   *148*
Hans Gmoser, Mr. & Mrs. T.Hindset, August 1968
By far the most popular route on the Crescent Towers, this climb ascends
the first vague buttress up the broken ground to the right of the base of the
broad, sandy southwest gully.

Wander up and right through the initial scree of the southwest gully.
The route starts a few metres uphill from a large white flake leaning against
the wall, near the start of the highest horizontal break that girdles the entire
face. The climb is difficult to describe due to the complex nature of the terrain.
Climb over blocks, flakes and ledges trending right for two shorter pitches
to gain the base of an inside corner system. Follow the crux corner pitch
(5.6) to the crest of the buttress. Climb broken ground to a slab, which is
followed up right to a steep step in two pitches. Climb left up the short,
steep step and follow the ridge for two pitches to the top of the Central
Towers.

57 Lions and Tigers   AD- 5.8   (6-7h)   6 p   *148*
Greg Jahn, Allen Mathews, September 1996
Lions and Tigers generally follows the depression between the buttresses
of *Lion's Way* and *Tiger's Trail*. The first ascent party described it as "following
blocks and cracks on the left side of the gully left of *Tiger's Trail*" (5.5). Climb
cracks on clean rock higher up (5.8) joining *Lion's Way* near the top.

58 Tiger's Trail   AD- 5.9   (6-7h)   6p *148*

Chris Atkinson, John Martinek, June 1988

Tiger's Trail follows the next vague buttress right of *Lion's Way* and left of the steep wall of the first Donkey Ear.

From the big flake at the base of Lion's Way access the block–covered ledge system running out onto the face. Scramble over blocks and past a gully to reach a corner system at the end of the ledge. This belay can also be accessed from the lower scree–covered ledge via a short, clean 5.8 crack. **1:** Follow cracks left of the corner past a small ledge to belay in blocks on a pedestal on the buttress crest (5.9, 50m). **2:** Follow a small left–facing corner in the middle of the vague buttress to blocks and short cracks and a flake belay at a short white wall (5.8, 50m). **3:** Climb up and left through flakes and cracks to where the buttress becomes very narrow. Traverse down left then back up right to regain buttress. Climb cracks to a boulder belay (5.6, 50m). **4:** Follow broken terrain to gain the Central Towers.

59 Lost in Space   AD+ 5.10   (6-8h)   9p *148*

Pete Amphlett, Neil Main, July 1994

This climb takes the gully system between *Tiger's Trail* buttress and beneath the steep wall of the first Donkey Ear. The pitches are short due to rope drag.

Locate the scree–covered ledge that gives access to the climbs on the south face of the Donkey's Ears. Follow the ledge to the first gully feature just past *Tiger's Trail* buttress. Follow cracks and corners up a vague gully system, trending right near the top, to gain the col between the Central Towers and the southern towers. Follow the South Tower descent routes.

South Tower

60 Thatcher Cracker *   D - 5.10   (6-8h)   7p *149*

C.Kenyon, T.Fields, August 1986

Thatcher Cracker climbs the steep left wall of the south face of the west Donkey Ear. It starts at the lowest point in the face right of the *Lost in Space* gully. This is a steeper and more sustained line.

1: From the lowest point of the face climb cracks a few metres left of a roof. Follow cracks up and right to the approach ledge that girdles the face (5.10-), or walk the ledge to this point. **2:** Climb a short pitch above the ledge to belay on a small terrace. This is the common second pitch with the *Edwards–Neufeld* (5.8). **3:** Climb cracks on the left edge of the terrace to the base of a clean, white corner. Follow corner and face crack to belay at a horizontal break (5.10). **4:** Continue above to black ramp. **5:** Follow ramp to base of upper dihedral. **6:** Climb dihedral with an offwidth section to belay near its top (5.10-). **7:** Climb and stem (poor protection) for 30m to the shoulder near the summit (5.10).

61 Edwards–Neufeld *   D- 5.10+   (6-8h)   8p *149*

Guy Edwards, Shaun Neufeld, August 1999

This route climbs the steep white wall right of *Thatcher Cracker* before moving right and joining *Ears Between* on the last pitch.

Access the short white wall at the lowest point of the face. **1:** Climb a crack to pass the right edge of a roof. Continue up cracks to belay on the approach ledge (5.9). **2:** This common pitch with *Thatcher Cracker* climbs a short pitch to belay on a small terrace (5.8). **3:** Gain a face crack to the right that splits the clean, white wall. Follow it to belay at a horizontal break (5.10+). **4:** Climb the crack above to belay on top of a pedestal (5.10+). **5:** Climb the crack to belay at another horizontal break (5.10-). **6:** Traverse the horizontal break out right to belay at the base of a small corner. (5.10). **7:** Climb the corner above, breaking out right under a roof to gain the main chimney of *Ears Between* (5.10+). **0.** Climb the chimney to a notch.

| 62 | **Ears Between** | * | AD | 5.7 | (6-7h) | 6p | *149* |

R.Lofthouse & CMC party, August 1968   *AAJ 16:414*

Ears Between climbs the broken ground in the middle of the south face of the Donkey's Ears to gain the chimney leading up to the notch between the ears. This is a well-travelled route with a great position on the upper pitches. Many parties traverse to the climb via the approach ledge that girdles the lower south face.

Direct start. From below the roof at the toe of the face walk 50m further east to locate two cracks forming a 5m high triangle. A sling often hangs in the left crack. Climb the crack in the centre of the triangle to an alcove under roof flakes. Step right around blocks and follow cracks and flakes to the approach ledge belay (5.8).

Classic Start. Walk the approach ledge past a large teetering flake. Belay about 30m past the flake where the wall turns black with lichen. Minor variations along this ledge are possible for the first two pitches. **1:** Climb a short pitch over broken ground. **2:** Continue up cracks over small ledges trending left to belay below a notch leading to a ramp (5.4). **3:** Struggle through the notch and an awkward mantle to gain the ramp that is followed to a belay at its end (5.7). **4:** Climb flakes to access the chimney and an alcove belay above (5.7). **5:** Follow the steep and airy chimney in one long pitch to the notch between the ears (5.7). **6:** Gain the East Ear via ledges and cracks on the north side.

| 63 | **Eyore** | | AD+ | 5.9 | (6-8h) | 5p | *149* |

Peter Oxtoby, Rose Reindl, August 1994

This route starts up the black, lichen covered rock from the end of the approach ledge to gain a buttress higher up leading to the top of the east ear. Minor variations are possible lower down.

As with *Ears Between* follow the approach ledge past the large jammed flake to the start of the black, lichen covered rock. **1:** Climb up to access a black slab and beyond to a boulder belay (5.5). **2:** Climb up blocks and flakes and move left to belay at the bottom of a sloping chimney (5.6). **3:** Follow chimney then move right across a slab to a boulder belay below the ridge-crest (5.7). **4:** Move up the ridge-crest to where it steepens: a few 5.7 moves. From here it is possible to downclimb and rappel on the left to pick up the southeast ridge descent route to the Crescent-Eastpost Col. **5:** Jam 5.8 and 5.9 cracks near the ridge-crest to the top of the east ear (5.9).

Cobalt Lake Spire   2689m

Cobalt Lake Spire is immediately south of Cobalt Lake, forming the southern rampart that cradles the lake. The peak consists of a small multi-gendarmed satellite that forms the Brenta–Cobalt Lake Spire Col, and the main peak that is slightly further east and 75m higher. The spire also forms the northern wall of the Cobalt–Crescent–Eastpost cirque, which contains a tarn that is often mistaken for Cobalt Lake. The rock is not of the same quality as the main Bugaboo Spires, it is shattered and more reminiscent of the Rockies. Routes described are on the main peak avoiding the satellite.

Approach: From the Kain Hut Basin and Applebee Dome access the Crescent–Eastpost Col via vague trails above the camping terraces. From Applebee Dome pick up small trails that head up and right above the tarns. Bypass the first trail branch that heads steeply up to the first col on Eastpost Spire. Continue north above the tarns until a trail branch heads up right to gain the lower col between East Post Spire and the Crescent Towers. From this col follow the drainage down about 500 metres until it is possible to bear left underneath the Whipping Post to the top of the first of several morainal bumps. From the first bump, Brenta Spire and the Brenta–Cobalt Lake Spire Col are visible. Descend down towards the tarn about 50m until possible to head up into the boulder–strewn basin that leads to the Brenta–Cobalt Lake Spire Col. To descend from this col to the outlet of Cobalt Lake and the Cobalt Lake Trail, steep and sometimes broken snow slopes must be negotiated. Ice axes, self-arrest techniques, and on occasion, crampons are needed. It is also possible to gain the Brenta–Cobalt Lake Spire Col from Cobalt Lake. From

COBALT LAKE SPIRE EAST SIDE

Peak   Satellite

Brenta
Spire

view from
Northpost Spire

the lake outlet follow the height of land on the southern shore to the slopes of Cobalt Lake Spire. Traverse slabs and scree to gain snow slopes, which are followed up to the col.

Descent: Descend down the *North Ridge* until possible to cut left down to the northwest face. Scramble down and left over third class terrain to gain snow. Traverse the snow slopes towards Brenta Spire to regain the Brenta–Cobalt Lake Spire Col.

64 Southwest Face   PD-   4th   (5-8h)   200m   *152*

M.Sherrick & party, July 1955   *Sierra Ann 41:91*

The *Southwest Face* route ascends the face seen from the Eastpost–
Crescent Col. The steep, narrow gully to the east of the summit can be nasty
when transitioning from snow to rock.

From the Eastpost–Crescent Col, gain the basin below Brenta–Cobalt
Lake Spire Col. From the basin below it, scramble up a right-trending gully
and ramp system underneath the south face of the western satellite peak.
This gully and ramp system gains the col between the satellite peak and the
main peak. Alternately, gain the Brenta–Cobalt Lake Spire Col and follow snow
and ice slopes underneath the north side of the satellite peak to gain the col
between the satellite peak and the main peak. From this col, follow the large
scree–covered ledge system that cuts down and across the southwest face
and underneath the summit. From the eastern end of this ledge system a
steep snow and rock gully ascends to the ridge–crest east of the summit.
Follow this narrow and steep gully to ridge–crest. Scramble the ridge to
summit. Difficulties will depend on the amount of snow the gully contains.

65 West Ridge   PD   low 5th   (5-7h)   120m   *152*

FRA Chris Atkinson, August 1990

The *West Ridge* runs from the satellite–main peak cols directly to the summit.
Following the ridge from the Brenta–Cobalt Lake Spire Col over the satellite
peak makes for an interesting technical diversion.

From the Brenta–Cobalt Lake Spire Col, follow snow–slopes on the
Cobalt Lake side around the satellite peak to gain the left of the two cols
between the satellite peak and the main peak. This col can also be gained
from the south side via a gully, ramp and scree. From this col follow the ridge–
crest directly to the summit. The initial slab or the left crack are mid fifth
class climbing with the upper ridge being fourth class. The satellite peak can
also be followed directly from the Brenta–Cobalt Lake Spire Col. It involves
climbing around numerous gendarmes. Fourth class with numerous short
fifth class sections. A single rope rappel gains the satellite–main peak col.

66 North Ridge   F   3rd   (5-7h)   150m   *152*

A.C.Faberge & ACC party, August 1946   *CAJ 36:99*

This was the line of the first ascent party, up the ridge that rises from Cobalt
Lake and is the usual line of ascent for most parties. It is often combined
with Eastpost Spire or Brenta and Northpost Spire for a day of fourth class
summits.

From the Brenta–Cobalt Lake Spire Col descend and traverse down
snow–slopes on the Cobalt Lake side to avoid the satellite peak of Cobalt
Lake Spire. Follow snow and ice east to gain the North Ridge on broken third
class terrain where the ridge begins to drop sharply down towards Cobalt
Lake. Follow more broken third class terrain up onto the ridge, which is
followed to summit. The north ridge can also be gained by traversing in higher
on the snow–slope and gaining the rock directly below the summit. Broken
third class terrain and ledges are followed up and left to gain the North Ridge
at about two thirds height.

Brenta Spire   2958m

Brenta Spire is the highest summit north and east of the main spires. Connected by third and fourth class ridges to Northpost Spire to the northeast, and Crescent Spire to the southwest, it forms the western wall of the cirque that cradles Cobalt Lake. The western walls descend nearly 750m to the lower Vowell Glacier. Although it is not as steep and imposing as the main spires, the rock on Brenta Spire is generally very good. The east face in particular is attractive for new route development.

Approach: Brenta is usually approached from one of two ways.

(1) **From the Kain Hut and Applebee Dome** gain the Crescent–Eastpost Col via vague trails above the camping terraces. Descend the drainage, cutting left under the Whipping Post just above a tarn. Scramble over loose boulders to gain the basin below the Brenta–Cobalt Lake Spire Col. The *South Ridge* can be reached from here via the Crescent–Brenta Col. From the basin, scree slopes lead to the Brenta–Cobalt Lake Spire Col for southeast face routes.

(2) **The approach to the *South Ridge*** is over Crescent Spire via the broad, sandy southwest gully to the summit and then descending the northeast ridge to the Crescent–Brenta Col. Brenta Spire can also be approached from Cobalt Lake.

Descent: Two descent options are used for Brenta Spire. Both involve descending the *South Ridge* to the Crescent–Brenta Col.

(1) **The *South Ridge* is mostly scrambling** with a short fourth

Cobalt Lake Spire
Satellite

Northpost
Spire

Crescent
Spire

Cobalt
Lake

BRENTA SPIRE EAST FACE

view from Cobalt Lake Spire

class step at the summit and another high on the ridge. From the col, most parties climb the connecting *Northeast Ridge* of Crescent Spire. This involves fourth class ledges and a short 5.6 step lower down on the north side of the ridge and easy scrambling higher up. From the summit of Crescent Spire follow the ridge down south to access the broad gully leading right down to the Crescent Glacier.

(2) **Another option from the Crescent–Brenta Col** is to descend the east side of the col to gain the basin that is followed down around the Whipping Post to gain the drainage leading back up to the Crescent–Eastpost Col. The descent down the col is complex and not obvious and entails some fourth class down-climbing. Generally, from the south end of the col work right down connecting slabs to find an arching handrail leading under the steep right wall. This gives access to a short corner and the start of ledge systems that are followed left down to the toe of the bluffs.

67 **South Ridge** *	AD- 4th	(6-8h) 450m *153*

Lawrence Coveney, Sterling Hendricks, Percy Olton, Polly Prescott, Marguerite Schnellbacher, July1938
AAJ 3:298

The *South Ridge* runs from the Crescent-Brenta Col to the summit of Brenta Spire. The lower half of the ridge is mostly walking with the upper half being very aesthetic third class climbing with a few fourth class steps mixed in. Combined with Crescent Spire and Northpost Spire it makes for 2½km of ridgeline one way. The *South Ridge* can be approached from the basin below the Crescent-Brenta Col or by descending the *Northeast Ridge* of Crescent Spire. The latter being the more popular and aesthetic route. To gain the col from the basin, access a third class ledge system that starts near the toe of the bluffs and makes a rising traverse left to where it ends against a steep wall. From the steep wall, follow a short fourth class corner to a hand rail that curves right to gain a slab. Follow the slab down to its end and wind up connecting slabs to the col. The Crescent-Brenta Col can also be reached by descending the *Northeast Ridge* of Crescent Spire. From the Crescent Glacier follow trails up the broad sandy gully to the col that divides Crescent Spire from the Crescent Towers and scramble left to the summit of Crescent Spire (third class). From Crescent Spires summit scramble down the blocky *Northeast Ridge* that drops towards the Crescent-Brenta Col. As the ridge levels off briefly pick up trails and ledges on the Vowell Glacier side of the ridge. Ledges on this side of the ridge are followed all the way to the col. Mostly third class there are several fourth class steps and one 3m low-mid fifth class step to downclimb. This col can also be accessed from the lower Vowell Glacier via a basin and fourth class gullies to the left of the col.

From the Crescent-Brenta Col follow vague trails up the boulder strewn lower slopes until the ridge levels off. The *Southeast Spur* joins the ridge here with the southeast face routes joining the ridge slightly lower. Follow the ridge over third class terrain with the occasional fourth class step. A final fourth class step right of the summit leads to the top.

68 Southeast Face   AD   5.9   (7-9h)   5p   *154*
Eran Philly, Bethan Martin, August 1998

This route follows a corner system starting below the Crescent–Brenta Col and trending right to gain the S*outh Ridge* below the south bump.

Gain ledges directly below the col and follow them right to the base of a corner system. Climb the corner in three pitches, the second pitch is the crux with a 5.9 chimney, followed by a 5.8 stemming pitch. Short fifth class sections and scrambling gain the *South Ridge* below the south bump.

69 Southern Comfort   AD   5.8   (7-9h)   5p   *154*
FA Eric Dumerac, John Setters, August 1997   *CAJ 1998*

This route climbs a right-trending corner and ramp system on the right side of the southeast face to join the *Southeast Spur* at three quarter height before gaining the *South Ridge* at the south bump.

Climb a short tongue of snow to gain the rock. A 5.7 pitch leads to a chockstone belay at 60m. Follow a right-trending corner at 5.8 for 75m to a small roof. Squeeze under the roof at 5.6 and climb broken ground to a belay. Continue up and left, crossing the broad gully to join the *Southeast Spur* where it steepens. Climb 5.6 steps to the south bump on the *South Ridge*.

70 Southeast Spur **   AD   5.6   (6-9h)   210m   *154*
FRA Chris Atkinson, August 1990

Another Bugaboo classic, the *Southeast Spur* rises directly from the Brenta-Cobalt Lake Spire Col to gain the *South Ridge* where it starts to level out and the good scrambling of the *South Ridge* begins. The spur offers nearly 300m of fourth class terrain before joining the *South Ridge* and if followed directly some steep and clean fifth class steps are encountered.

Gain the Brenta–Cobalt Lake Spire Col via the Eastpost–Crescent Col and the Cobalt Lake Route or from the Cobalt Lake Trail and Cobalt Lake. From the Brenta–Cobalt Lake Spire Col begin scrambling over large blocks directly up to the south ridge. Detours to the left of the spur can keep the climbing within the fourth class range. If followed directly the spur presents three or four low-mid fifth class steps on sound rock at about three quarters height. From the ridge–crest, follow the *South Ridge* to the summit. Descend via the *South Ridge*.

71 Another Fine Day in the Bugaboos * AD 5.7 (7-10h)   9p   *154*
Graham Dudley, Chris Ruthiem, Steve Hiopes, July1997   *CAJ 1998*

Another Fine Day follows the northeast spur to gain the *North Ridge*. The first ascent party described it as a pleasant outing. Approach via the Crescent–Eastpost Col, and the Brenta–Cobalt Lake Spire Col.

From the Brenta–Cobalt Lake Spire Col, traverse mostly snow–slopes past the toe of the east buttress to gain the northeast spur. Begin up cracks left of the spur's toe to gain the left side of a gendarme in three pitches. Climb cracks and a chimney, left of the spur proper for two pitches. Scramble and climb for two more pitches Climb the spur for a pitch followed by another pitch of scrambling to the north ridge which is followed up easy terrain to the summit. Descend via the *South Ridge*

---

72 **North Ridge**   AD   4th   (6-9h)   450m   *154*
D.P.Richards, I.A.Richards, August 1938   *AAJ 3:369*

This route is rarely climbed as an objective unto itself. Most often it is climbed as part of the Northpost and Brenta Spire traverse.

The *North Ridge* can be approached from either the traverse of Northpost Spire from the Cobalt Lake outlet or after having descended it to climb the *Southwest Ridge* of Northpost Spire. The Brenta–Northpost Col can be gained from the Brenta–Cobalt Lake Spire Col by traversing out from the col under the east face of Brenta Spire. Steep, loose talus basins can be followed up to gain the *North Ridge* above the col. This complex fourth class approach is rarely travelled and is gruelling.

The *North Ridge* is mostly third class and can be descended from the summit of Brenta Spire or climbed from the Brenta–Northpost Col without much difficulty. Cornices can linger on the ridge into July.

73 **Vockeroth Route**   AD   4th   (10-12h) 500m
Don Vockeroth & ACC Party, August 1990   *CAJ 1992:61*

Details of this route are limited, but it is believed to run up from the Vowell Glacier via an indistinct spur and gains the ridge just north of the summit.

Brenta–Northpost Grand Traverse: Combined with Crescent Spire, the traverse of Brenta and Northpost Spires makes for a Grand Traverse of over 3½km of high, moderate terrain. The most aesthetic linkage is to gain Crescent Spire from the Crescent Glacier via the *Southwest Gully–South Ridge*, descend to the Brenta–Crescent Col via the *Northeast Ridge* and follow the entire ridgeline over Brenta Spire and Northpost Spire, descending the *East Ridge* to finish at the outlet of Cobalt Lake. Very strong parties have added Cobalt Lake Spire and Eastpost Spire on the way back to the Kain Hut Basin.

The Gendarme of Bugaboo Spire.
The piece de resistance that took nearly two hours to negotiate was reached at an elevation of 10,000 feet and here the laggards again rejoined Conrad and John, who sat below it nonplussed at the sight of a veritable bugaboo, which immediately suggested to our minds the appropriateness of the name "Bugaboo" for this spire.

A.H. MacCarthy, Canadian Alpine Journal, 1917.

Northpost Spire   2919m

Northpost Spire is the northernmost peak of the Eastern Spires, and long with Brenta and Cobalt Lake Spires, it forms the catchment basin for Cobalt Lake. Brenta and Northpost share a long, high connecting ridge making for an ideal traverse. The 500m northwest face rises above the outwash plain of the Vowell Glacier and cannot be seen from the main Bugaboo group. The steep south face however, can be seen from many parts of the main spires but was not explored until 2002, producing some unique and exciting climbing.

Approach: Northpost Spire can be approached from three sides. From the Kain Hut Basin, Crescent Spire can be traversed to gain the *South Ridge* of Brenta Spire and onto the *Southwest Ridge* of Northpost Spire. The south face and east ridge can be accessed via the Crescent–Eastpost Col and the Brenta–Cobalt Lake Spire Col or via the Cobalt Lake Trail to Cobalt Lake. The northwest face routes are usually accessed from the Kain Hut Basin via the Bugaboo–Snowpatch Col and a descent of the lower Vowell Glacier to a camp on its outwash plain. Stay right at the icefalls and consider the cold outflow winds when choosing a campsite.

Brenta Spire

Cobalt Lake

NORTHPOST SPIRE SOUTH FACE

view from
Brenta–Cobalt Lake Spire Col

Descent: The easiest descent from Northpost Spire is down the *East Ridge.* From the summit follow broken, fourth class terrain down to snow. A short rappel may be needed. If camped at Cobalt Lake, or hiking out the Cobalt Lake Trail, follow the entire ridge over its flat section and down left to reach its end. If returning to the Kain Hut Basin it is possible to circle the lake high on the right side under Northpost and Brenta Spires. From the flats of the *East Ridge,* follow grassy slopes down towards the lake. Pick up goat trails heading right along a grassy ledge system. Follow these to regain snow–slopes under the Brenta–Northpost Basin and traverse them to the Brenta–Cobalt Lake Spire Col. If camped near the lower Vowell Glacier it is possible to descend the *Northeast Rocks* trending left towards the *North Ridge* via fourth class terrain.

74 Southwest Ridge   AD- 5.7   (8-11h)   450m   *142*
First ascent unknown

This is the long ridge that connects the summits of Brenta and Northpost Spires. It is rarely climbed on its own, but when combined with the traverse of Crescent and Brenta Spires and the descent down the *East Ridge* of Northpost Spire it makes for a Grand Traverse of over 3½km of moderate terrain. The Brenta–Northpost Col can be gained from the Brenta–Cobalt Lake Spire Col by traversing out from the col under the east face of Brenta Spire. Steep, loose talus basins can be followed up to gain the *North Ridge* of Brenta Spire above the col. This complex fourth class approach is rarely traveled.

From the summit of Brenta Spire, descend its *North Ridge* via west side ledges. Follow the ridge to a short rappel down a step and continue weaving left and right along the ridge. The crux section follows a crack system down the east side, traverses and then leads back up to the ridge–crest (5.7). Continue up the ridge, working difficulties on the left. At a large block and a final step in the ridge, follow an exposed ledge system around the west side to gain a scree gully, which leads to the summit. The ridge is mostly fourth class with several low-mid fifth class steps.

75 Fast Eddie Lives   D+ 5.10 C1   (10-12h)   5p   *157*
Chris Geisler, Kai Hirvonen, August 2002   CAJ 86:139

Fast Eddie Lives follows the left edge of the steepest section of white rock on the south face. The first ascent party climbed a short section of C1 on the second pitch due to lichen, which would likely go at 5.10 if cleaned. This route is easily viewed from the Brenta–Cobalt Lake Spire Col.

Access the base of the face up scree–covered ledges. **1:** Climb a right–facing corner on the left side of the face (5.9). **2:** Continue up the corner. At one third height step right into a hand–crack (C1, 5.10 if cleaned). **3:** Step left onto the left side of an arête and meander up rock above (5.7). **4:** Climb a steep corner to a ledge (5.7). **5:** Follow steep terrain, right of a gully, up right to a flake belay in a corner, just left of an obvious roof at the top of the face (5.7). **6:** Rail right on a flake and up exposed, broken terrain to the top (5.9).

76 **Free Heeling** *** D+ 5.10+ (10-12h) 5p *157*

Chris Geisler, Kai Hirvonen, August 2002 CAJ 86:139

This route climbs the centre of the steep white south face trending right near its top to pick up quartzite rock. The climb is steep, varied and sustained and is reported to be a high quality route that the first ascent party rated 5.10++. It is easily viewed from the Brenta–Cobalt Lake Spire Col.

Gain the base of the wall via scree ledges. **1:** Stem the right side of a pillar in the middle of the face (5.10, 45m). **2:** Follow various parallel cracks on a diagonal dyke feature to the left end of the first roof. Protection is dubious at times. One fixed knifeblade (5.10, 50m). **3:** Climb up a corner left of the roof, protect, then layback out a wild flake to an arête. Follow a flared finger–crack layback on the arête: brilliant position, fixed nut. Climb a handcrack to belay (5.10+, 50m). **4:** Mixed ground and rope drag lead up and right towards a black roof at the top of the face (5.9, 30m). **5:** Climb slab moves and head right on a ledge to the base of the cleanest quartzite corner (5.8, 30m). **6:** Follow corner, move right on a ledge and back left on a short ramp. Continue up through steep breaks to the top (5.9, 70m).

77 **East Ridge** PD 4th (7-9h) 490m *156*

First ascent unknown

The *East Ridge*, with its long flat middle section forms the northern retaining wall of Cobalt Lake and buts into the alp lands to the east. It ends very near to the Cobalt Lake Trail. The *East Ridge* itself is mostly walking with the fourth class section near the summit. It is most often done as a day trip up the Cobalt Lake Trail. An ice axe is often required for a minor snow–slope above the flats. The views into the main spires are commanding.

78 **Northpost Couloir** PD ice (4-6h fr. base) 700m

First ascent unknown

The *Northpost Couloir* is known mostly as a Canadian Mountain Holidays heli ski run in the winter. It can be accessed from the end of the Vowell Glacier outwash plain but is easiest to access from the Cobalt Lake Trail. From near the end of the Cobalt Lake Trail and the foot of the *East Ridge* of Northpost Spire traverse down right through talus and larch trees to gain a steep scree gully descending to the base of the couloir. The couloir tops out between the summit and the flats of the *East Ridge*.

79 **North Ridge–Northeast Rocks** PD+ 4th (4-6h fr. base) 700m

D.Richards, I.Richards, August 1938 AAJ 3:369

This was the line of first ascent of Northpost Spire. As with all the routes on the northwest side, it is accessed from the Vowell Glacier outwash plain.

From the toe of the north ridge follow the fourth class ridge to gain easier slopes leading up and left on third-fourth class terrain to the summit.

First Winter Ascents.

South Howser, Beckey–Chouinard. 1982, Scott Flavelle, Phil Hein.

Bugaboo, Northeast Ridge. 1985, Joe Buszowski, Bernard Ehmann.

80   In Search of the Northwest Passage AD 5.8   (5-7h fr. base) 3-4p
Cyril & Sandra Shokoples, August 1990   *CAJ 1992:61*
This route explores the large apron below the north ridge and northwest face,
giving great run–out friction climbing. The multi–pitch route is described as
following a series of water–worn weaknesses in the apron to a large ledge.
The first ascent party encountered deteriorating rock out left towards the ridge
and retreated. One bolt was placed on lead and several bolts and pins were
left as rappel anchors.

81   North by Northwest   AD+   5.8   (6-8h fr. base) 570m   166
Cyril & Sandra Shokoples, August 1990   *CAJ 1992:61*
This route follows the base of the apron up right to start up a left slanting
dihedral system on the left side of the northwest face proper. It joins the
north ridge at two–thirds height, with about eight pitches of mid fifth class
climbing on reasonable rock. The last crux pitch involves laybacks, stemming
and face climbing on lichen covered rock (5.8). The ridge provides about one
hour of climbing to the summit with the final step avoided by a rising traverse
out left on rotten rock.
    Bring a standard rack plus a 5inch cam and knife blades and lost arrows
for the belay stations.

82   Northwest Face   AD+   5.7   ♦ (6-8h fr. base) 520m   *155*
Fred Beckey, Gerry Fuller, August 1966   *AAJ 15:375*
This route follows the left side of the face to gain a vague buttress that joins
the north ridge just below the summit.
    Scramble along the base of the initial apron past the *North by Northwest*
dihedrals and gain a slabby depression. Climb up weaknesses to gain the
ramp at the base of the buttress. Follow buttress directly to the ridge. Avoid
the final step below the summit by a rising traverse out left on rotten rock.
The climbing is described as moderately difficult, often on down slabbing
rock. Protection is awkward at times and pins are probably useful.

83   Northwest Face, West Side AD+ 5.6 ♦ (6-8h fr. base) 420m *155*
John Alt, Stephen Arsenault, Volker Vogt, June 1967   *AAJ 16 :175*
This route ascends the steeper face directly below the summit. Follow the
slabby depression below the *Northwest Face* to the edge of a small snow
field. About one hundred metres of fourth and fifth class climbing lead up
left to a large ledge area. From here a corner is followed for 150-200m. with
the last two leads described as being very difficult (1967) fifth class jams
and laybacks. Broken terrain is followed directly to the summit.

First Winter Ascents.
Snowpatch Spire, Snowpatch Route. 1975, Heiri Perk, Walter Renner.
Snowpatch Spire, Kraus–McCarthy. 1999, Kirk Mauthner, Brad Shilling.

EASTERN SPIRES — VIEW TO THE WEST FROM NORTHPOST SPIRE

Eastern Spires →

Central Spires →

Bugaboo Glacier Peaks →

Cobalt Lake Spire

Eastpost Spire

Anniversary Peak   Rock Ridge Peak

Cobalt Lake

Cobalt Lake Trail
(page 24)

EASTERN SPIRES PANORAMA

EASTERN SPIRES INTRO: 113
MAP: 20

EASTERN SPIRES PANORAMA

NORTHPOST, BRENTA, CRESCENT AND BUGABOO SPIRE — NORTH SIDES

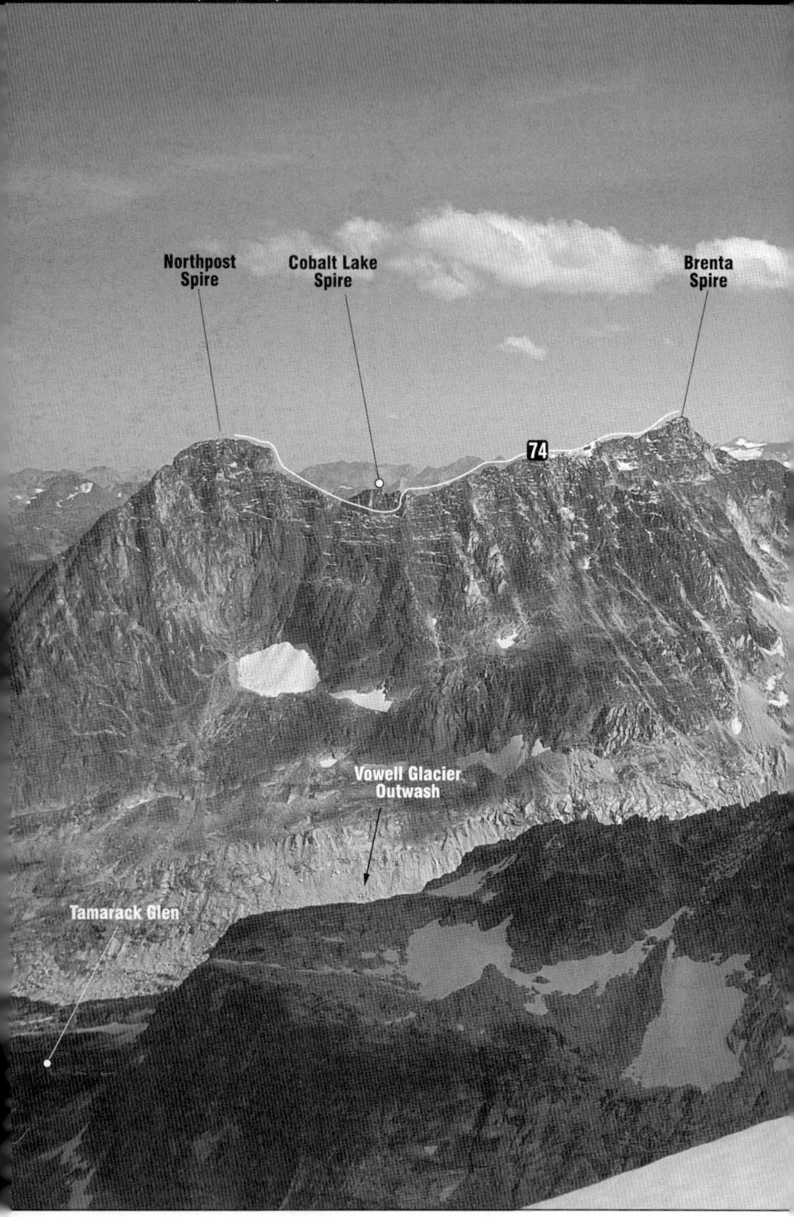
Northpost Spire
Cobalt Lake Spire
Brenta Spire
74
Vowell Glacier Outwash
Tamarack Glen

EASTERN SPIRES PANORAMA **ROUTE: 74** (137)

view from Vowell Group East Glacier cam

Snowpatch–
Pigeon Col

Brenta–
Crescent Col

Crescent
Spire

Bugaboo–
Crescent Col

Lower Vowell
Glacier Icefall

Bugaboo
Spire

Marmolata

EASTERN SPIRES PANORAMA

EASTPOST SPIRE – SOUTHWEST FACE

60m
11+ finger-crack
on arete

30

slab

29

27

60m

10+

layback

groove

mantel

28

29 30

Crescent
Spire

28

27

Applebee
Dome

29 30

Kain Hut

ROUTES: 27 28 (115)   **29 30** (116)

Eastpost
Spire

27

34

31

33

CRESCENT TOWERS — SOUTH FACE

Crescent Spire

North Tower

Central Towers

South Tower (Donkey's Ears)

See photo-topos on page 148-149

50

53 54 56 57 58

59 60 61 62 63

CRESCENT SPIRE — MCTECH ARETE AREA

Crescent Towers

Bugaboo Spire

36

See photo-topo on page opposite

37

38

39 40 41 42 43 44
45 46 47 48 49

ROUTES: **50** (125)   **36** (119)   **37** (120)   **38** (120)

CRESCENT SPIRE – MCTECH ARETE AREA

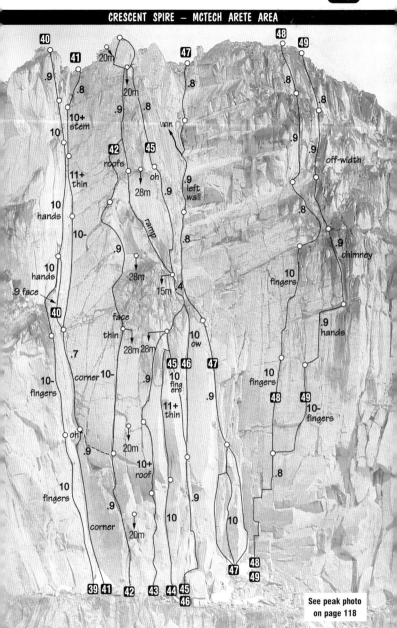

40
.9
10
10+ stem
11+ thin
10 hands
10-
10 hands
.9 face
40
.7
10- corner
10-fingers
oh!
10 fingers

41
.8

20m
20m
.9
42
roofs
.9
28m
face
thin
28m 28m
.9
20m
.9
corner
20m

45
.8
oh
28m
ramp
.9 left wall
.8
15m .4
10 ow
45 **46**
10 fingers
11+ thin
10+ roof
.9
10

47
.8
nn
47
.9

48 **49**
.8 .8
.9
off-width
.8
.9
chimney
10 fingers
.9 hands
10 fingers
48 **49**
10-fingers
.8

47
48
49

39 41   42   43 44 45 46

See peak photo on page 118

CRESCENT TOWERS – SOUTH FACE LEFT

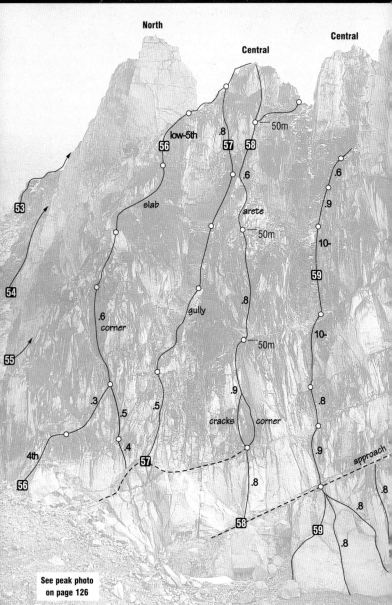

North

Central

Central

low-5th

56

.8

57 58

50m

.6

.6

slab

arete

.9

53

50m

10-

54

.6

59

corner

gully

.8

10-

55

.8

50m

.3

.5

.5

.9

.8

cracks

corner

.4

.9

57

4th

approach

56

.8

.8

58

59

.8

.8

See peak photo
on page 126

ROUTES: 53 54 55 56 57 (127) 58 59 (128).

CRESCENT TOWERS – SOUTH FACE RIGHT

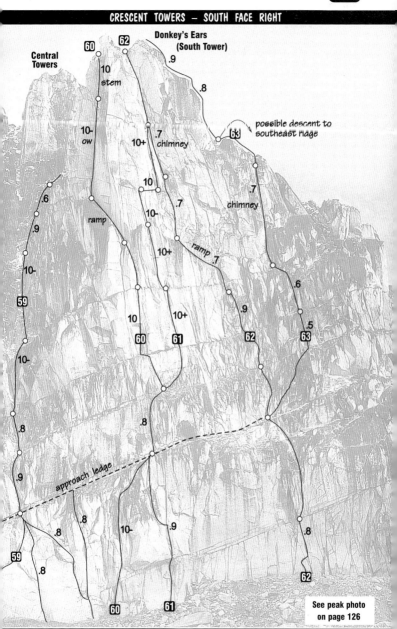

ROUTES: **59 60 61** (128) **62 63** (129).

Crescent Towers — North

South   Centre

Crescent Spire

Snowpatch Spire (behind)

Bugaboo Glacier (behind)

53

52

descent routes off Donkey's Ears (South Tower)

same place

Vowell Glacier Side

Brenta–Crescent Col

52

67

view from Brenta Spire summit
early July 2002

ROUTES: **52** (125)   **53** (127)   **67** (133)

Crescent Spire

Crescent–Brenta Col

Bugaboo Spire

Brenta Spire

52

95

52

67

view from approach basin

ROUTES: **52** (125) **53** (127) **67** (133)

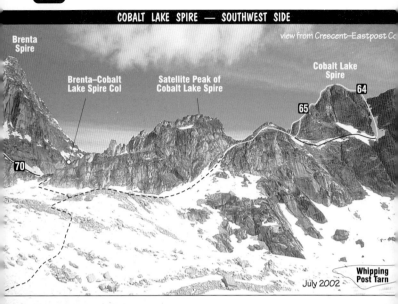

COBALT LAKE SPIRE — SOUTHWEST SIDE

Brenta Spire

view from Crescent–Eastpost Col

Brenta–Cobalt Lake Spire Col

Satellite Peak of Cobalt Lake Spire

Cobalt Lake Spire

64

65

70

Whipping Post Tarn

July 2002

COBALT LAKE SPIRE — NORTHWEST FACE

Cobalt Lake Spire

65

66

Cobalt Lake

66

July 2002

ROUTES: 64 65 66 (131) **70** (134)

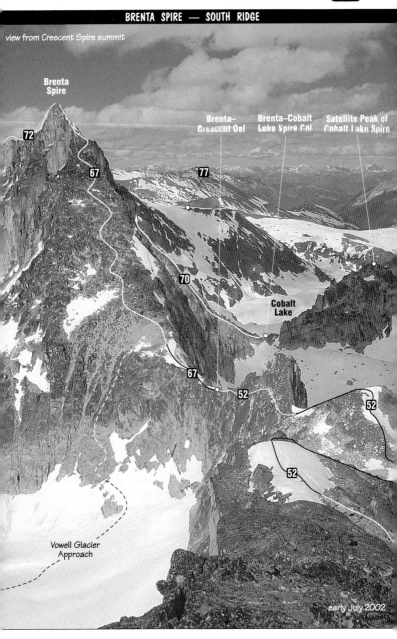

BRENTA SPIRE — SOUTH RIDGE

view from Crescent Spire summit

Brenta
Spire

72

67

70

67

52

52

52

Brenta–
Crescent Col

77

Brenta–Cobalt
Lake Spire Col

Satellite Peak of
Cobalt Lake Spire

Cobalt
Lake

Vowell Glacier
Approach

early July 2002

ROUTES: **52** (125)   **67** (133)   **70** (134)   **72** (135)   **77** (138)

BRENTA SPIRE – EAST FACE

Cobalt Lake Spire
Satellite Peak

67

70

72

68

69

71

Cobalt Lake Spire
–Brenta Col

Cobalt Lake
Basin

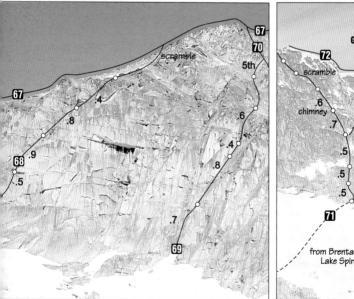

67

scramble

5th

67

.4

.8

.6

68

.9

.4

.5

.8

.7

69

70

Gendarme

72

scramble

.6
chimney

.7

.5

.5

.5

71

from Brenta–Cobalt
Lake Spire Col

ROUTES: **67** (133)   **68 69 70 71** (135)   **72** (135)

NORTHPOST SPIRE — NORTHWEST FACE

view from Vowell East Glacier camp

Northpost
Spire

74

83

82

81

79

80

Vowell Glacier Outwash Valley

Tamarack Glen

August 2002

ROUTES: **74** (137) **79** (138) **80 81 82 83** (139)

NORTHPOST SPIRE — SOUTH SIDE

view from Brenta–Cobalt Lake Spire Col

Northpost Spire

72 74

75 - 76

77

Cobalt Lake

COBALT LAKE AND EASTERN SPIRES — VIEW FROM THE EAST

nowpatch Spire

Cobalt Lake Spire

Pigeon Spire

South Howser Tower

Bugaboo Spire

Brenta–Cobalt Lake Spire Col

Brenta Spire

Northpost Spire

77

Cobalt Lake

ROUTES: **72** (135)   **74 75** (137)   **76 77** (138)

NORTHPOST SPIRE — SOUTH FACE

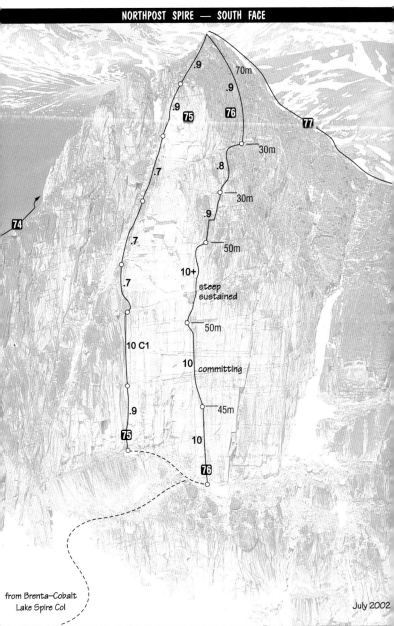

.9
70m
.9
75 **76**
.9
.9
77
30m
74
.8
30m
.9
.7
50m
10+
steep
sustained
.7
.7
50m
10 C1
10 committing
.9
45m
75
10
76

from Brenta–Cobalt
Lake Spire Col

July 2002

ROUTES: **74 75** (137) **76** (138)

Snowpatch Spire

Pigeon Spire

Bugaboo–Snowpatch Col

Bugaboo Spire

Crescent Glacier

Crescent Glacier

August 2002

THE CENTRAL SPIRES FROM THE EAST (CRESCENT SPIRE)

THE CENTRAL SPIRES FROM THE WEST RIDGE OF PIGEON

Bugaboo Spire

Northpost Spire

Brenta Spire

Crescent Spire

Crescent Towers

Bugaboo–Snowpatch Col

Snowpatch Spire (North Summit)

Pigeon Spire

Upper Vowell Glacier

early July 200

CENTRAL SPIRES

The Central Spires consist of Bugaboo, Snowpatch and Pigeon Spires, the most sought after and most frequently climbed peaks in the Bugaboos. Rising off the Crescent Glacier, above the Conrad Kain Hut and Applebee Camping Area are the imposing east faces of Snowpatch and Bugaboo Spires separated by the Bugaboo–Snowpatch Col, a heavily travelled passage that also provides access to the Upper Vowell Glacier. From here lies the approach to the popular *West Ridge* of Pigeon Spire, as well as the west face of Snowpatch Spire and the *Kain Route* on Bugaboo Spire. The Upper Vowell Glacier also gives access to the Western Spires and the Vowell and Conrad Groups.

The south face of Snowpatch Spire and the east face of Pigeon Spire are approached via the Pigeon Fork of the Bugaboo Glacier, around the southeastern toe of Snowpatch Spire.

Bugaboo Spire	South Peak	3204m	North Peak	3197m
Snowpatch Spire	South Peak	3084m	North Peak	3060m
Pigeon Spire	First Peak	3118m	Main Peak	3156m

Climbs: The climbs of the central spires are numerous and varied and the granite is some of the best alpine rock in the world. The eighty-four routes on these three peaks range in difficulty from the spectacular and technically easy *West Ridge* of Pigeon Spire to the numerous hard wall routes of Snowpatch Spire. Within this area are the popular Bugaboo classics of the *Kain Route* and *Northeast Ridge* on Bugaboo Spire, the *West Ridge* and *East Face* on Pigeon Spire and the *Surfs Up*, *Sunshine* and *Snowpatch Routes* on Snowpatch Spire.

Traverses and Enchainments: The central spires each stand isolated by the surrounding glaciers with no connecting ridgelines. This stark isolation is one of the most defining characteristics of the Bugaboos. There are two popular traverses; of Bugaboo Spire via the *Northeast Ridge* and down the *Kain Route*; and of Pigeon Spire via the *East Face* or *Wingtip Arête* routes and down the *West Ridge*.

Enchainment possibilities are good here. Strong parties can add Pigeon Spire to an ascent of either Bugaboo or Snowpatch Spires and all three have been climbed in a single day. Strong parties have also climbed multiple routes on the west face of Snowpatch Spire on the same day. The most popular enchainment is of *McTech Arete* on Crescent Spire with the *Northeast Ridge* on Bugaboo Spire.

BUGABOO   PAGES 160–177
SNOWPATCH   PAGES 178–219
PIGEON   PAGES 220–237

North Summit · South Summit

Bugaboo–Snowpatch C

Snowpatch Spire

Crescent Spire –Bugaboo Col

Vowell Glacie

Sept 20

BUGABOO SPIRE — NORTH FACE

BUGABOO SPIRE — SOUTHEAST FACE

South Summit · North Summit

North Howser Tower

Bugaboo–Snowpatch Col

Crescent Spire –Bugaboo Col

rockfall zone

Crescent Glacier

Crescent Glacier

Conrad Kain Hut

Sept 200

| **Bugaboo Spire** | 3204m (South Peak); 3197m (North Peak) |

This is the legendary peak from which the entire region gained its name. It was on Bugaboo Spire in 1916 that Conrad Kain made his famous first ascent of the south ridge, overcoming the then-formidable difficulties of the Gendarme high on the route. His ascent at the time was one of the most demanding climbs in the world.

From the Kain Hut and Applebee Camping Area the east face of Bugaboo Spire can be seen rising above the Crescent Glacier. The immensely popular *Northeast Ridge* forms the right-hand skyline leading to the north summit and the *Kain Route* forms the left-hand skyline ending on the south summit. The Bugaboo–Snowpatch Col forms the steep, narrow gap that lies at the base of the *Kain Route* and the steep north wall of Snowpatch Spire to the left.

Approach: Access to Bugaboo Spire is via the Crescent Glacier, directly above the Conrad Kain Hut and Applebee Camping Area. The trail leaves the hut above the outhouse boulders and climbs up the moraines towards Applebee Dome. At the first set of rock slabs (15–20 minutes) the trail branches left to the Crescent Glacier and the Bugaboo–Snowpatch Col. This col gives access to the *Kain Route* and the west and north face routes. The east face routes and the *Northeast Ridge* are accessed from the Crescent Glacier below the Bugaboo–Snowpatch Col or directly from Applebee Camp through the moraines on the left side of the tarns above camp. The slabs below the Bugaboo–Crescent Col give access to the start of the *Northeast Ridge.* The north face routes can also be accessed from this col by descending the Vowell Glacier side to a pocket glacier and traversing high and left to a scree ramp directly under the face.

Descent: Descent from all the routes on Bugaboo Spire is off the south summit of the peak, down the rappel anchors of the *Kain Route* (South Ridge). For the routes topping out on the north summit, including the *Northeast Ridge,* a very exposed third and fourth-class traverse must be made to the south summit.

Summit Traverse: Rappel slings can be found on a small flat area about 10 to 15 metres before the North Summit. Squeeze awkwardly through a vee-slot and rappel down the east face approximately 6 metres, go left behind a large boulder and gain easy ledges which are followed across and then up to the ridge crest. This point can also be gained from the summit via a short rappel. Follow the very exposed, fourth-class ridge crest for approximately 60 metres downward to a significant col. Traverse slabs close to the ridge-crest to a small notch against a vertical wall. The short, steep wall with horizontal cracks leads to the south summit (5.10, 8m). A very long reach or shoulder stand are required to reach the first horizontal crack. The south summit can be gained more easily by doing a very short rappel from the notch down the southern ramp to a small ledge. A blocky ledge and gully lead left and up to the south summit.

Rappel 1: From the south summit chain anchors lie about 8m to the south overlooking the gendarme, which appears as a blade of rock from above. A single rope rappel descends to a ledge leading to the gendarme rappel anchors.

Rappel 2: A single rope rappel drops down the left (east) side of the gendarme approximately 25m to a small ledge. Climb back up to the left to gain chain anchors in the notch behind a large flake. Rappelling down the right side of the Gendarme requires a very long pendulum and nasty rope jamming issues.

Rappel 3: Rappel 20m towards the south ridge (*Kain Route*) and along a ramp to gain another set of chain anchors.

Rappel 4: Rappel about 20m to another small ledge and climb back up left again to a comfortable area a few metres shy of the ridge crest. Scramble along the ridge-crest. Climb down a step in the ridge and onto a final knoll where the ridge drops off steeply towards the south. Chain anchors can be found on the left.

Rappel 5 & 6: Rappel two 25m pitches down the east side of the ridge to gain ledges, ramps and the start of the downclimbing. Scramble down the steep part of the ridge until it levels out and heads towards the south again. One set of chain anchors exists above a large jammed boulder. The rest of the descent stays on or near the ridge-crest until it is almost directly above the Bugaboo–Snowpatch Col.

Be forewarned, do not be drawn down the east side. Rappel stations, rock cairns and well-trodden descent trails lead down the east side in many places, but there is no access to the col or the Crescent Glacier without an epic.

Descent down the Bugaboo–Snowpatch Col can be made by downclimbing with crampons and an ice axe or by using either of two chain anchor rappel routes. The first anchors lead down the Bugaboo side of the snow via five rappels to clear the bergshrund. This is also the general line of ascent. Double ropes are required for the middle rappels and some rockfall danger from the *Kain Route* above exists. The second set of chain anchors lead down the

Snowpatch side of the upper snow slope. Two 25m, and one 30m rappel leads to the toe of the rock above the bergshrund. A fourth rappel leads around, over or through the bergshrund depending on the time of the season. This route avoids the normal line of ascent on the upper snow (page 172).

84   Kain Route (South Ridge)   **   AD 5.6   (6-12h)   450m   *170*
Conrad Kain, Albert & Beth MacCarthy, John Vincent Aug. 1916   *CAJ 8:25*

The *Kain Route* was the line of first ascent on Bugaboo Spire, over the famous gendarme. The lower half of the route from Bugaboo–Snowpatch Col is a scramble over scree and boulders. The next quarter ascends steeper third class terrain and the upper quarter of the route contains more difficult terrain. The climb is only committing from one pitch below the ridge leading to the gendarme, to the summit, so a reconnaissance in marginal weather is possible.

Approach from the hut or Applebee Camp via the Crescent Glacier and the Bugaboo–Snowpatch Col. Once at the top of the col follow scree trails right. A scree–covered ramp leads up right past the first rock scar or snow to a vague buttress. Wander up black, lichen–covered boulders to gain the ridge-crest as low as possible. Do not follow vague trails out into the scree of the lower slope as this bombards climbers below the Bugaboo–Snowpatch Col with rockfall. Follow the ridge over several short steps to where it dramatically steepens. Follow third class terrain over more steps right of the ridgeline, trending right to gain the base of a steeper, shallow chimney. Climb the chimney to the ridge crest (5.4, 50m). Scramble a flat section of the ridge, to where it steepens again. Ledges to the right and left help bypass a step in the ridge. From a small notch where the ridge bars progress, follow a ramp, ledges and short corners on the right side just below the ridge-crest to gain a small pedestal belay on the wall directly below the gendarme proper. Climb the short steep wall past horizontal cracks (fixed pins), to the crest of the ridge. Friction slightly down the other side to the top of a shallow corner and make a long reach out left to gain a crack (fixed pin) leading to a belay behind the gendarme (5.6, 25m). Follow the ledge behind the gendarme to a flaky corner system, which leads up to the south summit.

85   Herr² Route   D+   5.11   (10-14h)   13p   *173*
Hugh Herr, Hans Herr August 1979
This route follows the extreme left side of the east face. It offers good climbing but is exposed to rockfall generated by climbers on the *Kain Route* and the south summit.

Start near the bottom of the *Japanese Pillar*. The lower six pitches climb the series of flakes and ledges angling up left to the base of a right-leaning corner system that joins the south ridge just below the gendarme. These lower pitches are characterized by short, steep corners separated by ledges and short fourth-class sections. The final four pitches to the ridge crest involve continuous 5.10 crack climbing ranging from big fists to tipped off fingers. From the ridge crest the upper section of the *Kain Route* can be followed to the south summit

86 Japanese Pillar   TD-   5.12- (5.9 A3)   (8-10h)   6p   *173*

First ascent (1970s) unknown   *FFA Scott Cosgrove, Mark Bowling August 1992*

Known as the incomplete route with the most first ascents, this route was climbed to the top of the large pillar left of the *Cooper–Gran* some time in the early 1970s by a Japanese party. Freed in 1992, it follows face cracks and shallow corners for three pitches to the base of a right-facing corner system. This corner is followed for three more pitches to the top of the pillar.

87 Cooper—Gran (East Face)   *   TD   5.11 (12-16h)   12p   *173*

Ed Cooper, Art Gran August 1960
FFA Mike Tschipper, Tom Gibson August 1980   *CAJ 44:77, AAJ 12:383*

This was the first route up the east face of Bugaboo Spire, climbed over two seasons and many storms. From the left edge of the Balcony it follows shallow left-facing corners directly below the north summit exiting high on to the *Northeast Ridge*.

     Climb a pitch off of the Crescent Glacier to gain the Balcony directly below the *Midnight Route*. Traverse left for about 100 metres to the end of the ledge system and a shallow left-facing corner system. Follow corners and cracks for five pitches (5.10-) to a ledge below a bolt ladder. Aid the bolt ladder or free climb the bolt protected 5.11 face-climbing to the right to gain an offwidth. Climb a 5.10+ groove pitch followed by two easier pitches to gain a right-trending ramp leading to the northeast ridge.

88 Symposium   *   TD+   5.8 A2+   (18-24h)   15p   *173*

Alex McAfee August 2002   *CAJ 86:88*

From the Balcony, *Symposium* climbs the right-facing corner 60 metres right of the *Cooper–Gran*, through a series of overhangs and then traverses left into the *Cooper–Gran* at pitch five.

     Climb two short pitches from the Crescent Glacier to gain the left edge of the Balcony (5.6 and C1). Climb the corner for two pitches on A2+ beaks and C1 to a roof. Follow the roof out right to a belay requiring 5 inch cams. Traverse left on A1 blades to a belay and bivy ledge. Climb A1 cracks using button heads for one pitch past an overhang followed by A2 blades to a ledge belay. Climb left at A1 to pendulums left and an A1 crack leading to a ledge belay. Tension left to gain the *Cooper–Gran*, which is followed to the north summit.

     Bring a regular modern wall rack, 5 inch cams, extra blades and beaks.

89 Midnight Route   *   TD   5.9 A3   (14-18h)   12p   *173*

Jay Wilson, Peter Cole July 1981

The *Midnight Route* follows a left-facing flake–corner system 50 metres right of the *Symposium* corner.

     Climb flakes and cracks from the Crescent Glacier in one pitch (5.10 or A1) to gain the middle of the Balcony directly below the shallow flake–corner system. A few awkward A2 moves lead off the Balcony to gain the base of the corner, which is followed for two 5.9 pitches. Pitch three steps out right to nail a parallel left arching crack. Tension out an alcove along a dyke and regain the corner and a sling belay. An A3 pitch leads to a sling belay followed by a 5.9 A1 pitch exiting right as the corner arches left. The next four pitches involve 5.9 climbing interspersed with A2 and A3 aid climbing. These pitches lead up and right over convoluted terrain to gain the *Northeast Ridge* that leads to the north summit.

Bring a regular rack with extra small nuts and RPs and a small selection of KBs and LAs

90   Thanks for the Handout   D+   5.10- A2 (5.11)   (8-10h) 6p*173*

Alex McClure, Jason Magness, Andy Magness, Greg Huey August 1997

This incomplete route follows the next system right of the *Midnight Route*. From the Crescent Glacier climb the first pitch of the *Harvey Roach* to gain the extreme right edge of the Balcony. Scramble thirty metres up and left to gain the left of two dihedrals. Climb the 5.9 dihedral past a small roof, to gain a belay below the next roof. Turn the roof and climb 5.11- or A2 to a sling belay above the next big roof (20m). Stem (5.10-) to climb corner and cracks to top of dihedral (30m). Tunnel right through an alleyway behind a flake to another corner. The first ascent party suggested the route would follow the last corner and traverse to gain *Pretty Vacant* near the *Northeast Ridge*.

91   Harvey–Roach   D+   5.10+   (10-14h)   13p   *173*

Kennan Harvey, Scott Roach Sept. 1990

The *Harvey–Roach* climbs, in eight pitches, from the Crescent Glacier past the right end of the Balcony to join *Pretty Vacant* before gaining the *Northeast Ridge*.

Access the extreme right end of the Balcony via a right-facing corner. Scramble right and climb steeper ledges to a second dyke. Traverse right to below the corner system that is right of *Thanks for the Handout*. Layback a 5.10+ flake to gain a corner that is followed to gain flakes and ledges (5.9). Trend right to join in with *Pretty Vacant* and follow it to the *Northeast Ridge*. Finish up the *Northeast Ridge*.

92   Pretty Vacant   D+   5.10 (A1)   (10-16h)   13p   *175*

Joe Buszowski, Craig Thompson August 1983

Pretty Vacant ascends the prominent right-facing corner system 70 metres left of the *Northeast Ridge* rope up terrace and joins that route at about mid height.

As with the *Northeast Ridge* approach, leave the Crescent Glacier via steep slabs to gain the Bugaboo–Crescent Col and scramble up to gain the rope up terrace for the *Northeast Ridge*. Follow the dyke and terrace down and left to gain the base of the corner. Climb the corner and chimney system for three pitches, and follow 5.8 flakes for a pitch. At this point the route finding becomes confusing. A thin dyke on a slab leads up right to beneath a roof, above which the *Vacant and Obscure* variation is supposed to branch off. Tension down and right past a corner to gain face cracks which are followed for three pitches. A final right-trending 5.10 (A1) pitch climbs over convoluted terrain to gain the *Northeast Ridge*, which is followed to the summit.

Bring a regular long route free rack with extra small nuts and RPs and a small selection of KBs and LAs

93 Vacant and Obscure   D+   5.10   (10-16h)   13p   *175*
Hugh.Widdowson July 1989

This is a minor variation of *Pretty Vacant* that bypassed the aid climbing on that route.

On pitch five where *Pretty Vacant* descends right, continue more directly up, climbing connecting cracks for four pitches to gain the *Northeast Ridge*. Accounts are vague but both routes may share the final one or two pitches.

94 Where's Issac?   5.11+   (3-5h)   2p   *175*
Jonny Copp, Jeff Hollenbaugh July 2002

Where's Issac? is a two pitch route that climbs the wall below the dyke and terrace leading from the *Northeast Ridge* down to the *Pretty Vacant* corner. It can be climbed on its own with a descent down to the Bugaboo–Crescent Col or used as a direct start to *Pretty Vacant*.

From the Crescent Glacier find a ledge directly below the *Pretty Vacant* corner cutting up and right onto the face. Follow a thin left-facing corner for two 5.11+ pitches, exiting up and right to near the start of *Pretty Vacant*.

95 Northeast Ridge ***   D-   5.8   (8-16h)   12p   *175*
Dave Craft, David Isles, Richard Sykes, John Turner August 1958
FWA Joe Buszowski, Bernhard Ehmann 1985   *CAJ 44:77, AAJ 12:383*

The *Northeast Ridge* on Bugaboo Spire was made famous by Roper and Steck's book *Fifty Classic Climbs in North America*. Like so many Bugaboo climbs the climbing is varied, the rock good and the position spectacular. A word of caution though, more parties have been benighted on the *Northeast Ridge* than all the other routes in the Bugaboos combined. Traditionally only half the parties on this route make it back to camp before dark. Climbing the *Kain Route,* and scoping out the traverse between the summits and having an intimate knowledge of the descent route will increase a party's chance of 'success in a day'.

From the Bugaboo–Crescent Col the route follows fourth-class terrain to a terrace where three pitches lead up the left side to gain the ridge-crest proper. The rest of the route follows cracks and chimneys on the north side of the ridge to gain the north summit. A protracted traverse leads to the south summit and the rappels and descent of the *Kain Route* that ends at the Bugaboo–Snowpatch Col, which must also be descended.

Follow the Crescent Glacier beneath the east face of Bugaboo Spire towards its eastern end. From the base of the large corner systems that make up the McTech Area of Crescent Spire, follow the edge of the snow and ice up hill towards Bugaboo Spire. A few hundred metres along, a right-leaning slabby wall can be found. The rock of the slab takes on an orange-green-gray colour. Climb fourth-class with the occasional low–fifth class moves up the left side of the slab to exit left off of small ledges and steep blocks to the Bugaboo–Crescent Col. Scramble up the lower ridge to a terrace which is part of the white dyke–ledge system that girdles the right side of the east face and the *Northeast Ridge*. This is the start of the pitched climbing. The climb starts about 10m left of the actual arête in an alcove amidst some stacked flakes.

1: A strenuous 5.8 move on finger locks leads out of the alcove to gain hand-cracks. Climb up to follow the left side of a chimney/flake system. Near the top of the flakes traverse out left to gain small ledges below and right of a left–rising series of shallow, flaky grooves. **2:** Climb these grooves up and left to the top of a pillar (5.6). **3:** Climb down left for about 3m until it is possible to climb back up above the belay. Climb the right-arching dyke system back right on positive holds (5.7) to reach the belay immediately right of the ridge-crest. **4-5:** Climb 5.6 hand and fist-cracks on the immediate right side of the arete. A long pitch (60m) takes you to the higher belay ledge. **6-9:** Step out right and follow a chimney system over blocks and the occasional chock–stone (5.6). Snow is often present here. Belay at a good ledge on the ridge-crest above the chimney. Cracks very near the ridge-crest provide aesthetic variations at 5.8 and 5.9 and join the chimney line midway up. **10:** Climb cracks on the right side of the ridge over two short steps (5.7) to where the ridge kicks back. **11-12:** Climb a short fourth-class pitch along the ridge to gain a rappel station and an even shorter stretch of fourth-class around to the right to gain the North Summit.

　　To descend, traverse to the south summit and the *Kain Route* rappel anchors.

96　North Face Direct　　　TD+　5.10 A1 ♦ (12-16h) 650m　*176*
Ward Robinson, Bernhard Ehmann　early 1980s

This huge face sits hidden from view from the Kain Hut basin. The route follows the large left-facing corner system for about eight pitches to join the *North Face* at mid–height. From here it may also be possible to climb left onto the *Northeast Ridge*. The route has had very few ascents.

97　North Face　　　　　TD　5.7 A1 ♦ (12-16h) 700m　*176*
Layton Kor, Claude Suhl August 1960　　　　　　　　　　*CAJ 44:82*

Very little is known of this route. The first ascent party climbed the 700m face in nine hours and placed two bolts giving it the rating of 5.7 A1

　　The route most likely starts at the lowest point on the face and follows the broken terrain, which lies directly below both summits. At the end of the broken terrain a ledge system leads out left for two to three pitches to the middle of the face. Flakes and cracks were followed above to a pendulum from bolts. More crack systems, strenuous at times were then followed to gain the *Northeast Ridge* just 20m below the north summit.

The summit of Pigeon, which hundreds of climbers had stood upon, fell off in the winter of 1991, taking the register with it.

98 West Face   D+ 5.4 ♦   (10-12h) 600m *177*

Fred Beckey, Pete Geiser, Roman Sadowy Aug 1959   *AAJ 12:23*

This route ascends the face that looks across the Upper Vowell Glacier to the east faces of the Howser Towers. It is approached by descending the Vowell Glacier from the Bugaboo–Snowpatch Col and gains the south summit. Information on the two west face routes is vague and both climbs have seen very few ascents. The face presents many possibilities for route variations and it is likely the route grade is in the 5.8 range.

From a talus cone at the centre of the face, follow a ramp leading right for about 120m before breaking out left to traverse three or four rope lengths to a ledge system. From the far end of the ledge system a short steep section gives access to another right-trending ramp that sits directly below the steep, rotten, white wall. Follow the ramp to its end and cross into "a long, shallow, slabby trough". The route climbs up this trough and breaks out left to gain the thin ridge one pitch below the south summit.

99 West Face Direct   D+ 5.4 A2 ♦ (12-14h) 600m *177*

Ed Cooper, Elfrida Pigou August 1959   *CAJ 43:74*

This route was climbed in 1959 one week before the *West Face* and follows a very similar line. Follow the initial ramp and traverse to the ledge systems as with the *West Face*. The next ramp below the steep, white wall is gained sooner on this route and requires only minor aid up "a short overhang enclosed in a wide chimney" The ramp is followed to the gain the same slabby trough, but instead of breaking out left, it is followed all the way up and right to gain the *Kain Route* just below the gendarme. As with the *West Face*, this route is more likely in the 5.8 range.

BUGABOO SPIRE – SUMMIT RIDGE TRAVERSE

North Summit

Cobalt Lake

Climber: Kevin McLane

view to the east

NEAR THE SUMMIT OF BUGABOO SPIRE

Snowpatch   Rock Ridge Peak   Marmolata   Howser Peak

Climber: Kevin McLane

ROUTE: 84 (163)

BUGABOO SPIRE – KAIN ROUTE

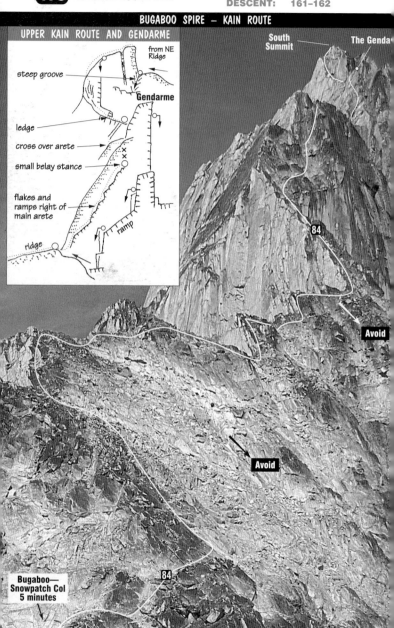

UPPER KAIN ROUTE AND GENDARME

from NE Ridge

steep groove

Gendarme

ledge

cross over arete

small belay stance

flakes and ramps right of main arete

ridge

ramp

South Summit

The Genda

84

Avoid

Avoid

Bugaboo— Snowpatch Col 5 minutes

84

ROUTE: **84** (163)

BUGABOO SPIRE — UPPER KAIN ROUTE

South Summit

The Gendarme

Climber: Cathy Dunlop
on the ridge leading to
the Gendarme

BUGABOO SPIRE — KAIN ROUTE GENDARME SECTION

South Summit

The
Gendarme

climbers

84

ROUTE: 84 (163)

BUGABOO—SNOWPATCH COL – EAST SIDE APPROACH FROM CRESCENT GLACIER

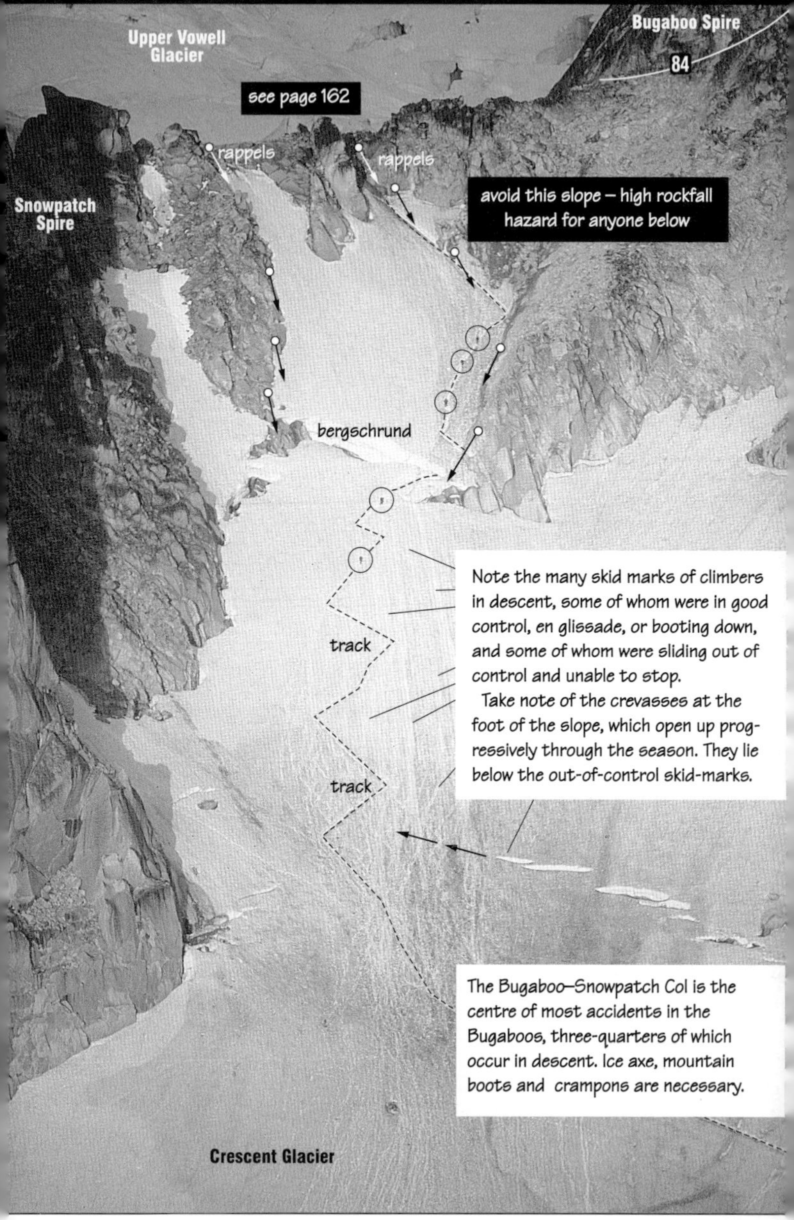

Upper Vowell Glacier

Bugaboo Spire

84

see page 162

rappels

rappels

Snowpatch Spire

avoid this slope – high rockfall hazard for anyone below

bergschrund

track

track

Crescent Glacier

Note the many skid marks of climbers in descent, some of whom were in good control, en glissade, or booting down, and some of whom were sliding out of control and unable to stop.

Take note of the crevasses at the foot of the slope, which open up progressively through the season. They lie below the out-of-control skid-marks.

The Bugaboo—Snowpatch Col is the centre of most accidents in the Bugaboos, three-quarters of which occur in descent. Ice axe, mountain boots and crampons are necessary.

BUGABOO–SNOWPATCH COL

BUGABOO SPIRE – EAST FACE

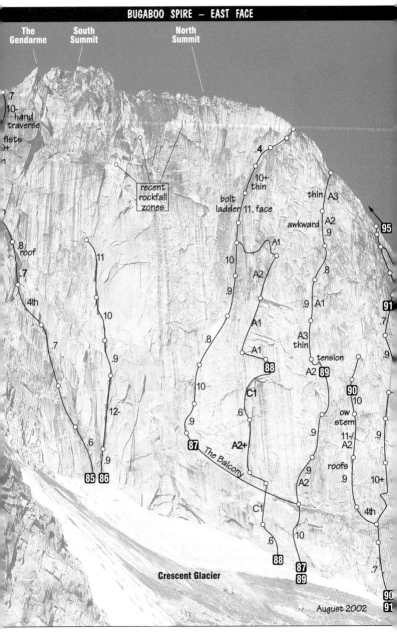

The Gendarme

South Summit

North Summit

.7

10-
hand traverse

fists +

.8 roof

.7

4th

.7

recent rockfall zones

.4

10+ thin

bolt ladder 11. face

thin A3

awkward A2 .9

.8

.9 A1

A3 thin

tension A2 **89**

10

ow stem

11-/ A2

roofs .9

10+

4th

.7

95

91

.7

.9

90

91

10

A1

A2

.9

A1

A1 **88**

C1

.8

10

.9

.6

A2+

The Balcony

87

C1

.6

10

88

87 89

11

10

.9

12-

.6

.9

85 86

90

Crescent Glacier

August 2002

BUGABOO SPIRE — NORTHEAST RIDGE

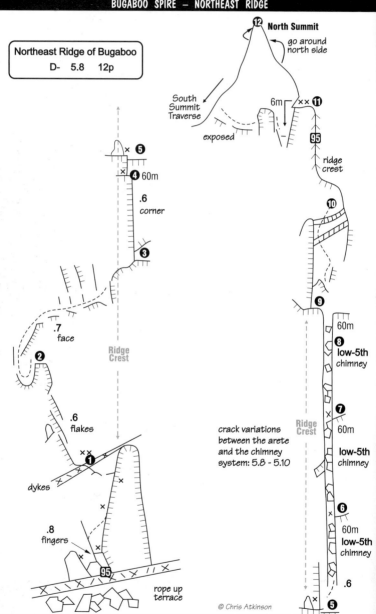

Northeast Ridge of Bugaboo
D-   5.8   12p

North Summit

go around
north side

South
Summit
Traverse

6m

exposed

ridge
crest

.6
corner

Ridge
Crest

.7
face

crack variations
between the arete
and the chimney
system: 5.8 - 5.10

Ridge
Crest

.6
flakes

60m

low-5th
chimney

60m

low-5th
chimney

dykes

.8
fingers

60m

low-5th
chimney

.6

rope up
terrace

© Chris Atkinson

ROUTE: 95 (166)

BUGABOO SPIRE — NORTHEAST RIDGE

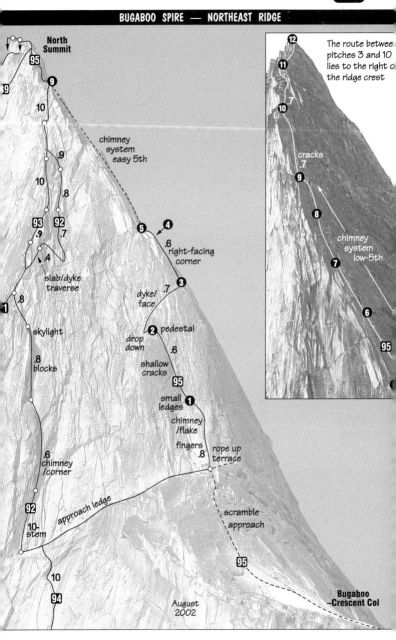

North Summit

95

9

9

10

.9

10

.8

93 .9

92 .7

.4

slab/dyke traverse

1 .8

skylight

.8 blocks

.6 chimney /corner

92

10-stem

10

94

chimney system easy 5th

5 4

.6 right-facing corner

3

dyke/ face .7

2 pedestal

drop down

.6

shallow cracks

95

small ledges 1

chimney /flake

fingers .8 rope up terrace

approach ledge

scramble approach

95

Bugaboo –Crescent Col

August 2002

The route betwee
pitches 3 and 10
lies to the right o
the ridge crest

12

11

10 .7

cracks .7

9

8

chimney system low-5th

7

6

95

BUGABOO SPIRE — NORTH FACE

North
Summit

South
Summit

95

97

98

99

96

rockfall
zone

97

from Bugaboo–
Crescent Col

from Bugaboo–
Snowpatch Col

Vowell Glacier

ROUTES: **95** (166) **96 97** (167) **98 99** (168)

BUGABOO SPIRE — WEST FACE

South Summit

Vowell
Glacier

August 20C

ROUTES: **84** (163)   **98 99** (168)

Tom Egan Wall

East Face (partly hidden)

North Face

West Face

Upper Vowell Glac

Bugaboo–Snowpatch Col

view of Snowpatch Spire from the north, near the summit of Bugaboo Spire

Snowpatch Spire   3084m (North Peak); 3060m (South Peak)

Snowpatch Spire rises out of the Crescent Glacier directly above the Conrad Kain Hut and to the left of Bugaboo Spire. It hides the view of Pigeon Spire and the Howser Towers and casts an early afternoon shadow over the Kain Hut basin. Conrad Kain after his ascents of Bugaboo Spire, Mount Robson and Mount Louis wrote, "… I feel inclined to prophesy that this pinnacle will be the most difficult in the Canadian Alps", and he was right. First climbed in 1940 by Jack Arnold and Raffi Bedayn via the *Snowpatch Route*, Snowpatch Spire was the last of the major summits in the Bugaboos to be climbed and is the most difficult. With over fifty routes, it is also the most extensively explored.

The routes run from the six to eight pitch 5.9 to 5.12 climbs on the west face to the twelve to fifteen pitch wall routes on the east face. Hard, sustained free routes exist on all four faces.

There has been much confusion amongst climbers over the names of the *Southeast Corner* and *Southwest Ridge* routes, mostly because the *Southeast Corner* is a ridge and the *Southwest Ridge* is a corner. Because of this confusion the guidebook uses the names *Snowpatch Route* and *Surfs Up* to avoid confusion. The most popular and busiest routes are: *Snowpatch Route, Surfs Up, Kraus–McCarthy* and *Sunshine Crack*.

Approach: Much of Snowpatch Spire's popularity is due to the short approaches. The east face and north wall can be gained in forty minutes from the Conrad Kain Hut and less than thirty minutes from Applebee Camp.

East Face and North Wall. From the hut follow the trail to Applebee Dome for about 15–20 minutes taking a trail left above the rock slabs at a faint junction. From Applebee Camp faint trails contour towards the east face to join the trail on the flats above the rock slabs. Follow the drainage up to gain the Crescent Glacier and the east face and north wall.

To reach the west face, continue up the Bugaboo–Snowpatch Col, usually passing the bergshrund on the right side where it pinches onto the rock. At the top of the snow–slope traverse left to exit up a short gully in order to avoid the very loose scree on the right. From the col, head up a short snow or ice slope on the left to gain the base of the west face.

***Snowpatch Route* and south face routes.** These are approached via the Bugaboo Glacier. From the Conrad Kain Hut follow rough

trails behind the largest boulder up towards the southeast toe of
Snowpatch Spire. From the toe, drop down around rock slabs to gain
the edge of the ice. For the *Snowpatch Route* follow the ice a short
distance around the slabs and cut back right to follow the base of
the bluffs up to a broken gully leading to a notch between Snowpatch
Spire and its small satellite bluffs known as Son of Snowpatch. The
rock slabs can also be scrambled directly to avoid the steep but easier
ice. *Lightning Bolt Crack* is located in this small basin on the upper
left side. To reach the south face, bypass the first basin by staying
on the ice. Follow the glacier up onto the flats directly below the
south face of Snowpatch Spire and the east face of Pigeon Spire.
Crevasses often extend to the rocks on this route.

Descent: Two established rappel routes exist off Snowpatch
Spire, both are down the west face, and both are six or seven double
rope rappels in length. The *Kraus–McCarthy* rappel route, fixed with
chain anchors, descends from the south summit (page 213) and the
Beckey–Greenwood rappel route, fixed with slings, descends from the
north summit (page 212). *Sunshine Crack* also has an established
rappel route fixed with slings from the top of the north wall, and
avoids having to gain the north summit (page 194).

From the base of the west face, two options exist to return to
the Kain Hut Basin; via the Bugaboo–Snowpatch Col or the Pigeon–
Snowpatch Icefall rappels. Mountain boots, ice axes and crampons
are recommended for both due to the glacier travel.

For climbers camped at Applebee Dome, descent by the
Bugaboo–Snowpatch Col is fastest. For those who wish to avoid
downclimbing, there are two chain anchor rappel routes, one down
the ascent line on the Bugaboo side and one down the Snowpatch
side of the upper snow slope. The latter requires only a single 60m
rope and avoids the ascent line.

For climbers at the base of the west face routes and wishing to
return to the Kain Hut, an alternative to going down the Bugaboo–
Snowpatch Col is the rappel route of the Pigeon–Snowpatch Icefall.
To reach them, head to the south end of the west face and follow
the edge of the glacier down to exit left onto a flat rock promenade.
Chain anchors can be found on the wall. Six 25m rappels reach the
Bugaboo Glacier. Cross the glacier flats under the south face and
follow the ice down two steep rolls to the toe of Son of Snowpatch.
A traverse beneath the rock slabs leads to a short uphill section to
gain the Kain Hut Basin and a short descent to the hut.

Snowpatch Spire: East Face

The east face of Snowpatch Spire is the broad, high face that rises off the Crescent Glacier above the Conrad Kain Hut. The east face is approximately 500m high and is bounded on the south side by the famous snowpatch of the southeast face and on the north by the *Bugaboo Corner* route of the north wall.

The face can be divided into three sections; the left or south section where the routes lead to the south summit; the central section where the routes lead to the north summit; and the Tom Egan Wall section on the right or north end where the routes lead to the top of the north wall before merging to climb the final towers of the *Buckingham Route* to the north summit.

The Climbs: With the exception of the *Snowpatch Route* on the southeast side, all the routes on the east face are big wall in nature. The face is vertical and mostly aid climbing, for the lower half while the upper half of the face tends to be free climbing in the 5.8 to 5.10 range. Some hard free or mostly free climbs exist on the Tom Egan wall with sustained 5.11-12 climbing. There is much potential for free climbing the wall routes of the east face, continuous and linked crack systems are commonplace.

A section low down on the central face fell off in the winter of 1998. This affects *Deus ex Machina, Les Bruixes ex Pentinum, Parker–Brashaw* and *Sunshine Wall*. A direct approach from the first pitch of *Les Bruixes ex Pentinum* appears possible. A traverse where the top of the now-disappeared flake was may require a short bolt ladder.

The routes on the Tom Egan wall are the most popular of the east face routes. It has steeper and cleaner rock and offers shorter but generally harder and more continuous lines. The original *Beckey–Mather* route of 1959 and the *Deus ex Machina* continue to be popular, with moderate aid and free grades.

Descent: None of the east face routes are set up as rappel routes although some of the routes on the Tom Egan Wall have been rappelled. Here are three descent options off the east face.

(1) For south-end routes that reach the south summit the *Kraus–McCarthy* rappel route down the west face is used (page 213).

(2) For routes that reach the col between the north and south summits, or for routes that reach the north summit, the *Beckey–Greenwood* rappel route down the west face is used (page 212).

(3) Routes on the Tom Egan Wall that reach the flats above the north wall can rappel *Sunshine Crack* (page 194).

SNOWPATCH: EAST FACE PHOTO–TOPOS 188 – 193

Son of Snowpatch is the satellite bluff that runs off the southeast corner of Snowpatch Spire. On the approach to the *Snowpatch Route* numerous cracks and corners are passed. Many of these have been climbed, most of them being 5.8 to 5.10. A multi–pitch route also ascends the southeast crest of Son of Snowpatch, being about 5.8.

100 **Snowpatch Route** *** D- 5.8 (10-16h) 19p *189*

Jack Arnold, Raffi Bedayn, August 1940 *AAJ 4:219*
FWA Heiri Perk, Walter Renner, winter 1975

This is another Bugaboo classic. The *Snowpatch Route* on the southeast corner of Snowpatch Spire was the line of first ascent, with Fritz Wiessner and C.Cranmer pioneering the lower part of the route in 1938. It is a long, aesthetic and moderate route with the crux being up high and the descent down the west face rappel route. The route is technically moderate but is long and many parties have problems with the routefinding.

Approach via the Bugaboo Glacier. From the Conrad Kain Hut follow rough trails behind the largest boulder up towards the southeast toe of Snowpatch Spire. From the toe, drop down around rock slabs to gain the edge of the ice. Follow the ice a short distance around the slabs and cut back right to follow the base of the bluffs up to a broken gully leading to a notch between Snowpatch Spire and its small satellite bluffs known as Son of Snowpatch. From the base of the gully several direct corners lead up left at about 5.9. Above these are the dihedral and spur pitches that lead to the Weisnner Overhang.

1-2: From the notch at the top of the gully, contour down the Kain Hut Basin side slightly until able to scramble up broken ground bypassing two small pinnacles on the ridge to gain the ridge-crest proper where it steepens. Several off–route variations exist to the right of the ridge at about 5.9 and gain the ridge higher up. **3:** Cross the crest back to the Bugaboo Glacier side and follow a descending ledge system to gain the base of a dihedral overlooking the approach gully.

4-5: Climb the dihedral for one low–fifth pitch, then low–fifth cracks on the right wall to gain the spur and a belay at the base of the steeper wall known as the Weissner Overhang. **6:** Drop down right to follow a rising mid–fifth class handtraverse on the white slab below a bulging black wall. Belay at its end on a small ledge below the snowpatch. **7:** Climb straight up to gain the slabs below the snowpatch. **8-11:** Four long pitches lead up the slabs left of the snowpatch. The climbing is easy fifth class but protection and ledges are scarce. **12-13:** Follow broken ground for two more low–fifth class pitches, trending steadily right to a belay behind a large flake known as the Inverted Pear. The *Direct Variation* leads left up ramps and short walls in five pitches to 5.9 (A.Hall, C.Hall, C.Boeking August 1986). **14:** Continue along the ledge system for one more pitch to the base of a left-facing white corner. The harder climbing starts here.

These upper pitches are not long but the route–finding is convoluted and rope drag is a concern. **15:** At the start of the white corner, slings out right in another corner mark the off route *Honeymooners Variation* (Leslie

Benoliel, Alex Hamilton August 1989) which leads in four 5.7 pitches to the saddle north of the south summit. Climb the first corner past fixed pins to a flake and friction out left below a bulge to a slab belay below a short dyke and an offwidth.**16:** Either face-climb or offwidth the short, steep wall above at 5.6 to another slab and a belay at its top. **17:** Climb a short section up steep flakes to a hand–traverse left past fixed pins. Make an awkward move left around a jutting flake and climb the hollow 5.7 cracks up the short, steep white wall past fixed pins to a ramp. Shuffle right along the ramp to a belay. **18-19:** One or two easy pitches lead to the south summit.

Descent is down the *Kraus–McCarthy* rap route on the west face. Bring a standard free rack with a piece for the offwidth and extra single and double slings.

101 **Beckey–Mather Route** * TD+ 5.10 A2   (1-2 bv)   16p *190*
Fred Beckey, Hank Mather, August 1959   *AAJ 12:17*

This route was the first of the big walls to be climbed in the Bugaboos and a bold undertaking for 1959. It climbs the left side of the east face to the south summit.

The route starts below a long, slender pillar. **1-2:** Climb an A2 crack to a belay ledge. Continue up an A1 crack to another ledge. **3-6:** Aid the A2 crack with occasional free moves past good belay ledges to the highest ledge. Aid a loose flake then move right to a corner and aid cracks past roofs. Tension to the left edge of a large dark roof and continue on aid over it to a series of ramps and a sling belay below a larger roof. (A2). **7-9:** Climb a series of strenuous overhanging corners to an alcove. Aid above and then free climb a low–angle gully to a good ledge. Aid a left-leaning corner to a ledge. **10-13:** Move down left and aid a 10m pillar. Traverse down left and step across to a crack system. Climb to double cracks and flakes in a right-facing corner below a chimney. Go left into the chimney and up 10m to aid the right crack to a belay ledge. Climb a flaky roof to a right-facing corner and belay in a black, flared corner. **14-16:** Move left and face-climb a ramp to another flared corner. Climb a fist-crack in a low–angled corner to 25m below the summit block and continue up easy slabs to the summit.

A standard wall rack with extra knifeblades and lost arrows and two or three large cams is needed.

102 **Vertical Party** *   TD+ 5.9 A2   (1-2 bv)   15p *190*
Marc Arbos, Jaume Clotet, August 1993   *AAJ 1994:177*

This route follows the next major crack system right of the *Beckey–Mather*. It heads left to join that route for pitch five and then splits right above the overhangs and climbs the upper wall to the col between the summits.

Like most routes on the east face, the lower section is predominantly A2 climbing with the upper section being mostly free climbing to 5.9-10 and the occasional easy aid section.

A standard wall rack including hooks and copperheads with extra knifeblades and lost arrows is needed.

103 **East Face Diagonal** *   TD+   5.7 A3   (1-2 biv)   13p   *190*

Peter Carman, Yvon Chouinard, Doug Tompkins, August 1971   CAJ 55:79

An appropriate name, this route follows a left-trending diagonal crack through
the first two thirds of the face before straightening up to gain the col between
the summits.

Details are unknown but continuous nailing up the diagonal crack with
mixed free and aid climbing on the upper wall is likely.

There are no bivy ledges on the lower wall. The grade is from the 1970s.

Likely a standard wall rack with extra knifeblades and lost arrows

104 **In Harm's Way** *   TD+   5.9 A3   (1-2 biv)   13p   *190*

Peter Cole, M.Richey, R.Rouner, August 1975

In Harms Way starts just right of *East Face Diagonal* in the beginning of the
massive flake system that climbs up and right across the lower face into
the Tom Egan Wall.

The route ascends cracks to gain the right side of a ledge and then
climbs the right of two left-facing corners. It crosses the right end of the
long overhang that runs right from the *Beckey–Mather*. Above this the route
joins into *Deus ex Machina* and follows corner systems directly to the north
summit. Predominantly aid climbing on the lower half with mixed free and
aid on the upper half.

105 **Deus ex Machina** *   TD+   5.9 A3   (1-2 biv)   15p   *190*

Mike Jefferson, Dennis Jefferson, Dennis Saunders, August 1974   AAJ 20:472

Deus ex Machina originally started with a 5.9 offwidth at the base of the
large flake system that ran up and right. A large section of the flake has since
fallen off and a more direct start is now up the first pitch of *Les Bruixes ex
Pentinen*, which is part of the left-trending diagonal crack that forms the lower
half of *Deus ex Machina*.

Aid the diagonal crack for five or six pitches to below a roof (5.9 A3).
Continue over the roof to where it gains the upper corners and *In Harms
Way*. Follow corners past good bivy ledges up mixed free and aid climbing
to a black, dirty, overhanging A3 slot. Aid over slot and continue directly to
the north summit.

106 **Deus ex Machina Variation**   TD+   5.10+ A2   (1-2 biv) 15p*190*

Pat Littlejohn, D.Llato, August 1976

A minor variation on *Deus ex Machina*, which climbs the parallel diagonal
weakness to the right of pitches three through five.

107 **Les Bruixes Es Pentinen** *   TD+   5.10+ A3 (1-2 biv)   12p   *190*

Roger Besora, Jordi Bou, Felix Queipo, August 1997

This route starts just right of the fresh white scar on the lower face. It climbs
cracks and flakes stepping right initially to climb diagonal left over ledges
before trending back right to climb a vague tower left of a gully system. Pitch
two nailed right under the hollow flake that has since fallen off hence the
current status of the pitch is unknown. A bolt kit and hooks may be needed.
The route is mixed aid and free climbing throughout.

Take a standard wall rack with extra angles, lost arrows and small cams.

108 **Parker–Brashaw**   TD   5.10 C1 ◆   (16-20h)   11p   *192*

P.Brashaw, A. Parker, July 1977

The *Parker–Brashaw* is a major variation to Sunshine Wall.

Start as for Sunshine Wall to gain the long traverse. The Parker–Brashaw climbs up off the ledge system midway along the traverse to gain a steep, black–stained corner immediately right of a larger left-leaning corner. Above the black corner follow cracks and corners up to the start of a gully system. Avoid this system by a rising left traverse to cracks and corners, which lead to the top of *Les Bruixes ex Pentinen*. Little is known of the route but it is likely free at 5.10 with short sections of A1 or C1

109 **Sunshine Wall**   TD   5.10 ◆   (16-20h)   11p   *192*

Art Higbee, David Breashers, July 1975

Very little is known about this line, which was far ahead of its time when it was put up as the first free route up the east face. Given the era the climb was put up in, and the history of the first ascent party, the climbing is probably in the 5.11 range. Bring a larger rack, heavy on the bigger sizes.

Start as for the original *Deus ex Machina*, following cracks and corners up and right to ledges between *Deus ex Machina* and *Les Bruixes ex Pentinen*. This section did involve 5.9 climbing before the fall of the great flake but now a blank section exists which may require a short aid section or bolt ladder. From ledges above the missing flake, a short rappel descends to a traversing section along ledges and flakes. Follow this ledge system through short sections of 5.9 to its end at a long, white, left-facing dihedral. Climb the dihedral in three pitches of 5.10; hands to chimneys. Continue up trending left through more 5.9 and 5.10 climbing to gain slabs leading right to the top of the north wall and the *Sunshine Crack* rappel route.

110 **Warrior's Way** **   TD   5.10 A3+   (1-2 biv)   11p   *193*

Steve Grossman, Keith Johnson, July 1993

Warrior's Way climbs left-facing corners from the left side of the Tom Egan Wall to gain steep, long, clean cracks between *Sunshine Wall* and *Tom Egan Memorial*. The route joins the *Tom Egan Memorial* at the pendulum at the top of the shield.

The lower three or four pitches are continuous aid climbing to A3+ before merging into the hard free climbing of *Sweet Sylvia* and *Hockey Night in Jersey*, which can be followed to the top of the north wall and the *Sunshine Crack* rappel route.

Bring a standard wall rack including hooks with extra knifeblades, lost arrows and larger cams as well as three sets of RPs.

Three times in it's history, the Kain Hut has been hit by substantial avalanches sweeping down the Crescent Glacier.

111 **Hockey Night in Jersey** ** TD 5.9 C3 (1-2 biv) 11p *193*
Steve Grossman, Keith Johnson, July 1994

This route has the same first ascent team as *Warrior's Way* and is a similar line. *Hockey Night in Jersey* starts in cracks between *Warrior's Way* and *Tom Egan Memorial*. It climbs three pitches of face cracks at A2 and A3 before merging into the steep ramp running up from the *Tom Egan Memorial*. The route continues up to join with *Warriors Way* and the steep cracks that meet the *Tom Egan Memorial* at the pendulum pitch. It follows that route for a pitch before breaking out left on an awkward traversing pitch, which leads to the base of a right-curving crack on the left side of the striking white headwall. A challenging pendulum at the end of the curving crack leads to easier climbing and the top of the north wall.

The first ascent party rappelled *Warrior's Way* but the *Sunshine Crack* rappel route on the north wall provides a more established descent.

Bring a standard clean wall rack including many wires, three sets of cams and at least one 5 inch cam. The first ascent party placed only one knifeblade and one bolt.

112 **Sweet Silvia** *** TD 5.12 (14-18h) 11p *193*
Will Hair, Kennan Harvey, Brad Jackson, Craig Luebben, July 1997 AAJ 40: 239

Sweet Sylvia climbs parts of *Tom Egan Memorial*, *Hockey Night in Jersey* and *Warriors Way* and offers a very long, hard and sustained free route.

1: Climb a 5.8 offwidth to a left-leaning dihedral. **2:** Start up the dihedral and exit right past a bolt to gain a steep finger-hand-crack that leads to a good ledge (5.12-). **3:** From the left edge of the ledge climb the right-facing corner (5.10-, 55m). **4:** Continue up the corner past loose flakes to a large detached flake (5.11-, 45m). **5:** Climb a steep and slightly right-leaning hand-offwidth crack to a ledge (5.11+, 50m). **6:** Climb a left-facing corner to a small stance, going from fists to offwidth and back to hands (5.11-, 55m). **7:** Climb through a chimney then around a flake, right and then back left to a left-leaning finger-crack (5.12- 60m). **8:** Climb an overhanging corner to gain a slabby ramp (5.11+, 55m). **9:** Continue straight up a flared 5.10- hand and fist-crack to the top of the north wall and the *Sunshine Crack* rappel route.

Bring a large free rack of all sizes including RPs, small TCUs, cams to 6 inches and two #1 Bigbros. A 60m rope is required.

113 **Tom Egan Memorial Route** *** TD 5.9 A3 (1-2 biv) 13p*193*
Darrel Hatten, John Simpson, August 1998

This is a varied and aesthetic aid line complete with an El Cap shield-like crack. The line climbs left-trending cracks to gain the intersection of the left and right-trending corners of *Sweet Sylvia* and *Power of Lard*. It then follows the face crack up the overhanging headwall before merging with the more convoluted terrain and chimneys of the upper wall. The route ends on top of the north wall and the *Sunshine Crack* rappel route.

1: From the broken ledges at the base of the wall climb a right-facing 5.8 chimney and offwidth. **2:** Follow a left-trending crack on easy aid. **3:** Free climb up a left-trending corner at 5.8 to a ledge at the base of the headwall. *Sweet Sylvia* and *Power of Lard* also reach the ledge via 5.12+ climbing. **4-**

6: Aid the shield-like crack above for three pitches. The crack is fairly uniform in size from knifeblades and lost arrows to one inch. Bees have been known to nest in the crack so be aware. Near the end of the third pitch a bolt is reached. Pendulum left from the bolt to gain a crack and a belay below an offwidth. **7:** Climb the offwidth at 5.11- or 5.9 A3 to a belay and bivy site on a block in the chimney. **8:** (**7:** *Sweet Sylvia*) Chimney above using flakes and squeeze through a slot to a ledge. *White Ducks in Space* chimneys right towards the top of *Bugaboo Corner* on the north wall. **9:** Head left, chimney some more to a pinch then go left again. **10-12:** Follow a crack to a corner, which is aided to another crack to blocks, then climb over right to a belay. **13:** Free or aid a crack to the top of the north wall and the *Sunshine Crack* rappel route.

Bring a standard wall rack with at least ten each of knifeblades, lost arrows and angles to three quarters of an inch. Extra small cams and nuts to one inch for the headwall as well as large cams and big bros for the offwidth are useful.

114 White Ducks in Space Variation TD 5.7 A3 (1-2biv) 12p *192*
Rob Orvig, Jock Richardson, July 1987

White Ducks in Space is a variation to the upper pitches of the *Tom Egan Memorial*.

Climb the Tom Egan Memorial to the seventh belay on the blocks inside the chimney. Instead of climbing the chimney, walk back into it for about 10m and tunnel up through a skylight to a belay. Aid a left-arching crack then go back right to a belay below a roof. Climb up left over the awkward roof to a belay. Continue up a crack to a large ledge belay. Free and aid above to the top of the north wall and the *Sunshine Crack* rappel route.

115 The Power of Lard ** TD 5.12+/13- (14-18h) 10p *193*
Gunter Dengler, Toni Lamprecht, August 1996   *CAJ 80:4*

This climb gains the base of the *Tom Egan Memorial* headwall and then follows the right slanting corner to gain the top of *Hobo's Haven* before continuing up to traverse into *Bugaboo Corner*. As with *Sweet Sylvia* it is a hard and sustained free climb.

1: Climb the first pitch of *Tom Egan Memorial* to a belay in a left-leaning dihedral (5.8, 40m). **2:** Exit right past a bolt to gain a steep finger-hand-crack that leads to a good ledge (5.12-, 15m). **3:** Face-climb straight up past bolts to gain the base of the headwall. Start up the beginning of the right-trending corner to a belay (5.11+, 40m). **4:** Continue up the corner to a ledge belay (5.11-, 15m). **5:** Continue up the corner for a long pitch to a belay on *Hobo's Haven* (5.10+, 55m). **6:** Follow Hobo's Haven up and left and exit up to the *Hobo's Haven* bivy ledge (5.11+, 35m). **7:** From the right end of the ledge climb a sustained crack to a belay (5.12+/13-, 35m). **8:** Traverse right 10m to the *Bugaboo Corner* chimney (5.10, 10m). Finish up *Bugaboo Corner* or rappel one pitch and continue up *Banshee* to *Sunshine Crack*. The route can also be rappelled.

116 **Hobo's Haven**   TD-   5.7 A4   (12-16h)   6p   *193*

J.Beyer (solo), August 1976

Hobo's Haven climbs six pitches from the right end of the Tom Egan Wall to a large ledge, where *Power of Lard* continues in two more pitches to *Bugaboo Corner*.

From the base of *Tom Egan Memorial* continue up right for about 30m to a short left-trending ramp. **1:** Scramble left across fourth-class rock to the base of a right-facing corner. **2:** A4 and sustained A3 leads to a sling belay before the corner arches right. **3:** Step left out of the corner to another crack and aid at A1 to a sling belay. **4:** Aid up the crack to a roof. Aid out right under the roof at A3 and continue right on hooks to gain a left-facing corner and continue up to another sling belay. **5:** Follow the crack as it curves left to a common belay with *Power of Lard*. **6:** Aid and free out left until it is possible to climb up and back right to *Hobo's Haven* ledge. Rappel the route from the right end of the ledge or continue up *Power of Lard*.

Bring a standard wall rack including hooks. A double set of cams to four inches, extra RPs, twelve knifeblades and 24 lost arrows are needed.

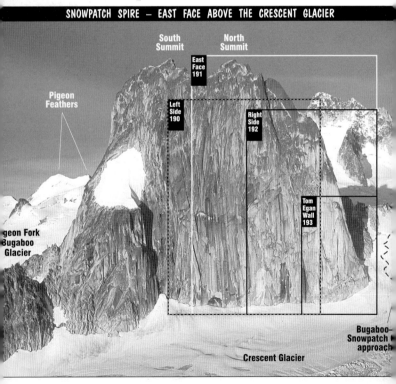

SNOWPATCH SPIRE – EAST FACE ABOVE THE CRESCENT GLACIER

South Summit
North Summit
East Face 191
Pigeon Feathers
Left Side 190
Right Side 192
Tom Egan Wall 193
geon Fork Bugaboo Glacier
Bugaboo–Snowpatch approach
Crescent Glacier

SNOWPATCH SPIRE SOUTHEAST FACE — SNOWPATCH ROUTE

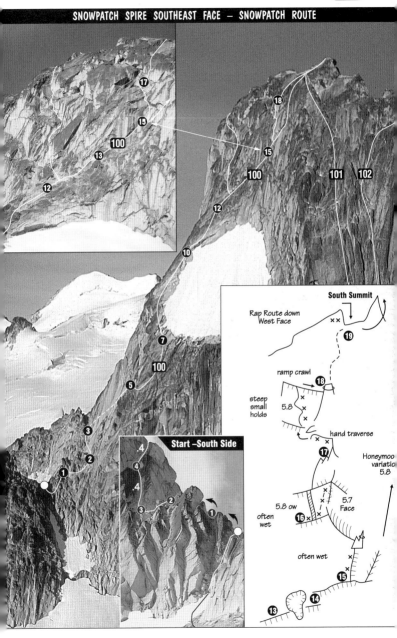

South Summit

Rap Route down West Face

ramp crawl

steep small holds

5.8

hand traverse

Honeymoo variatio 5.8

5.8 ow

5.7 Face

often wet

often wet

Start –South Side

SNOWPATCH SPIRE – EAST FACE LEFT

.7
101
102
.9
103
.9
105
A3
107
A1

.9
A2
A1
.8
A1
tension
.9
tension roof/chimney

bivy
.8
A1
A1
terrace
10
.9
.9
A1
A1
A1
.9
A1
.8

.9
A2+
loose blocks

A2
roofs
tension A2+
hooks
.7
A2
A1
A3
roof

bivy (sloper)
.6
106
bivy

A2
shallow
cracks
.9
A2
.8
A3
10+
A1

A2
A3+
.9
A2
105

A1
A2+
A3
.9
.9
107
.9

A2
.9
squeeze
?
recent
rockfall
?

101
102
103 104 105
.9
ow
A3
107

ROUTES: 101 102 (183) **103–107** (184)

SNOWPATCH SPIRE — EAST FACE RIGHT SIDE

North Summit

103 105 107

109

111 113 114

102 104 108 113 115

105 106 107 108 109 110 113 115 116

112
113
115

109 107

rockfall

rockfall

116

113
111 112
115

1 102 103 104 105 106
107

110

Tom Egan W:

ROUTES: **101 102** (183) **103–108** (184-185) **111–113** 186) **114–116** (184)

SNOWPATCH SPIRE – EAST FACE RIGHT

TOM EGAN WALL

tension
A1

terrace
.9
A1

A2+
loose blocks

bivy

10+
A1

.9

.9

.9

recent
rockfall

?

?

A3

see photo-topos
page 188, 191

105

109

106

105

109

109

107

108

113

109

111

113

113

114

113

110

111

112
115

113

116

SNOWPATCH SPIRE – EAST FACE TOM EGAN WALL

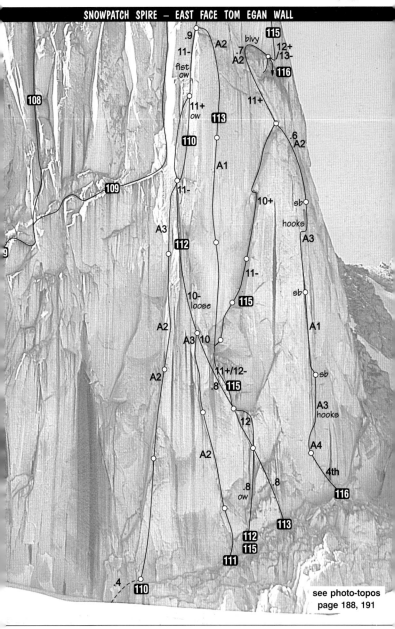

ROUTES: **111–113** (186) **115** (187) **116** (188)

SNOWPATCH SPIRE – NORTH WALL

North Summit

Son
Sum

boulder move 10   10+

10

.8

119

tunnel in behind to East Face

117

.9   .9 flakes

.9   same place

.9 stem

.9

118

11- roof   .9

chimney

roof

118   .9 fist/OW

.9   .7   roof

squeeze   10

.9 roof

squeeze ow

.9 layback

.9   **119**

117

.10 hand rail

.9

10 ow

119
117
118

horn belay   10

121

same place

start

30m

30m

25m

bergschrund

photo: early July 2002

Bugaboo–Snowpatch Col
north-side slope

ROUTES: 117 118 (197)   **119** (198)

Snowpatch Spire: North Wall

The north wall of Snowpatch is the narrow face that rises steeply out of the east side of the Bugaboo–Snowpatch Col, extending from near the Tom Egan wall on the east face to the *Buckingham Route* on the west face of Snowpatch. The north wall ends at a large flat area below the lower towers of the *Buckingham Route,* which can be ascended to gain the true north summit.

The Climbs: There are four routes on the wall, three of which (*Banshee, Bugaboo Corner* and *Sunshine*) share the same initial pitches. All end on top of the wall and do not make the north summit proper. It is possible to climb from the flat area on top of the north wall out left onto the east face to join up with the *Buckingham Route* as it climbs out onto the northeast side of the summit towers. The wall stays in shadow until late afternoon making the belays cool at times.

The four climbs are all technical, sustained routes. *Sunshine Crack* is the most aesthetic and popular climb and accounts for more than 90% of the ascents here. *Banshee* and *Bugaboo Corner* are both worthy free climbs but require many large cams or big bros to protect the offwidths and squeeze chimneys. The one aid climb on the wall is the incomplete *Dark Side of the Sun,* offering thin, hard nailing. New route possibilities lie on the central and righthand sides of the wall, but the nature of new climbs will lean towards intricate aid routes.

Descent: There are two options.

(1) The most popular and simplest is to rappel *Sunshine Crack.* All stations are fixed but most of the stances are very small or semi-hanging. Double 50m ropes are required for the seven double rope rappels and double 60m ropes will bypass some intermediate stations. This descent ends very near the base of the climbs so no snow or glacier travel is required and no mountain boots, axes or crampons have to be hauled up.

(2) The second option is to continue to the north summit proper. From there, walk and scramble south down to the col between the south and north summits, where the fixed rappel stations down the *Beckey–Greenwood* can be found. Five or six double 50m rope rappels gain the glacier beneath the central section of the west face. An easy walk back north along the glacier gains the top of the Bugaboo–Snowpatch Col, north of the first wind roll. To descend the col either downclimb the upper snow slope on the Bugaboo Spire side (requiring mountain boots, ice axes and crampons), or rappel. Two chain anchor rappel routes exist down each side of the upper slope. The Snowpatch side descent requires only a single 60m rope and avoids the ascent line.

117 **Bugaboo Corner** *   D+   5.10-   (8-10h)   5p   *194*
E.Davies, P.Derouin, I.Rowe, July 1971   *CAJ 55:78*

Bugaboo Corner was the original line on the north wall. It climbs the crack on the left edge of the wall that widens into a chimney and forms a sharp pinnacle on the edge of the east face.

Ascend the initial snow-slopes at the bottom of the Bugaboo— Snowpatch Col to gain the scree at the base of the wall. The route starts at the far left side of the wall in a short right-facing corner capped by a small roof. **1:** Climb the short corner and go over a 5.10 roof to a face crack. Continue up to a horn belay. **2:** Continue up the widening crack through a 5.10 offwidth section and a belay below a roof. Two 4 1/2in cams are useful on this pitch. **3:** Climb left around the 5.9 overhang, past the *Sunshine Crack* handrail which heads right and continue up through a 5.9 offwidth and squeeze section. Belay below a roof. **4:** Climb through the roof at hard 5.9 and continue past the bulging right wall at 5.9 to a belay. *Banshee* heads right to another crack from this belay. **5-6:** Continue up the widening chimney into the darkness. This is where *White Ducks in Space* and the *Tom Egan Memorial* routes join. It is possible to follow any of those routes to the top of the north wall and the *Sunshine Crack* rappel route or continue up to the *Buckingham Route* or *Parker–Brashaw* to the north summit Most climbing parties rappel the route.

A large free rack is required and there is often protection inside the chimneys for small to medium size gear. Bring extra large cams to 4 1/2in for the offwidths.

118 **Banshee** **   D+   5.10   (8-10h)   9p   *194*
Art Higbee, M.Kosterlitz, July 1974

Banshee follows *Bugaboo Corner* for the first four pitches then breaks out right, crosses *Sunshine Crack* and then joins back to that route on pitch eight.

1-4: Climb *Bugaboo Corner* to the belay at the top of pitch four. **5:** Climb up right to gain a short left-facing corner that soon becomes a face crack. Follow the crack up to a belay on the steep slabs. **6:** Climb out right at 5.7 and up past small ledges and cracks to a horizontal crack and a belay at the junction with *Sunshine Crack*. **7:** Continue traversing right to climb a 5.9 crack around the right side of the roof and a belay in a corner below a headwall. **8:** Climb the short corner above at 5.9 to a small slab. Head up and left over flakes and belay just before the left-facing corner system (5.9). **9:** Gain the corner system (*Sunshine Crack*) and follow it to a belay (5.9). **10-12:** Follow *Sunshine Crack* for three pitches of 5.8 to 5.10 to the top of the wall and the rappel route.   A large free rack with extra 3½-4½in cams is needed.

In the mid-1980s a tyrolean traverse was set up between the summits of the Crescent Towers and Eastpost as a search and rescue exercise.

119 **Sunshine Crack** *** D+   5.11-   (8-10h)   9p   *194*
Alex Lowe, S.Scott, July 1980

Sunshine Crack is by far the most travelled route on the north wall and one of the better climbs in the Bugaboos, with steep, clean, continuous climbing, and a rappel route straight back to the base. *Sunshine Crack* follows *Bugaboo Corner* for two pitches before heading out right to gain cracks that head straight up, splitting numerous overhangs on the way to the top of the wall.

1-2: Climb *Bugaboo Corner* for two pitches of 5.10. **3:** Continue up the *Bugaboo Corner-crack* left around an overhang at 5.9 and gain a handrail heading out right. Follow the handrail to its end and make a 5.10 layback up a crack to a belay. **4:** Follow the crack to a 5.9 layback and a belay. **5:** Continue up the crack over the first 5.9 roof. Climb either the shallow corner or the right–hand-crack to the next 5.10 roof. Belay above the roof in the right crack. **6:** Follow the crack above over another, easier, roof and belay on the upper slab where Banshee crosses. **7:** Climb up the slab and over a 5.11- roof then step right to belay. **8:** Climb a longer pitch up the steepening crack above to the corner system, flakes and a belay at its end (5.9). **9:** Continue up the ramp into a groove up left which steps over a small roof into a face crack. Belay above in an alcove (5.8). **10:** Climb the 5.10 crack above the alcove to a belay where the crack forks. **11:** Either make a 5.10 boulder move left to gain a 5.8 crack or climb the crack out right which curves back left near the top at 5.10+. Both options gain the top of the north wall.

It is possible to gain the *Buckingham Route* and follow it to the north summit, however most parties rappel the route.

Bring a large free rack of all sizes with extra 3½-4½in cams.

120 **Dark Side of the Sun**   D-   A4   (6-8h)   2p
Joe Buszowski, John Simpson, August 1980

This short aid climb starts part-way up the gully beneath the north wall.

Face-climbing leads to hooks and continuous A4 nailing. It awaits a finish. Bring a regular aid rack, heavy on the smaller stuff, including hooks, copperheads, beaks and RURPS.

The Gendarme on Bugaboo Spire.

Our route was completely blocked by a most formidable gendarme, whose base completely spanned the width of the ridge. It's wall on the west side ran up in prolongation of the mighty cliffs that rose from the glacier far below, and it's top edge rose sharply like a horn to the point where it joined the high sheer east wall.

A.H. MacCarthy, Canadian Alpine Journal, 1917.

Snowpatch Spire: West Face

The west face of Snowpatch Spire is a broad, steep face approximately 300m in height. The face rises out of the middle Vowell Glacier and looks out onto the north side of Pigeon Spire and the east faces of the Howser Towers. The west face runs from the top of the Bugaboo–Snowpatch Col across to the Snowpatch–Pigeon Icefall. The face is roughly divided into three sections. The southern section rises from a short scree slope and contains the climbs that end on the south summit. The middle section rises directly from the glacier and contains the climbs that finish between the north and south summits. The north section rises directly from the glacier and contains the climbs that end on the north summit.

Climbs: The west face is fairly uniform in height with all of the routes being approximately eight pitches in length. Nearly all the west face routes are free climbs ranging from 5.9 to 5.12. Most of the climbing is sustained in the 5.8 to 5.9 range with the *Kraus–McCarthy* and *Surfs Up* being the easiest and most popular climbs at 5.9. Most of the routes on the west face have several minor variations. The rock is generally very good quality with the less travelled routes having some lichen cover.

Although new routes are possible, most of the obvious lines have been climbed and nearly all the routes freed.

Descent: There are three descent options. All require mountain boots, ice axes and crampons to be used from the foot of the face back to the Conrad Kain Hut. Note, however, that the rappel descents off the west face finish on scree or easy snow, allowing the mountain gear to be left at the base of the climbs.

(1) For all climbs reaching the south summit the *Kraus–McCarthy* rappel route is used. It consists of six chain anchor rappels that require double 50m ropes.

(2) For all climbs reaching the col between the north and south summits or the north summit proper, the *Beckey–Greenwood* rappel route is used. Six or seven double 50m rope rappels are encountered. Stations are fixed but replacement webbing and rappel rings may be needed.

(3) The *Buckingham Route* can be descended from its first tower, via five double 55m rope rappels, all from slung blocks and flakes. The climb is only 5.7 up to that point.

121 Buckingham Route: The Enjoyable Way * AD+ 5.8 (7-9h) 8p 210

This is a very pleasant and non-intimidating climb that follows mostly 5.6 and 5.7 cracks and flakes to the lower tower north of the main north summit.

Start from the extreme left side of the west face at the top of the Bugaboo–Snowpatch Col. Climb approximately 70m of 5.6 cracks to gain the depression leading up and left. Follow 5.6 cracks and flakes up the depression past a large pillar on the right wall for three pitches to belay in a dihedral system. Climb out right from the dihedral following flakes and weaknesses parallel to the ridge-line and left of a black pinnacle for two long 5.7 pitches. A shorter pitch climbs straight up cracks, ledges and 5.8 face (some lichen) climbing past two old bolts to gain the top of the tower. The complete *Buckingham Route* descends onto the east face via a rappel before regaining the ridge-crest near the north summit.

Seven 50m rappels descend the route with stations being slung blocks or flakes. The initial rappells drop straight down, regaining the depression lower down

122 Buckingham Route D 5.10+ (8-12h) 12p

William Buckingham, Arnold Guess, Robert Page, Earle Wipple July 1958
CAJ 42:53, AAJ 11:311

The Buckingham route follows *The Enjoyable Way* up 5.6 and 5.7 cracks and flakes to the lower tower north of the main north summit, before descending onto the east face to gain cracks leading to the main north summit.

Follow *The Enjoyable Way* to the north sub-tower (8p, 5.8). Rappel into an ice-choked gully on the east face to gain a dihedral in the south wall. Aid at C1, or free at 5.10+, a short section past a fixed pin to easier climbing and a belay at the base of the final tower. Follow a curving ledge on the east side to a short scramble and the main north summit.

Bring a standard free rack with extra ½ to 2 inch nuts and cams, and extra slings if aid climbing the 5.10+ pitch.

To descend follow slabs down to the *Beckey–Greenwood* rappel route.

123 Gran–Hudson D 5.7 A2? (8-12h) 12p 211

Art Gran, John Hudson, August 1961 AAJ 13:242

The *Gran–Hudson* ascends the long and prominent chimney ending at a sharp notch between the Buckingham Tower and the north summit

Below the chimney system lies a lower-angled snow slope guarded by a slabby face. Climb flakes on either side of the face to gain the base of the snow (5.4–5.6). Continue up to the base of the chimney system. Slabs to the right or left can be used to avoid the snow. Follow the chimney for two pitches then step left into a more prominent chimney. Climb main chimney in three pitches to the notch, passing the major chock-stone to the right

Details are unknown but it is suspected the route to the notch goes free at around 5.9. From the notch it is possible to either rappel back down the route or to rappel east down a gully to gain the 5.10+ or C1 dihedral of the *Buckingham Route*, which leads to the north summit. Be prepared to make rappel stations if descending the route.

124 **Quasimodo**   D   5.9 A1   ♦   (8–12h)   10p

Dave Nichols, Eric Weinstein, August 1975

Quasimodo possibly lies somewhere between the *Gran–Hudson* and *Flamingo Fling*. The route has not been marked on the photos because of the ambiguous nature of route information.

From the little that is known, gain the base of the *Gran–Hudson* chimney. Move right and down to cracks, pass over a small 5.8 roof and work up right. Climb a widening crack from 5.5 layback to 5.8 offwidth. Move right and up a right-leaning crack to an overhanging 5.8 chimney/flake. Hand traverse left to a blocky section and climb 5.9 cracks on a white wall to a roof. Pendulum right twice to reach easier blocky ground that is followed to a large ledge below a chimney. Climb the chimney to broken flakes, moving slightly right to a 5.8 layback, back left to a boulder and right again to a 5.5 layback and the summit. Good luck.

125 **Flamingo Fling** *   D   5.10-   (7–12h)   10p *210*

R.Accomazzo, Tobin Sorenson, August 1975   FFA Chris Atkinson, Yosemite Alf, August 1988

Flamingo Fling is a fine climb that sees very little activity. It follows a line left and parallel to the long white cracks of *North Summit Direct*.

1–3: Climb cracks and flakes to gain the right edge of the *Gran–Hudson* snow–slope. From the far right edge of the snow, climb flakes to a belay below a shallow corner. **4:** Climb 5.8 layback cracks and jamming, with a few 5.10- moves to a small ledge belay. **5:** Climb a left-leaning 5.7 crack to more broken terrain, 5.8 cracks and a belay below a corner capped by a large roof. **6:** Climb a 5.9 hand-fist corner-crack to a sling belay at the right side of the roof. **7:** Reach out right to gain a 5.10- finger-crack that widens to 5.9 hands and into a 5.7 chimney. Belay amongst blocks on a ledge. **8:** Climb 5.6 hand-cracks on the right wall past the left side of a 5.5 layback flake to a ramp belay. **9:** Easier ground leads right to the summit.

126 **North Summit Direct** *   D+   5.11+   (8–14h)   8p *211*

P.Morand, J.C.Sonnenuye August 1979   FFA Tom Gibson, Rob Rohn, August 1981 CAJ 65:84

This is a steep and sustained aesthetic climb on good rock up long right-slanting cracks through white rock directly to the north summit.

Begin in white rock at the right edge of the *Gran–Hudson* and *Flamingo Fling* slabs. **1:** Squeeze up a flake to a 5.9 layback trending right and a ramp belay. **2:** Climb out right to a 5.10 corner that ends with an awkward overhang and a ledge belay above. **3:** A 50m pitch leads over flakes and into the left of several corner-crack systems. Start up the shallow corner at 5.11- to a sling belay. **4:** Follow the sustained corner-crack at 5.11+ for 50m to a small ledge belay. **5:** Climb a short 5.9 offwidth then climb right across one corner to gain a second thin corner, which is followed at 5.11 to a sling belay. The first free ascent party suggested a better finish would continue up and left from the top of the offwidth. **6:** Continue up the thin 5.10 corner to its end then climb left to a wide crack. Exit left to gain a hand-crack in the next corner. Follow that to a ledge belay. **7:** Easier climbing leads to the summit.

Take a large free rack with extra finger-to-hand size protection. To descend, scramble down slabs to a notch and the *Beckey–Greenwood* rappel.

127 **Tower Arête** *   D+ 5.12-   (8-14h)   8p *211*

Rod Gibbons, Randall Green, Chris Hecht, July 1986
FFA Topher Donahue, Patience Gribble, August 2000

This is another aesthetic Bugaboo climb. *Tower Arête* ascends the right side of three vague towers to just right of the north summit.

Start 10m left of the main corner that leads to the notch between the summits. **1:** Originally A2, a thin 5.11+ crack leads past a fixed pin through overhangs to an alcove belay. **2:** Climb 5.8 cracks to a belay in flakes near the first tower. **3:** Continue up 5.9 flakes to a ledge belay on top of the first tower. **4:** Follow right-curving cracks (5.12-) right of a wide dirty crack past fixed nuts to a sling belay in an alcove. **5:** Climb over the second tower to a ledge belay below a hand-crack and a large detached flake. **6:** Climb the 5.9 hand-crack past a thin 5.10- section. **7:** Trend right over thin 5.8 flakes to a crack and a ledge belay. **8:** A thin 5.9 layback leads to a 5.11- section and a 5.9 flake leading right to the ridge just below the north summit. To descend, follow slabs down to a notch and the *Beckey–Greenwood* rappel route

128 **Super Direct** *   D 5.10   (8-11h)   8p *212*

Nils Preshaw, R.M.Preshaw, July 1992

The *Super Direct* is a direct and logical start to the upper half of the *Beckey–Greenwood* and follows the huge right-facing dihedral from the glacier directly to the notch between the north and south summits. Of all the west face routes it receives the most sun.

1: Climb a 20m 5.9 pitch past a fixed pin to a sling belay in the main corner. **2:** Continue up the thin 5.10 corner past more fixed pins to near its end before exiting right to a belay in broken ground at 55m. **3-5:** Climb three 5.7 pitches up the main corner to a belay at the base of the yellow headwall. **6:** Climb horizontally right on a crack below the rusty bolts to a 5.9 arête with a fixed pin. Follow the arête to a belay at a rappel station. **7:** Climb horizontally left and down (5.9) to regain the main corner. Follow the corner at 5.10 for 50m to the notch between the summits. The north summit can be gained over easy slabs.   To descend, rappel the route.

129 **Beckey–Greenwood Route** D 5.10   (7-11h)   10p *212*

Fred Beckey, Brian Greenwood, July 1959   *CAJ 43:73, AAJ 12:21*

The *Beckey–Greenwood* follows a long rising terrace system for five pitches to gain the huge dihedral at mid-height. The original route aided out on bolts and pins from the base of the yellow headwall before regaining the corner.

Locate a crack right of a short left-facing corner at the base of the long left-trending weakness that is the *Beckey–Rowell* route. **1-5:** Climb a 5.7 crack for one pitch to gain ledges and slabs leading left. Follow an ascending traverse over fourth and low fifth class terrain to gain the huge corner. **6-8:** Climb the 5.7 corner to a belay at the base of the yellow headwall. **9:** As with the *Super Direct,* climb horizontally right on a crack below the rusty bolts to a 5.9 arête with a fixed pin. Follow the arête to a belay at a rappel station. **10:** Climb horizontally left and down (5.9) to regain the main corner. Follow the corner at 5.10 for 50m to the notch between the summits. The north summit can be gained over easy slabs. To descend, rappel the route.

130   **Tam-Tam Boom-Boom Pili-Pili**   *   D+   5.11+C1   (8-14h)   8p   *212*

P.Faivre, J.Lemoine, P.Tanguy, August 1987

This clean and appealing line climbs thin cracks and corners up the middle of the face between the *Beckey–Greenwood* and the *Wildflowers* corners.

Locate a face crack in a white slab that leads to a short, shallow right-facing corner. **1:** Climb a crack to gain the shallow right-facing corner that leads to a small ledge belay (5.11+). **2:** Climb out right from the corner on 5.0 face cracks to gain a chimney that is followed to a belay just below the *Beckey–Greenwood* terraces. **3:** Continue over easier 5.4 ledges to a belay at the base of a shallow left-facing corner. **4:** Climb the corner at 5.10+ around a small roof to a ledge belay below a white, right-facing dihedral. **5:** 5.10+ face-climbing leads into the dihedral and a belay. **6:** Continue up the corner moving around a roof to a belay above. All but 10m of this pitch have been free climbed at 5.10+. **7:** Follow the 5.9 corner to the ridge then go right to the south summit.

Bring a larger free rack to four inches with extra smaller cams and nuts or a few lost arrows for the ten metres of aid climbing.

Scramble down east and then south to gain the *Kraus–McCarthy* rappel route.

131   **Beckey–Rowell Route**   *   D+   5.10+   (8-12h)   9p   *212*

Fred Beckey, Galen Rowell, August 1967
FFA Andrew Bowers, Guy Edwards, August 1997   *AAJ 16:173*

It is uncertain where the original line actually went but it is believed to follow the left-trending weakness that runs from the base of the Beckey–Greenwood terraces to just left of the south summit block. This is the line of the first free ascent.

Locate a face crack left of the base of the *Wildflowers* corner and right of a short left-facing corner. **1:** Climb a 5.7 crack to a belay where the *Beckey–Greenwood* terraces lead out left. **2:** Continue up the 5.7 weakness to a belay at the start of a dihedral. **3:** Climb an awkward 5.8 layback pitch. **4:** Climb an arête then go left into a corner (5.9+). **5:** Continue up awkward 5.9+ stemming and laybacking. **6:** Climb a corner and over an unlikely 5.9 roof. **7:** Continue up a chimney and offwidth to a difficult traverse left and up a corner (5.10+). **8:** 5.8 climbing leads to the ridge.

Scramble down east and then south from the south summit to gain the *Kraus–McCarthy* rappel route.

Was a good year.
In 1961, the year of the first ascent of the Beckey–Chouinard, the Salathe Wall on El Cap and the Central Pillar of Freney on Mont Blanc were also climbed. And at Squamish, the Grand Wall of the Chief.

132 **Wildflowers** *   D   5.9   (8-12h)   8p *212*

B.Dougherty, Art Higbee, August 1974

Wildflowers is a popular climb up the large left-facing flake/corner system that leads to the top of a huge pillar before finishing at the south summit.

Locate the huge pillar that lies directly below the south summit. The first five pitches follow the left-facing corner system that makes up the pillar's left edge. **1:** Start in a blocky area directly below the corner and follow a faint crack system through fourth-class blocks and ledges to a belay below a small right-facing corner. **2:** Climb the small 5.7 corner past a flake and over blocks to the base of the main left-facing dihedral. **3:** A pitch of wider 5.9 jamming leads to a belay. **4:** Follow the narrowing 5.9 crack. **5:** Move right to continue up the main corner where wide 5.9 jamming and stemming leads to a belay. **6:** Continue up the thinner 5.9 corner to flakes, cracks and finally blocks which lead to a large ledge belay on an arête. **7:** Climb a shorter 5.7 pitch up cracks right of the arête. **8:** Follow wide rounded 5.9 cracks and grooves up the right side of the arête to the south summit.

Scramble down east and then south from the south summit to gain the *Kraus–McCarthy* rappel route.

133 **Kraus–McCarthy Route** * D- 5.9   (7-10h)   8p *213*

Hans Kraus, James McCarthy, August 1956   *AAJ 10:229*
FWA Kirk Mauthner, Brad Shilling, February 1999

The *Kraus–McCarthy* was the first route on the west face and is used as the rappel route from the south summit. It follows a broad, shallow gully system immediately right of the south summit.

On the right end of the west face lays a section of scree–covered terraces. Scramble up the far left side of the terraces to the base of the broad and shallow *Kraus–McCarthy* gully. **1-2:** Climb easy fifth class cracks to belay at the start of a steep ramp leading left into the large corner. **3:** Climb the ramp and continue over a 5.8 roof to cracks and a ledge belay in the corner. This pitch is often wet but does not hinder progress. **4:** Follow an easier ramp up right. Climb left across rounded 5.6 grooves to another belay in the corner. **5:** Follow another ramp up right to 5.8 rounded cracks on the steepening wall and a small ledge belay. **6:** Climb up steep cracks and opposing corners at 5.6 to another small ledge belay. **7:** Continue up into a narrow 5.8 chimney. Where the chimney turns into an offwidth it is possible to continue up the 5.8 offwidth or traverse out right to a short 5.8 hand-crack. The pitch gains the ridge at the rappel chains. The south summit can be gained by scrambling out right and then up over a short step to the summit slabs.

134 **Mark Stewart Variation**   D   5.11 C1   (8-12h)   8p *213*

Mark Stewart et al, August 1999

This route follows cracks up the right side of the *Kraus–McCarthy* gully.

Climb the first two pitches of the *Kraus–McCarthy*. Follow disconnected cracks, corners and ledges for six pitches, staying on the steeper right side of the broad, shallow gully to rejoin the *Kraus–McCarthy* at the top of the last pitch. The climbing is mostly 5.10 with moves of 5.11 and C1. Many variations are possible.

135 Furry Pink Arête *   D   5.10+   (8-12h)   8p *213*
Peter Croft, Greg Foweraker, August 1981

Furry Pink Arête is an enjoyable climb that loosely follows the arête right of the *Kraus–McCarthy*, with a fine, classic seventh pitch.

1: The original first pitch climbed a 5.9 crack right of the arête but the more popular line follows a hand-crack starting on the left side of the arête. Both options lead to a ledge belay on the arête. **2:** Climb 5.7 cracks just left of the arête to another belay on the arête. **3-4:** Climb 5.9 cracks up a narrow face on the tip of the arête to a blocky ledge belay. Continue over 5.8 broken terrain to a belay below the 'white nose'. These two pitches can be combined. **5:** Climb a 5.9 crack right of the 'white nose' passing left by an overhang and continuing up the left side of the arête via a 5.9 crack, past a small stance to exit right to a big, blocky, belay ledge. **6:** Climb a straight–in crack to a belay ledge below a clean, white, left-facing crescent crack. **7:** Climb right into the crescent crack and follow it as it curves left through 5.10+ fingers and laybacks into an easy chimney and a ledge belay at its top. **8:** Climb out right on clean cracks to the flat ridge-crest. Scramble left to find the *Kraus–McCarthy* rap route in a notch and the south summit beyond.

Bring a standard free rack with extra nuts and small cams for the crux finger-crack.

136 Which Way   D   5.10   (8-12h)   8p *213*
C. Copeland, T.Thomas, August 1987

Which Way follows the vague corner system right of, and parallel to the *Furry Pink Arête* joining that route at its crux seventh pitch. Described by the first ascent party as "sustained, strenuous climbing on good rock," this route is less popular then it deserves.

1: Start to the right of the base of *Furry Pink Arête*. Climb a long pitch up flakes and cracks into the vague corner system. **2:** Climb 5.9 cracks up the main depression. **3:** Continue up 5.9 and 5.10 ground over cracks and flakes trending right. **4:** Follow 5.10 cracks and corners, thin at times, still in the vague corner/depression. **5-6:** Continue up, trending slightly right then back left to gain a ledge belay at the base of the clean, white, right-facing crescent crack on pitch seven of *Furry Pink Arête*. **7–8:** Climb the last two pitches of *Furry Pink Arête* (5.10+). Scramble left to find the *Kraus–McCarthy* rap route in a notch and the south summit beyond.

A larger free rack with RPs, extra nuts and small cams is needed.

137 Degringolade   D   5.10   (8-12h)   8p *213*
Sibylle Hechtel, Jon Jones, July 1973   *AAJ 19:166*

Details of *Degringolade* and its variation *Rock the Casbah* are sketchy and ambiguous. *Degringolade* follows the face right of *Which Way* to gain left-facing corners right of the upper pitches of *Furry Pink Arête*.

A small one-pitch pillar lies against the wall right of the *Furry Pink Arête* and *Which Way*. **1:** Gain its top via either side (5.7). **2-3:** Climb cracks and flakes straight up, then trend slightly left to a belay (5.9). **4:** Climb right to the base of the upper, left-facing corner. **5:** Climb the 5.9 corner and chimney to a belay. **6:** Continuing up the corner and chimney to where it is possible

to exit right and belay. **7:** Exit right out of the corner and climb down a
chimney. Step right around to a black slab and belay at its top. **8:** Climb right,
up a 5.7 groove, to pass right around an overlap to a slot and the south ridge.
Scramble over slabs up the ridge then step down into the notch with the
Kraus–McCarthy rappel route. The South Summit is a short scramble around
its right side.

138 Rock the Casbah   D   5.10   (8-12h)   8p *213*
Randy Atkinson, Craig Thompson, August 1984
Rock the Casbah is a major variation to *Degringolade*. It follows weaknesses
and cracks to the right of *Degringolade* for four pitches to gain *Degringolade*
at the base of the upper, left-facing corner system.

   1: Gain the top of the small pillar that marks the top of pitch one of
Degringolad.e **2–3:** Follow the ramp up right until able to climb back left and
belay below a steeper wall. **4:** Climb 5.9 flakes and cracks to gain the base
of the upper corner and the top of pitch four of *Degringolade*. Follow the
last four pitches of *Degringolade* to the top.

139 Attack of the Killer Chipmunks D 5.10 (8-12h)   8p *213*
Geoff Crieghton, Craig Thompson, August 1986
Attack of the Killer Chipmunks ascends the face between *Rock the Casbah–
Degringolade* and *Southwest–Surfs Up* routes. Because of the convoluted
and complex nature of the terrain, details of this route are unclear. Approach
it as an adventure.

   The route starts right of *Degringolade–Rock the Casbah* (5.8) to gain
the right-trending terrain near the second pitch of *Rock the Casbah*. Continue
up right-trending weaknesses to gain the steep terrain left of the alcove belay
on *Surfs Up* (5.9). Climb wide cracks up left-facing corners past a roof, then
straight up to exit right onto the ridge-crest (5.10). Follow the ridge to the
notch with the *Kraus–McCarthy* rappel route. The South Summit is a short
scramble around its right side.

140 **Surfs Up Direct**   D   5.9   (7-12h)   9p *213*
E.Davies, P.Derouin, August 1971   *CAJ 55:78*
The *Surfs Up Direct* is a direct finish to the original *Surfs Up* (Southwest Ridge)
route. It climbs the first three pitches of *Surfs Up* then continues straight up
to gain the ridge, avoiding the more aesthetic upper pitches of *Surfs Up*.

   1-3: Climb the first three pitches of *Surfs Up* to the alcove belay. **4:** Climb
the left-leaning 5.7 corner above the alcove to a ledge belay below steeper
white rock. **5:** Climb a short pitch up a 5.8 crack to a smaller ledge belay. **6:**
Climb a short, very steep 5.9 wall to gain a ramp. **7:** Follow the ramp right to
the ridge-crest. Follow the ridge as with *Surfs Up* to the *Kraus–McCarthy*
rappel route and the south summit.

The Beckey–Chouinard has been climbed fewer than 100 times in 42 years.

141 **Surfs Up** **   D   5.9   (7-12h)   9p *213*
Brian Greenwood, George Homer, August 1971   *CAJ 55:78*
Surfs Up (the "Southwest Ridge") is a deservedly popular climb. The crack
pitches above Surfs Up Ledge are stellar. The route lies at the far south end
of the west face, up a left-facing dihedral system before breaking out right
around the crest, and down to a sandy ledge on the south face. Clean and
aesthetic cracks lead to the broad ridge crest that is followed to the south
summit.

Gain a small saddle at the south end of the west face. Scramble about
60m to belay at the base of a deep north-facing dihedral system. It is less of
a distinct corner, appearing more as a series of big stacked flakes. **1:** Climb
30m of fourth and easy fifth up shallow, lower-angled corners stepping left
to a sandy pod (possible belay). Continue for 30m up cracks and flakes until
4m left of the corner, then gain a horn belay near the orange/white overhangs
where the dihedral becomes more pronounced (5.8). **2:** Follow the steepening
dihedral for 40m of cracks and flakes past an awkward 5.8 bulge to a flake
belay (5.8). **3:** Continue up the dihedral for 30m to the 5.9 crux move right
and over a bulge on finger-locks. Gain an alcove belay. **4:** From the alcove
belay climb a short finger-crack up and right until it is possible to step right
around blocks and the crest of the spur at about 10m. Descend down a ramp
for about 10m to Surfs Up Ledge and belay at its far end. **5:** Follow the
obvious face crack rising off the ledge, 5.9 layback and hand-jams lead to an
awkward jutting block. Pull over it and belay just above at 30m. It is also
possible to climb the short corner at the end of the ledge up 5.7 cracks for
two pitches to bypass the 5.9 and 5.8 pitches to the right. **6:** Clean 5.8 hand
jams and a few wider moves lead to a pedestal belay at 30m. **7:** Climb 20m
of 5.7 cracks, stepping right to avoid shallow rounded cracks, to gain a boulder
belay on the ridge crest. From the boulder belay, follow the ridge for about
150m to the south summit. Two short steps exist along the ridge that may
require a belay. As the ridge flattens a short step down on the right leads
back left to the chain anchors for the *Kraus-McCarthy* rappel route, found on
a small north facing wall overlooking the west face. To gain the south summit,
follow small ledges on the right to a 2m step. Scramble up left to the summit.

Descend down the *Kraus–McCarthy* rappel route.

142 **The Beach**   D   5.10+ C1   (8-12h)   9p *213*
Chris Atkinson, Marc Piche, August 2002
The Beach follows flakes and cracks directly to Surfs Up Ledge.

Start from the extreme right edge of the west face at the base of the
actual wall. **1:** Follow flakes out right onto the south face and up to belay
below a short chimney (5.8). **2:** Climb up into the chimney to where it begins
to overhang. Climb down right around the edge to gain cracks on a face (5.10).
Gain the corner to the right and follow a wide crack to a sling belay (5.10+).
3: Continue up and left on cracks to a belay in a corner below a roof (5.10+,
C1). **4:** Climb over the roof and up left to a belay below Surfs Up Ledge
(5.10+). **5–7:** Climb to Surfs Up Ledge and up the 5.8 cracks of *Surfs Up*.

A larger free rack to six inches. Pitches two and three are sustained.

SNOWPATCH SPIRE — WEST FACE

North Summit

123 125 126 127 128

128

127

130

121
22

123

125

126

Bugaboo–Snowpatch Col

Upper Vowell Glacier

ROUTES: 121 122 123 (200) **125-126** (201) **127 128 129** (202) **130** (203)

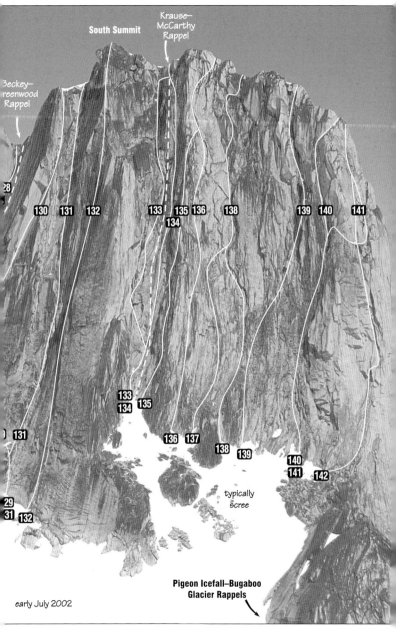

South Summit

Krause–
McCarthy
Rappel

Beckey–
Greenwood
Rappel

typically scree

early July 2002

Pigeon Icefall–Bugaboo
Glacier Rappels

ROUTES: **129** (202) **130-134** (203-204) **135-140** (205-206) **141-142** (207)

SNOWPATCH SPIRE — WEST FACE FAR LEFT

.8
face
25m

.7
45m

long
wide
chimney

.7 50m

45m .6

.2 50m

.5

45m

.6 25m

.4 40m

125

.6

.7 chimney

.9 hands

10 fingers

sb

.9
fist

.8

.8
hands

125 short 5.10
section

.8
lb

125

12

see photo-topo
page 208–209

July 2002

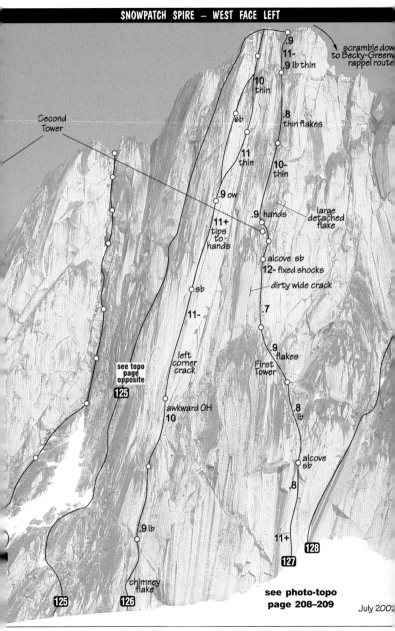

SNOWPATCH SPIRE – WEST FACE LEFT

scramble down to Becky-Green rappel route

.9

11-

.9 lb thin

10 thin

sb

.8 thin flakes

Second Tower

11 thin

10- thin

.9 ow

.9 hands

large detached flake

11+ tips to hands

alcove sb

12- fixed shocks

dirty wide crack

sb

.7

11-

.9 flakes

left corner crack

First Tower

see topo page opposite **125**

.8 lb

awkward OH 10

alcove sb

.8

.9 lb

11+ **128**

127

chimney flake

see photo-topo page 208–209

125

126

July 200?

SNOWPATCH SPIRE — WEST FACE CENTRE

Beckey–Greenwood rappel route

129
↓40m
10
✗ bolts
.9 ✗↓35m
.7
chimney + stemming
55m ↓ .7
129
55m↓
.7
↓55m
✗
✗10 thin
↓20m
✗
.9
28

4th + 5th terraces

chimney

.9

11+ 12-

130

see photo-topo page 208–209

130 **131**
.8
.9
.8
traverse left 10+ chimney ow
10m A1
10+
10+
.4
.9
.9+ stem lb
.9+
131
.8 lb
4th + 5th terraces
.7
129
.7

rounded grooves
.9
cracks up right of arete
132
.7
rounded grooves
.9
wide jamming and stemming
.9
move right
slings
crack narrow
.9
some face climbing
.9
.7
13
1

July 2C

ROUTES: **128 129** (202) **130 131** (203) **132** (204)

SNOWPATCH SPIRE – WEST FACE RIGHT

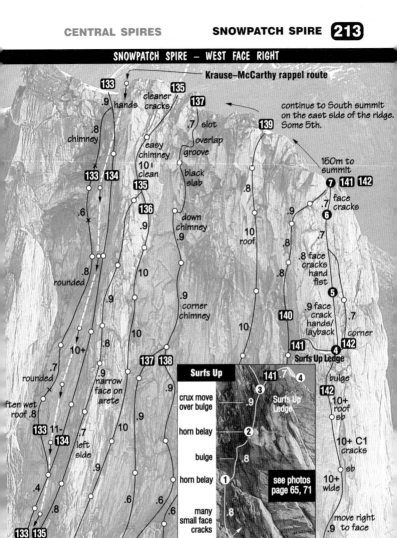

Krause–McCarthy rappel route

133

.9 hands

cleaner cracks **135**

137

.7 slot

139

continue to South summit on the east side of the ridge. Some 5th.

.8 chimney

easy chimney

overlap groove

10' clean

133 **134**

135

black slab

.8

150m to summit

7 **141** **142**

.7 face cracks

6

.6 ×

.9

down chimney

.9

10 roof

.7

136

.8 face cracks hand fist

.8

10

8

rounded

.9

.9 corner chimney

.8

.9 face crack hands/layback

140

10

5

.7

10

.9

.8

10+

137 **138**

10

.8

10

141

corner

142

Surfs Up Ledge

.7 rounded ×

.9 narrow face on arete

.9

4

Surfs Up

141 .7

4

ften wet roof .8

133 11-

134

.7 left side

10

.8

.9

137 **138**

.9

crux move over bulge

3

.9

bulge

142

Surfs Up Ledge

10+ roof sb

horn belay

2

.8

bulge

.4

.8

.6

.6

.6

horn belay

1

.8

see photos page 65, 71

10+ C1 cracks

sb

133 **135**

many small face cracks

10+ wide

.8

136

.7

.8

avoid big stacked flakes

easy

move right .9 to face

137

138

139

140 **141**

.8

140
141

142

see photo-topo page 208–209

ROUTES: **133 134** (204)   **135-137** (205)   **138-140** (206)   **141 142** (207)

Snowpatch Spire: South Face

This is a very steep white wall rising off the Pigeon Fork of Bugaboo Glacier, over twice the height of the west face. It faces Marmolata and the Hound's Tooth and the east face of Pigeon Spire, bounded on the west by the Snowpatch–Pigeon Icefall and the east by a toe of broken rock that separates it from a small cirque containing *Lightning Bolt Crack* and the approach gully to the *Snowpatch Route.*

Climbs: There are four full–length wall routes on the expanse of the southern walls; long, technical and sustained with the free version of the south face sustained at 5.11 and 5.12. The white rock of the south face is different from the rest of Snowpatch; although solid it has a thin, friable coating in places. All south face routes merge into the south ridge at the top of *Surfs Up* followed by 150m of easy terrain leading to the south summit and the *Kraus–McCarthy* rappel route. *Lightning Bolt Crack* is a two-pitch crag route that hides in the small cirque between the south face and the *Snowpatch Route.*

Descent: All full–length south face routes end on the south summit of Snowpatch Spire and use the *Kraus–McCarthy* rappel route down the west face for descent (page 213). From the base of the rappel route two options exist for a return to camp.

(1)   For Applebee it is quickest (if no gear left at the base)to traverse the glacier north, beneath the west face of Snowpatch to gain the top of the Bugaboo–Snowpatch Col. Descent down the col requires mountain boots, crampons and ice axes.

(2)   If heading to the Kain Hut, the best option is down the Snowpatch–Pigeon Icefall rappel route to the Bugaboo Glacier and the base of the south face (page 218). Scramble down scree beneath the *Kraus–McCarthy* rappel route to gain the snow and ice. Descend the few hundred metres of snow and ice down and left, hand-railing the small rock bump that descends from the base of *Surfs Up* towards the Snowpatch–Pigeon Icefall. Gain the flat area of this satellite rock just before it drops into the icefall proper. Chains are on the left wall. Seven 25m (single 50m rope) rappels descend the rock and over the bergshrund to the Bugaboo Glacier, from which the base of the south face is easily attained. Although snow and ice will be encountered, the base of the south face routes can be reached with approach shoes. The descent from the base of the rappels back down around the base of Son of Snowpatch towards the Kain Hut Basin requires mountain boots, ice axes and crampons. However, a convoluted, complicated and loose route can be made through the scree, talus and slabs on the east side of the glacier that avoids nearly all of the snow and ice. Be aware of loose scree and steep rock slabs.

In February of 1999 Kirk Maunthner and Brad Shilling climbed high on the south face via a new line (page 217) until storms and very cold temperatures forced a retreat. The two then made the first winter ascent of the *Kraus–McCarthy Route* on the west face.

143 South Face Left   TD+   5.8 A2 ♦ (1-2 biv)   16p   *217*

Chris Jones, Jeff Lowe, August 1973   *CAJ 55:78 AAJ 18:146*

This route follows right-trending cracks on the far left side of the south face. It involves extensive aid climbing on decomposed rock.

On the far left side of the main south face locate a steep triangular slab directly below a dark chimney system leading to a low shoulder. Climb the right edge of the slab and follow cracks out right to gain right-facing and right-trending cracks and corners. These are followed all the way up the left side of the south face to gain the south ridge where *Surfs Up* enters. The first ascent party made one hammock bivy.

144 ASTA *   TD+   5.9 A3   (1-2 biv)   17p   *217*

Jerome Blanc–Gras, David Jonglez, August 1996   *CAJ 80:93*

This extensive aid climb ascends the middle of the south face via a serpentine route, sharing three pitches with *South Face Direct*.

Start at the middle of the south face below a cluster of overhangs perch 30m above the glacier. Climb cracks that lead to a belay above and just right of these overhangs. Follow right-trending cracks for four pitches to a belay below a large roof level with the top of the fourth-class approach terrain off to the right that leads to the *South Face Upper*. Climb out right under the roof to join the cracks of the *South Face Direct* and belay above. Follow the *South Face Direct* cracks for two more pitches before breaking out left. Follow cracks and pendulum left to a ledge. Climb three pitches trending left to avoid overhangs joining *South Face Left* one pitch below the summit ridge.

145 South Face Direct   TD+   5.8 A2 ♦ (1-2 biv)   17p   *217*

H.Abrons, G.Millikan, July 1965   *Harvard 1967:63*

This was the first route up the lower south face. Details are unclear but the route involves extensive aid climbing.

Locate a shallow left-facing corner just left of parallel cracks that start on the right side of the south face where the snow sits slightly higher. Follow corners and cracks straight up for four pitches to a belay below and right of the roof where *ASTA* joins. Continue for two more pitches to where *South Face Upper* joins in from the right. Above this point *ASTA* can be followed for eight pitches as a continuation of the aid line or *South Face Upper* can be followed for nine pitches up to 5.12- as a free climb.

Grizzlies and Wolverines have been seen a number of times on the Vowell Glacier, sometimes following each other.

146 **Edwards—Jessup**   ED1   5.12-   (16-20h)   18p   *217*

Guy Edwards, Micah Jessup, August 1999   *AAJ 2000:229*

This route included a new free ascent line on the lower face and followed the *South Face Upper* giving the first free ascent of the complete south face. It is a long, serious and sustained free climb. The first ascent party made a bivy at the top of the approach terrain to *South Face Upper*. Strong parties will require a long day to complete the route.

Locate a crack right of the *ASTA* start, and just left of where the snow curves back up to the start of *South Face Lower*. **1:** Climb a very run–out 55m pitch at 5.11+ to a ledge belay. **2:** Climb right up a run–out open corner at 5.11- to belay near the *South Face Direct* cracks. **3:** Continue climbing right dropping down to under–cling a blocky roof at 5.11. Continue right to a ledge belay. **4-6:** Follow the edge of the white rock up run–out and featureless rock to belay at the top of the approach terrain to the *South Face Upper* (5.11, 5.9, 5.8). Escape is possible from here. Follow *South Face Upper* at 5.12- for ten pitches to the south ridge where *Surfs Up* enters.

147 **South Face Upper**   TD-   5.12-   (12-16h)   13p   *217*

J.Hudson, A.Leemets, R.Williams, July 1966
FFA Tom Gibson, Rob Rohn, August 1980   *AAJ 15:283*

South Face Upper follows the broken fourth-class terrain to the right of the lower south face to gain the technical climbing on the upper south face. The upper face was freed at 5.12- by Tom Gibson and Rob Rohn in 1980, a remarkable feat for that era.

From the glacial flats below the south face scramble up a loose gully that leads to broken fourth-class terrain curving up left to gain the right side of the upper south face. **1:** From the top of the broken terrain climb a 5.10- flake up and left to a ledge belay in a right-facing corner. **2:** Follow the corner to a ledge belay, past where it turns into a thin and sustained 5.11+/5.12- face crack. **3:** Start up a thin 5.11- right-facing corner following it left. Climb down left around a small overhang to gain a right-facing crack that leads to a belay. **4:** Step right into a left-facing crack. Climb the 5.10+ crack making a scary 5.10+ traverse left to a ledge belay atop a right-facing corner and below a small overhang. **5:** Climb a left-facing crack into a 5.10 offwidth past fixed protection to a pedestal belay. **6:** Follow a 5.10+ arête to a crack through blocks and left under a small roof to a belay at 40m. **7:** Climb a short section left at 5.6 to change corners. **8:** Follow 5.9+ cracks up and left to a ledge belay near *Surfs Up*. **9:** Climb 5.7 cracks to the top of the south face and the easy ground of the south ridge that leads in about 150m to the *Kraus–McCarthy* rappel route and the south summit.

148 **Lightning Bolt Crack**   5.10   2-3p

Gordon Banks, Lyel Dean, Neal Beidleman, August 1981

This is a 2–3 pitch cragging route located on the left side of a small cirque between the south face and the *Snowpatch Route* on the southeast ridge. It is approached as per the *Snowpatch Route (page 182)* and can be seen opposite the approach gully to that route. The route ends part way up the approach terrain of *South Face Upper*. The line is appealing but dirty.

SNOWPATCH SPIRE – SOUTH FACE

143 South Summit
.7
A1 10
A3
144 10+
143 10 OW
A2+
10+
142 A2 11 thin
A1
143 144 147
7 A1 12-
(5.8 A1) 11
A1 10- hands
A3 .8
144 4th and 5th scramble approach
A2 A1
.9 147
A3+
5.8 A2 A2+ 146 147
11
143 11- R
A1 R
11+
A1
many parallel cracks
view from Bugaboo Glacier 143 winter attempt 144 146 145

ROUTES: **142** (207)   **143 144 145** (215)   **146 147** (216)

SNOWPATCH SPIRE — SOUTH FACE

RAPPEL ROUTE — PIGEON–SNOWPATCH COL

25m

25m

25m

25m

25m

15m

Pigeon–
Snowpatch Icefall

147

same place

143 144 146 145

Kain Hut
Basin

Pigeon Fork Bugaboo Glacier

ROUTES: 143 144 145 (215) **146 147** (216)

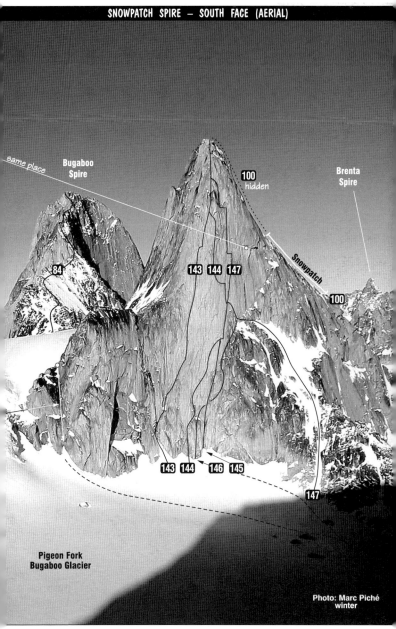

SNOWPATCH SPIRE – SOUTH FACE (AERIAL)

Photo: Marc Piché
winter

Pigeon Feathers

Pigeon Spire

South Howser Tower

Central Howser Tower

North Howser Tower

Pigeon– Howser Col

Upper Vowell Glacier

Bugaboo– Snowpatch Co

Snowpatch–Pigeon Col Icefall

view from Snowpatch Spire

PIGEON SPIRE — EAST SIDE, WITH THE HOWSER TOWERS BEYOND

PIGEON SPIRE — NORTHWEST SIDE

East Face

West Ridge

Pigeon– Howser Col

Bugaboo– Snowpatch Col

September 200

view from the summit of Bugaboo Spire

photo: Kevin McL

Pigeon Spire	3156m

Pigeon Spire sits west of Snowpatch Spire guarding the approach to the Howser Towers and the East Creek Basin and dividing the Bugaboo and Vowell Glaciers. The immensely popular and classic *West Ridge* runs from the col with the Howser Towers over Pigeon Spire's three progressively higher summits. The north buttress and northwest face are easily viewed from the Bugaboo–Snowpatch Col and from the approach up the Upper Vowell Glacier en route to the *West Ridge*. The much taller east face and south faces are viewed and approached from the Pigeon Fork of the Bugaboo Glacier. The east face is home to the long, elegant *Cooper–Kor* route. The short and relatively unexplored southwest bluff known as the Pigeon Feed Wall sits hidden just below the start of the *West Ridge* on the Bugaboo Glacier side. It has potential for numerous three pitch harder free climbs, all leading to the first summit.

Approach: There are two approaches to Pigeon Spire from the Kain Hut. For routes on the north side, northwest face, *West Ridge* and Pigeon Feed Wall, the Bugaboo–Snowpatch Col and Upper Vowell Glacier approach is used (**1**). For routes on the east face, southeast face and south side, use the Bugaboo Glacier approach (**2**).

(**1**) For the Bugaboo–Snowpatch Col approach (page 172), leave the Conrad Kain Hut and follow the trail heading up towards Applebee Dome for about 15–20 minutes, taking a trail left above the rock slabs at a faint junction. Follow the drainage up, to gain the Crescent Glacier and the base of the Bugaboo–Snowpatch Col. From Applebee Camp faint trails contour towards the east face of Snowpatch Spire to join the trail on the flats above the rock slabs, or trails above the camp lead around the left side of the tarns to gain the glacier below Bugaboo Spire which is followed to the base of the col. Continue up the Bugaboo–Snowpatch Col, usually passing the bergshrund on the right side where it pinches onto the rock. At the top of the snow–slope traverse left to exit up a short gully in order to avoid the very loose scree on the right. Ascend a short glacial slope above the col, avoiding the crevasses out left. After about 100m Pigeon Spire and the approach up the Upper Vowell Glacier comes into view. *Wingtip Arête* is immediately across from the West Face of Snowpatch Spire. Ascend the Upper Vowell Glacier parallel to the north wall of Pigeon Spire staying a few hundred metres to the north to avoid the crevasses that form under Pigeon's north wall. Follow the glacier up to the base of the *West Ridge*. The actual Pigeon–Howser Col and access to the East Creek Basin leads down and right from the *West Ridge* access. The Bugaboo Glacier is easily gained from the start of the *West Ridge,* making a loop circuit from the Kain Hut Basin a scenic and enjoyable option.

(2)   For the Bugaboo Glacier approach follow rough trails behind the largest boulder beside the Conrad Kain Hut up towards the southeast toe of Snowpatch Spire. From the toe, drop down around rock slabs to gain the edge of the ice. Follow the right–hand edge of the glacier up onto the flats directly below the south face of Snowpatch Spire and the east face of Pigeon Spire. Crevasses often extend to the rocks on this route. Continue up the glacier swinging around the base of the east face to gain the routes of the east and south faces. The glacier can be followed up beneath the Pigeon Feed Wall and onto the start of the *West Ridge.* The glacier travel is straightforward but some long, large crevasses can pose problems later in the season.

Descent: Descent for all routes is down the *West Ridge.* The entire route can be downclimbed with only a few sections of low fifth class climbing, however two single rope rappels from the main summit, down the northwest side, will bypass the 5.4 crux section. The first rappel chains can be found just west of the summit block on the northwest side. The first 25m rappel leads over the slabs to a short, steep wall and ends on a ramp with chain anchors on the wall. The second 25m rappel ends on the *West Ridge* traverse ledges near the col with the middle summit. The rest of the descent route follows the *West Ridge.* Follow the ledge system across to the col between the main and second summits. Blocks and flakes on the north side lead up to the second summit. Just west of the second summit a dihedral is followed down the north side for about 5m to small ledges leading back to the ridge-crest proper. Follow the ridge down to the col between the second and first summits, up over the first summit and down to the end of the ridge where the upper Vowell or Bugaboo Glaciers can be reached.

Return to the Kain Hut Basin.   Three options exist: down the Bugaboo–Snowpatch Col; the Snowpatch–Pigeon Icefall Rappel Route, or the Bugaboo Glacier descent.

(1)   **The Upper Vowell Glacier can be descended** to either the Bugaboo–Snowpatch Col or the Pigeon–Snowpatch Icefall rappels. For climbers camped at Applebee Dome, the Bugaboo–Snowpatch Col is fastest. Two chain anchor rappel routes exist, one down the ascent line on the Bugaboo Spire side and one down the Snowpatch Spire side of the upper snow–slope. The latter requires only a single 60m rope and avoids the ascent line.

(2) **For climbers staying at the Conrad Kain Hut**, an alternative is to descend the Pigeon–Snowpatch Icefall rappels. Contour down beneath the west face of Snowpatch Spire to access a small flat rock promenade below the shoulder that extends towards Pigeon Spire just above the main icefall. Chain anchors can be found on the wall. Six 25m rappels reach the Bugaboo Glacier. Cross the glacier flats under the south face and follow the ice down two steep rolls to the toe of Son of Snowpatch. A traverse left underneath the rock slabs is followed by a short uphill section, which gains the Kain Hut Basin and a short descent to the hut.

(3) **To descend the Bugaboo Glacier,** exit from the start of the *West Ridge* south onto the glacier and follow the wind roll beneath Pigeon Feed Wall down and east to the glacial flats below the south face of Snowpatch Spire. The Pigeon–Snowpatch Icefall rappels join here.

149 **West Ridge**   ***   PD   5.4   (6-10h)   500m   *229*
Eaton Cromwell, Peter Kaufmann, August 1930   *AAJ 1:297*

The *West Ridge* of Pigeon Spire is one of the most appealing and enjoyable climbs in the Bugaboos. The route is neither technically difficult nor sustained but the position is truly superb and the line classic.

Follow the Upper Vowell Glacier to its highest point near the beginning of the ridge. Scramble a short distance to the rock crest where ice axes, crampons and extra gear can be stowed. The climb to the first summit follows very near to the ridge-crest proper. Starting up the left side, gain the ridge, climbing sometimes on the right and sometimes on the left but never more than 3 or 4m away from the crest. A narrow section of the ridge two-thirds up is best done *au cheval* style. From the first summit, descend slabs on the south side to gain the saddle with the second summit. The climb to the second summit appears steep and intimidating but coarse rock, ramps and cracks make it no more than fourth-class climbing. Stay very close to the actual crest until a short, steep step forces the route across cracks on the north side into a corner system that leads up to the second summit. From the second summit low fifth class flakes and blocks on the north side lead down and right to the col with the main summit. From the col, icy ramps beneath the summit block lead out left. Follow the blocky ramp system down, across, and back up to the base of a slab heading up right, a short chimney straight above, and a narrow gully full of small blocks to the left. Scramble up the left-hand gully for about 5m, to a left slanting ten inch crack. Step right to the back of a big flake and chimney back left. Follow a small 5.4 hand-rail left for 4m, make a reach above, and scramble up and right over easier terrain to the main summit.

To descend, retrace the route. From the summit, two single rope rappels can be used to bypass the 5.4 crux section and regain the route near the main and second summit col.

150 **Tail–Feather Pinnacle Right**   *   D-   5.10-   (7-10h)   4p   *233*

Joe Benson, Gene Klein, Randall Green, August 1987

On the northwest face below and right of the second summit, lies a pinnacle.
Tail–feather Pinnacle Right follows the right side of the pinnacle to gain face-
cracks that lead to the ridge near the second summits.

Gain the base of the pinnacle from the Upper Vowell Glacier approach
to the *West Ridge*. The bergshrund is usually passable somewhere close to
the bottom of the route. Start at the base of the corner that makes up the
right side of the pinnacle. **1:** Climb either the main corner or a shallower corner
in stacked flakes a few metres left, trending left to a small ledge. Belay near
the actual arête where the main corner becomes a defined white dihedral
(5.7). **2:** Climb 5.10- hand-cracks on the main face of the pinnacle to a blocky
belay. **3:** Continue up 5.9 blocks and flakes and easier face-climbing to a belay
at the top of the pinnacle. **4:** Traverse right on a small ledge for about six
metres to gain a vertical dyke that is followed to the *West Ridge* (5.6, little
protection). A direct route up the main corner for pitches two and three is
possible and will likely be in the 5.10 range.

151 **Tail–Feather Pinnacle Left**   D-   5.10-   (7-10h)   5p   *233*

Chris Atkinson, Lindsay Eltis, Trish Fodor, August 1989

This route follows the left side of the pinnacle to gain the right-facing corner
high on the face that is followed to the second summit.

Gain the base of the pinnacle from the Upper Vowell Glacier approach
to the *West Ridge*. The bergshrund is usually passable somewhere close to
the bottom of the route. Start slightly left of the base of the pinnacle proper.
1: Climb flakes and cracks to gain a shallow left-facing, right-leaning crack
system that merges into the main left corner of the pinnacle (5.7). **2:** Follow
the shallow corner system to the base of the steep corner (5.8). **3:** The main
corner can be climbed directly by a wild 5.10+ layback, but is often wet. As
an alternative, climb out right on steep flakes to gain the face of the pinnacle
and follow 5.10- cracks up the left side to a ledge belay. **4:** Follow 5.7 cracks
and face-climbing up and slightly left to gain the hanging, right-facing corner
system. **5:** Follow the corner system to where the *West Ridge* traverses in
from the right and continue up the corner to the second summit (5.4).

152 **Feather Fallout**   D   5.7 A2   ◆   (8-10h)   6p   *233*

L.Johnson, S.Mikesell, R.Skelding July 1974

Feather Fallout starts about 20 to 30 metres left of *Tail–Feather Pinnacle Left*
and follows face cracks and shallow corners directly to the second summit.
Although still rated 5.7 A2 the route would likely go free in the 5.10 range.

Follow the Upper Vowell Glacier approach to the *West Ridge* and
traverse to the base of the northwest face directly below the middle summit.
Find a small open book marking the beginning of a vague crack system that
leads up towards the right edge of the upper slabs below the main summit.
Climb connecting face cracks and shallow corners straight up for three or
four pitches to the right edge of the upper slabs. Either continue straight up
over broken ground and a gully to the middle summit, or angle left across
the slabs to gain broken ground leading to the col between the middle and
main summits where the *West Ridge* is joined.

153 Northwest Face   D   5.7 A3 ♦   (8-10h)   6p *232*

Fred Beckey, Yvon Chouinard, August 1961   *CAJ 45:127, AAJ 13:242*

The actual position of this climb is uncertain but it is said to follow a fairly direct line that is usually wet or icy to the main summit.

   The route is described as following "a twenty–five metre aid crack to a section of slabs and cracks leading to a wide solitary crack". It then works over a bulge and up a layback to a belay ledge. A left-trending, vertical corner with jutting holds leads to two pitches of easier ground, past the snow/ice patch and on to the main summit.

154 **Wingtip Arête**   *   D   5.10-   (7-10h)   8p *232*

Chris Atkinson, Randall Green, August 1987

Wingtip Arête climbs a corner immediately right of the actual north buttress and then follows a vague buttress to the main summit. The route has a variety of climbing and good position.

   From the flat glacial area above the Bugaboo–Snowpatch Col contour into the base of the north buttress. The route starts in a steep corner just right of the toe of the north buttress. **1:** Climb the steep 5.9 corner up a widening crack. Step right as the corner turns to a 5.10- offwidth and follow flakes to a ledge belay near the crest. **2:** Continue up the 5.9 crack as it widens from fists to a 5.7 chimney and belay on the crest at the base of a slab. **3:** Follow easy cracks in the slabs around the left edge of a small roof and belay above at a horn (5.6). **4:** Follow cracks and shallow corners up a second slab to a belay below a roof and left of the ridge-crest. **5:** Step right under the roof and climb up onto a small, sharp arête that is climbed *au cheval* (5.6, no protection) to a ledge belay. **6:** Follow 5.6 cracks and shallow corners to a blocky belay. **7-8:** 100m of broken ground lead to the main summit.

   Bring a standard free rack with one or two larger cams for the offwidth on pitches one and two.

155 **North Face**   AD+ 5.7 A2   (6-10h)   8p *232*

Fred Beckey, Joe Hieb, Ralph Widrig, July 1948   *CAJ 32:50, AAJ 7:134*

To the left of *Wingtip Arête* lies a steep narrow gully. The *North Face* follows this gully to gain a small Y shaped snowpatch that leads to the upper pitches of either the *Cooper–Kor* or *Wingtip Arête* routes. Fifty years ago the gully was all snow except for one short pitch of 5.7 A2 to gain the upper snowpatch, but is now entirely mixed climbing. The grade varies with conditions but is generally around 5.9 WI4.

   From the flat glacial area above the Bugaboo–Snowpatch Col contour down past the base of the north buttress to gain the start of the gully above the bergshrund. Follow the gully for two pitches to a short, steep wall below the upper snow patch. Early parties aided this short section, but modern parties should be able to find a 5.9 route over it. Once the upper snowpatch is reached either follow the right branch to merge with *Wingtip Arête* at pitch five or follow the left fork to merge with the *Cooper–Kor* at pitch fifteen. The *Cooper–Kor* option involves one pitch of 5.6 to the ridge-crest followed by about 200m of broken ground to the main summit.

   Bring a standard free rack with a few pins and mixed climbing gear.

156 **Millar–Shepard**   AD   5.6   (6-10h)   8p   *232*

S.Millar, S.Shepard, July 1961

The *Millar–Shepard* is a variation of the *North Face* that follows the rock to the left of the gully, joining the *North Face* at the upper snowpatch.

From the flat glacial area above the Bugaboo–Snowpatch Col contour down past the base of the north buttress and the *North Face* gully until below a notch beside the small pinnacle called the *Pigeon Toe*. Climb to the notch and follow the edge of the slab right to a short, steep wall. Climb the wall on the right end to gain the ridge-crest at the edge of another slab. Continue right to climb a sharp arête that leads to the start of the upper Y-shaped snowpatch on the *North Face*. Climb the snow patch to either of the *North Face* options or continue up cracks left of the snowpatch and gain the *Cooper–Kor* option to the *North Face* above the snowpatch, there-by avoiding the snow and ice.

Bring a normal free climbing rack and an ice axe and crampons if climbing the snowpatch option.

157 **Pigeon Toe**   AD-   5th   (5-6h)   3p   *232*

David Bernays, James McCarthy, July 1954

The *Pigeon Toe* is usually climbed for entertainment during foul weather or as a bonus to the *Millar–Shepard*. The views across the east face are grand.

Approach as per the *Millar–Shepard*. Climb to the notch and continue up the righthand wall to the west summit.

158 **Cooper–Kor**   ***   TD-   5.10   (5.9 A0)   (10-14h)   18p   *235*

Ed Cooper, Layton Kor, August 1960
FFA Ed Drummond, P.Buchanan, July 1974   *CAJ 44:75, AAJ 12:385*

This classic line follows a long and devious route up the elegant east face. What it lacks in directness of line it makes up for with the bold and intricate nature of the headwall pitches. This route is **challenging for the second** due to its traversing pitches.

Approach via the Pigeon Fork of the Bugaboo Glacier to gain the left edge of the east face. **1–3:** Climb diagonally right up a flake and a crack to a belay (5.7). Zigzag up a short 5.4 pitch and continue up to gain the left end of the fourth-class ledge system that cuts across the face (5.6). **4–6:** Traverse right, past a crack system (variation) to the far end of the ledge. **7:** Undercling up and right to a layback crack curving back left to the start of the long left-trending chimney system (5.7). **8–9:** Follow the fourth and low fifth class chimney system over loose blocks to belay at its end. The variation cracks (5.8) passed on the traverse and parallel variation cracks above the chimney system (5.8) join here. **10:** Climb straight up over a small 5.7 roof continuing up the crack to belay above another small roof near the base of the headwall (5.7). **11:** Climb the short distance up the crack to the headwall and traverse right along the slab–headwall junction past a shallow corner system and descend to a small ledge belay. Protection is only possible in three places on this friction pitch, which can make it intimidating for the second climber (5.8). **12:** Continue right and up a short crack past a fixed pin to a small ledge with fixed pins. Downclimb or tension down and right from the pins to gain a shallow corner that is followed up to a fixed pin belay on a ledge (5.8, A0). **13:** Tension right from the belay to gain a crack and grooves that are followed up the steepening wall past fixed pins to a belay at the higher of two ledges (5.9). This pitch is often wet. **14:** Follow easy cracks above, past a patch of snow to a flake belay. **15:** Climb left, switching cracks to gain a corner and a belay at the ridge-crest (5.6). Follow broken ground, right of the ridge-crest, for about 200m to the main summit.

159 Cleopatra's Alley   *   TD   5.10 A2   (12-16h)   13p   *235*
Dave Knox, Tom Thomas, Gil McCormick, August 1987

This route climbs the left edge of the east face in a straight line to the main summit. There are only two short sections of aid on the climb that will likely go free.

Approach via the Pigeon Fork of the Bugaboo Glacier and follow the first three pitches of the *Cooper–Kor* to the fourth-class ledge system. **4–6:** Climb straight up the left edge of the face following low-mid–fifth class cracks to gain the base of the headwall. **7–8:** Climb two pitches of mixed free and aid up connecting cracks to a ledge belay below the large slab (5.9, A2). **9– 10:** Continue up cracks and over small ledges (5.9) to gain the big slab. Climb up the left side of the slab to a belay left of a big wet corner. **11:** Climb a pitch of sustained 5.10 finger-cracks to a ledge belay. **12:** Continue up right and climb a 5.10 offwidth right of a wet chimney to a ledge belay. **13–14:** Follow fourth-class terrain to belay below a 5.9 finger crack, which is followed to the ridge-crest very near the main summit.

160 Southeast Buttress   TD   5.8 A2 ♦   (12-16h)   11p   *235*
Fred Beckey, Steve Marts, July 1963   *AAJ 14:199*

This route climbs the buttress-like face between the great east face and the broken south face that lie below the main and middle summits respectively. The exact location of the line is uncertain.

Approach via the Pigeon Fork of the Bugaboo Glacier and ascend the right side of the broken slabs that lie left of the east face. Follow gullies and slabs to a large terrace beneath the steep upper face. Follow a steep aid corner beginning with an overhang for 100m to a ledge belay. Cracks and easier aid climbing lead out right to gain a small bivy ledge. A long solitary aid crack leads up to mixed free and aid pitches, then eases off in difficulty. A final short, steep wall leads to the summit.

161 Southeast Slabs   AD   5.6 ♦   (8-10h)   11p? *237*
D.Davis, G.Markov, August 1972

This route follows the *Southeast Buttress* up the lower slabs to gain the terrace. It then traverses scree ledges left to gain the long slab below the middle summit that is followed to the col between the first and middle summits. It is accessed from the Pigeon Fork of the Bugaboo Glacier.

162 South Face   D   5.6 A1   ♦   (8-10h)   10p   *236*

Hans Kraus, James McCarthy, John Rupley, August 1956   *Harvard 1957:34*

This route follows the slabby drainage between the *Southeast Buttress* slabs and the Pigeon Feed Wall to gain scree ledges below the steeper upper wall. It then leads up the cracks and corners that make up the large corner system that ends at the col between the main and middle summits. Halfway up the upper wall the route angles left over easier terrain to the left of two notches. The upper *West Ridge* can be followed to the main summit. The first ascent party used aid on the first pitch above the scree ledges. Access is from the Pigeon Fork of the Bugaboo Glacier.

The following three climbs, as described, end on the First Summit of the *West Ridge* of Pigeon

163 Parboosing Route   AD   5.5   ♦   (7-9h)   5p   *237*

Lorentz, Simon Parboosing, July 1988

This route starts at the toe of rock between the drainage gully of the *South Face* and the Pigeon Feed Wall. It climbs a large silver slab and continues for five short pitches of low and mid–fifth class climbing to gain the left edge of the giant slab leading up to the first summit. Access is quickest from the Pigeon Fork of the Bugaboo Glacier.

164 Lambrice Tour   AD   5.8   ♦   (7-9h)   3p   *237*

D.Deglise, D.Ossola, G.Valenti, July 1988

Approach from either the Bugaboo Glacier or the Upper Vowell Glacier over the *West Ridge* to the Pigeon Feed Wall.

This route starts at the right end of the Pigeon Feed Wall just up from the end of the scree. A short section of 5.7 face-climbing leads to a chimney that is followed for a short distance before breaking out right on 5.8 cracks to a belay below a roof. A bolt marks the 5.8 roof that leads to the *Parboosing Route* which is followed up the giant slab to the first summit.

165 Turk–Seashore   AD   5.9   (7-9h)   3p   *237*

Chris Seashore, Jon Turk, August 1991

This route climbs the little-explored Pigeon Feed Wall to the first summit. Approach via the Upper Vowell Glacier and over the start of the *West Ridge* to the base of the Pigeon Feed Wall.

1: Climb a series of flakes and cracks starting at the highest point of scree (5.9). **2:** Continue up cracks towards a roof formed by two flakes. Angle through the roof on the face to avoid the overhang and belay above on a ledge (5.9). **3:** Follow an easy traverse left to a dihedral that is followed to the *West Ridge* (5.9).

Guy Edwards climbed the West Ridge of Pigeon, solo and naked, in 19 minutes up and down; August 1999.

PIGEON SPIRE – WEST RIDGE, NORTHWEST FACE

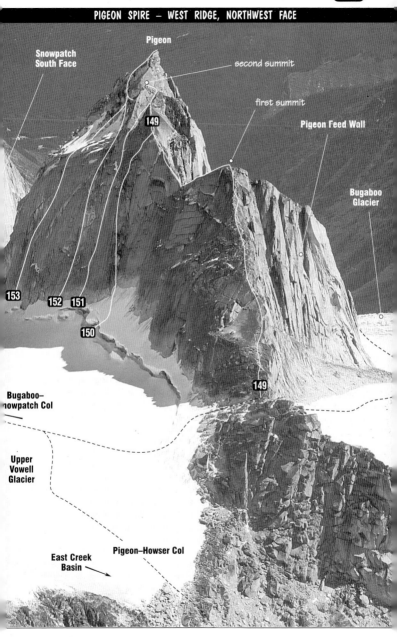

Snowpatch South Face
Pigeon
second summit
first summit
Pigeon Feed Wall
Bugaboo Glacier
149
153 152 151
150
Bugaboo–Snowpatch Col
Upper Vowell Glacier
Pigeon–Howser Col
East Creek Basin
149

ROUTES: 149 (223) **150 151 152** (224) **153** (225)

PIGEON SPIRE — WEST RIDGE, FIRST SUMMIT

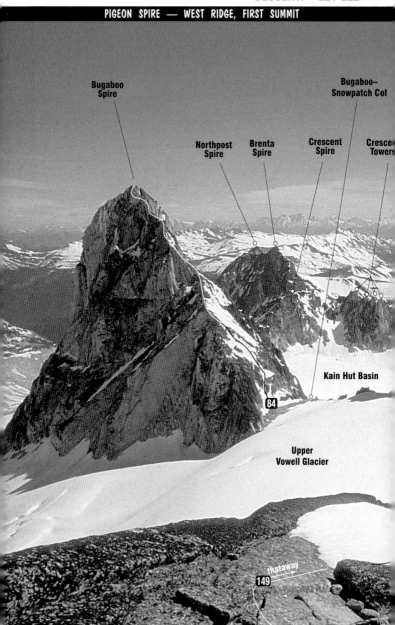

Bugaboo
Spire

Bugaboo–
Snowpatch Col

Northpost
Spire

Brenta
Spire

Crescent
Spire

Crescent
Towers

Kain Hut Basin

Upper
Vowell Glacier

84

thataway

149

ROUTES: **84** (163) **149** (223)

Snowpatch Spire (North Summit)
second summit
Pigeon Spire

ROUTES: 84 (163) **149** (223)

PIGEON SPIRE – NORTH SIDE

Main Summit

second summit

156 155 154

Pigeon Toe

157

154

156

155

view from Snowpatch Spire

July 2002

ROUTES: **153–155** (225) **156 157** (226)

PIGEON SPIRE – NORTHWEST FACE

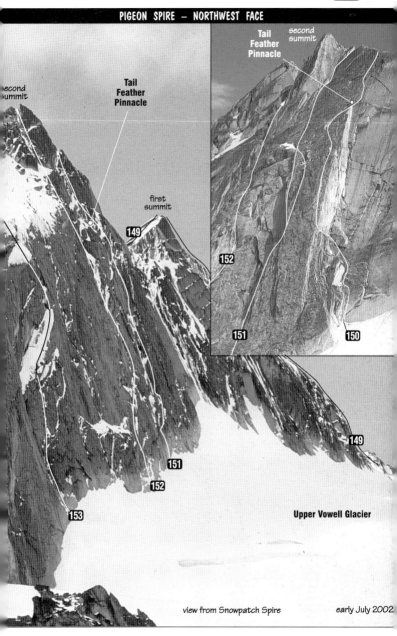

view from Snowpatch Spire   early July 2002

ROUTES: **149** (223)   **150** **151** **152** (224)   **153** (225)

PIGEON SPIRE – SOUTH FACE

cleopatra's alley

156

Pigeon Fork
Bugaboo Glacier

159

158

158
159

view from Snowpatch
West Face

Pigeon–Snowpatch
Icefall

ROUTES: 155 (225), **156 158** (226), **159** (227)

PIGEON SPIRE – EAST FACE

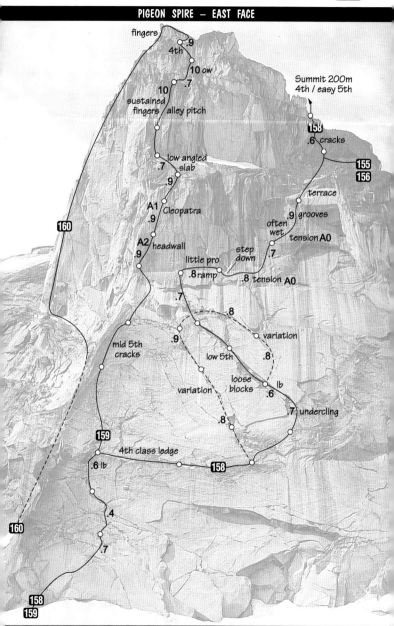

fingers
.9
4th
10 ow
10 .7
sustained
fingers / alley pitch

Summit 200m
4th / easy 5th

`158`
.6 cracks

`155`
`156`

low angled
slab
.7
.9
A1 | Cleopatra
.9
A2 | headwall
.9

terrace

.9 grooves
often
wet
tension A0
.7

little pro
.8 ramp

step
down

.8 tension A0

`160`

.7

.8

.9

variation

mid 5th
cracks

low 5th

.8

loose
blocks
lb
.6

variation

.7 undercling

.8

`159`

4th class ledge

.6 lb

`158`

`160`

.4

.7

`158`
`159`

PIGEON SPIRE – SOUTH SIDE

second
summit

main
summit

161

162

160

160
161

162

ROUTES: 160 161 (227) **162** (228)

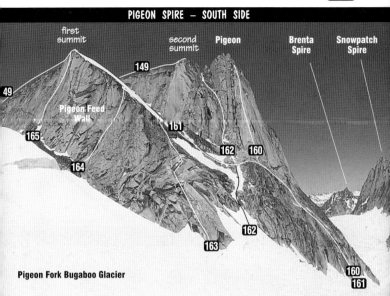

PIGEON SPIRE – SOUTH SIDE

first summit
second summit
Pigeon
Brenta Spire
Snowpatch Spire

149
49
Pigeon Feed Wall
161
165
162   160
164
162

163
160
161

Pigeon Fork Bugaboo Glacier

PIGEON SPIRE – PIGEON FEED WALL

first summit

165

164

Pigeon Fork Bugaboo Glacier

July 2002

ROUTES: **149** (223) **164** (228) **160 161** (227) **162** (228)

Approaching the *Beckey–Chouinard*,
South Howser Tower.
climber: Marc Piché

WESTERN SPIRES

The Western Spires consist of the Howser Towers, the steep western walls of the Pigeon Feathers, Crossed Fish Peak and Little Snowpatch, all located west of the Central Spires and the Bugaboo Glacier Peaks, and accessed via those areas. The Western Spires contain the longest routes in the Bugaboos as well as the majority of the harder, big wall routes. The much sought after *Beckey-Chouinard* on South Howser Tower and *All Along the Watchtower* on North Howser Tower reside here.

The climbs in the Western Spires are generally more committing and involved than those in the main Bugaboo Group, and run from the shorter but rarely-travelled climbs on the east faces of the three Howser Towers to the huge routes of the west face of North Howser. Some approaches such as that to the west face of North Howser are long, strenuous and committing while others such as the approach to the Minaret are a short stroll from an East Creek Basin camp. Although the *Beckey-Chouinard* can see up to four parties on a busy day, the majority of the climbs here have seen fewer than a handful of ascents and more than half have yet to be repeated.

The committing nature of the climbs and the wild and inaccessible valleys to the west make this area feel very remote. Many of the climbs require a camp in the East Creek Basin or a bivy at the base, and/or on the route. Camping at the Pigeon–Howser Col is inside the park and is prohibited by B.C. Parks, but a good bivouac site exists outside the park beneath the Minaret in the East Creek Basin.

Howser Towers

North Tower		3412m
South Tower		3364m
Central Tower		3344m
Minaret (South Tower)		3140m

Pigeon Feathers

West Peak	Fingerberry Tower	2930m
East Peak	Main	2990m
East Peak	Lost Feather Pinnacle	2900m
Southeast Peak	Wide Awake Tower	2950m

Crossed Fish Peak
2836m

Little Snowpatch
2915m

| Howser Towers | 3412m (North), 3344m (Centre), 3364m (South) |

The highest of all the Bugaboo Spires, the three towers that comprise this majestic peak stand high above the head of the Vowell Glacier and dominate the view to the west of the Central Spires.

The Howser Towers have three very distinct aspects: their east/northeast faces that rise above the Upper Vowell Glacier; the remote and hidden north/northwest faces; and their great west faces. The towers are linked to Pigeon Spire to the east by a low col, and drain to the west down into the forks of East Creek.

The western wall of North Howser Tower is the most impressive of all the Bugaboo walls and was unclimbed until 1971 with the ascent of *The Seventh Rifle*. It now sports eight ED2 climbs, and ranks with the great alpine rock-walls of the world.

Conrad Kain made the first ascent of the North Tower (the highest) in 1916 via the *South Ridge,* guiding H.Frind, Albert and Bess MacCarthy and John Vincent. This was a remarkable ascent accomplished in only twenty hours return from a camp near the present day CMH Lodge, before any trails existed.

Climbs on the east/northeast faces of the Howsers sit above the Upper Vowell Glacier, looking down and across to the Central Spires. They dominate the view from the Bugaboo–Snowpatch Col and the Central Spires and although not far away, they see very little climbing activity. Their nature is more one of alpine mountaineering rather than pure rock, and as a result, many fine climbs go un-travelled.

Due to a longer glacier approach, a problematic bergshrund and the high, exposed elevation, the climbs have a much more alpine feel than those on the surrounding spires. The ridge routes are classic fifth-class alpine terrain with short, difficult steps and mixed snow. Two mixed lines exist on the east face; *Perma Grin* and *The Big Hose*; these are in their best shape in September and October. Pure rock routes such as the *Thompson–Turk* routes exist, although the bergshrund and its hanging ice field must be negotiated to reach them. The North Tower offers moderate lines to the highest summit in the Bugaboos but sees few climbers. All these things considered, these climbs deserve more attention then they have received so far.

Times given for the routes on the east and northeast faces of the Howsers are round-trip from the Kain Hut Basin. If camped in East Creek (page 264) subtract about two hours.

Approaches: There are three approaches to the Howser climbs, dependant on the particular face and side of the three summits: Upper Vowell Glacier (page 242) for climbs on the east/northeast faces; North Shoulder Col (page 252) for the west face of the North Tower, and East Creek (page 265) for climbs on the west and south sides of the Central and South Towers.

Descents: The standard descents for all routes on the Howser Towers, including the big west face routes, are down the east faces.

(1) **South Tower:** The best rappel route off the South Tower is fixed, and roughly follows the *Northeast Face* route. The first rappel anchors can be found about 20m south of the summit, overlooking the east face. A short rappel leads down and right along a ramp to a slung block. Four double rope rappels lead down the left-facing dihedral system ending at a rappel station in the lower-angled terrain 15m above the snow. A double 60m rappel usually makes it over the bergshrund. All stations are slung but may require new webbing, and a V-thread kit may be needed to cross the bergshrund.

(2) **Central Tower:** Downclimb and rappel to the far end of the North–Central Col. Make one double rope rappel through the rocks to the snowslope and continue down in two double rope rappels to clear the bergshrund. Existing rappel anchors may be hard to locate. Carry rock gear and a V-thread for above the bergshrund.

(3) **North Tower:** The North Tower descent route follows the *East Face–North Ridge* route. From the summit downclimb the *North Ridge* to a col overlooking the north end of the east face. Make three double rope rappels down broken terrain to the snow. One or two double rope rappels will make it over the bergshrund. Existing rappel anchors may be hard to locate. Carry rock gear for the stations and a V-thread for above the bergshrund.

Traverses and Enchainments: Because most of the peaks are more isolated and the climbs very long, enchainments opportunities are limited. As of 2002 however, the *Beckey–Chouinard* has been the focal climb on two occasions for one-day enchainments variously involving Pigeon, Snowpatch, Bugaboo and Crescent Spires.

In 1965 Yvon Chouinard, Jock Lang, Eric Rayson and Doug Tompkins traversed all three of the Howser Towers north to south: a true Grand Traverse. The south to north version of the traverse is easier and for a strong party it can be done in a day. Another attractive traverse is the Flattop–Crossed Fish–Little Snowpatch enchainment, which although technically easier is still very involved.

Howser East Sides approaches: The east and northeast faces of all three towers are gained in a very straightforward manner from the Kain Hut Basin via the Bugaboo–Snowpatch Col, then up the Upper Vowell Glacier, past the Pigeon–Howser Col and the rock knoll that was the traditional bivouac area and up the glacier to the base of the face.

South Howser Tower — *East Side*

This section describes climbs that start off the Upper Vowell Glacier and ascend the east face of the South Howser Tower.

166 **East Ridge Integral**   D+   5.8 A1 ♦   (12-16h)   9p   *246*
Michael Heath, Bill Sumner, August 1970   *CAJ 54:77, AAJ 17:389*

This route gains the east ridge at the top of the Pigeon–Howser Icefall and follows it to join the *East Face–Ridge* higher up.

Traverse in on the glacier to cross the bergshrund at the top of the Pigeon–Howser Icefall. Cross the bergshrund and gain a 5.7 chimney that leads to the ridgecrest. Climb two or three pitches up low fifth-class rock, mostly on the south side, to the base of a slab. Follow small 5.7 cracks on the left side of the slab to a steep chimney that the first ascent party used aid to overcome. Two more 5.4 pitches lead to the where the *East Face–Ridge* gains the ridge.

167 **East Face–Ridge**   D+   5.9   ♦   (12-15h)   8p   *246*
Lloyd Anderson. Helmy Beckey, Lyman Boyer, Tom Campbell, August 1941
CAJ 28:37, AAJ 4:421

This route ascends the snow and ice field on the left side of the east face to gain the ridge-line that is followed to the summit. This was the line of first ascent and was originally rated 5.6 A1.

The bergshrund can usually be crossed directly below the left side of the ice-field. Climb the left side of the ice-field to gain a short flat section of the ridge. The upper ridge is difficult to describe accurately but can be summarized as moderate ground broken by short, steep walls that are usually climbed on the right.

168 **East Face Variation**   D+   5.8   (12-15h)   8p   *246*
William Buckingham, Peter Geiser, August 1961   *CAJ 45:126, AAJ 13:243*

This is a minor variation to the *East Face-Ridge*.

Cross the bergshrund and climb the ice-field trending right. Gain a small snowfield right and level with the top of the main ice-field. Ascend the smaller snowfield followed by a strenuous chimney that gains the ridge crest and the *East Face-Ridge*.

169 **Thompson–Turk**   *   D+   5.10R   (12-16h)   7p   *246*
Gray Thompson, Jon Turk, August 1990   *AAJ 1991:183*

This route follows a vague buttress that starts where the bergshrund comes closest to the rock; left of the *Perma Grin* depression.

Cross the bergshrund where possible and gain the rock about 20m right of its lowest point. Climb two 5.7 pitches to gain the base of a shallow 120m long dihedral. Two long 5.8 pitches gain a comfortable niche near its top. A short offwidth leads to a steep, left-trending crack that is followed past a small ledge and up a 5.9 finger-crack to a belay. A hand-crack can be seen 10m right of the belay. Either pendulum to the crack or climb unprotected 5.10 face moves to gain the 5.7 crack higher up, which is followed to the top of the buttress. A low fifth-class scramble leads to the summit.

170 **Perma Grin** **   D ǀ M5, Wi4 ⊓ (12-14h)   7p 246

Sean Isaac, Scott Semple, Brian Webster, October 2002   *CAJ 86:137*

Perma Grin is a mixed line that follows the left side of the depression that lies directly below the summit. The first three pitches roughly follow the *Northeast Face*, which is also the rappel route. The amount of ice will depend on the year but September and October usually see it iced-up.

1: Cross the bergshrund where possible and ice-climb to the base of the depression left of the *Big Hose*. 2: Climb a runnel up and left to a belay. 3: Move right to gain thin runnels. Little protection (WI4,R 50m). 4: Continue up to a flake rappel station and climb left up another runnel to a horn belay (60m). 5: Continue up through a groove and up a corner (M5, 50m). Options exist to the right. 6: More broken terrain leads to the ridge (40m). 7: Follow the ridge up right to the summit.

Bring a mixed rack of screws, including stubbies, nuts and cams.

171 **Northeast Face**   D+ 5.7 A2   (12-16h)   7p *246*

Fred Beckey, Yvon Chouinard, August 1961   *CAJ 45:127, 48:139, AAJ 13:241*

This route shares the same first four pitches with *Perma Grin* but then follows the left-facing corners on the right side of the depression. The route has seen few ascents, but is well-used as the standard rappel route from the South Howser Tower.

Cross the bergshrund where possible and ice-climb to the base of the depression left of the *Big Hose*. Follow flakes and cracks up left for a short pitch to a belay. Follow cracks and weaknesses up and slightly right for two pitches to where the depression widens. Climb left-facing corners up and right over steep bulges for two or three pitches to gain a left-trending ramp one pitch below the summit. Follow the ramp left and exit onto the ridge a short scramble below the top.

172 **The Big Hose** **   D+ 5.9 Wi4, M5 (10-15h)   7p *246*

Jon Krakauer, June 1978   *AAJ 22:208*

The Big Hose follows a deep and narrow chimney system on the right side of the east face. It was first climbed solo in 1978 and is now a popular mixed route. It is usually climbed in September and October, and although it may be wet in July and August some years it is climbable all summer for those who are determined.

Cross the bergshrund and ice-climb to the base of the hose. Difficulties will depend on the amount and quality of the ice but most pitches are WI3 with 5.8 moves around chockstones. Once the ridge is reached, a pitch of rock with a short, steep 5.8 crack leads to the summit.

HOWSERS EASTSIDE: PHOTO–TOPOS 246 — 247

173 Thompson–Turk Right   D+   5.10   (12-16h)   9p   *246*

Gray Thompson, Jon Turk, August 1991   *AAJ 34:145(1992)*

This route climbs crack systems to the right of *The Big Hose*.

Cross bergshrund and ice-climb to a belay 10m short of the hose. Climb right to gain a 5.8 crack that leads to a small 5.9 roof. Climb right around roof and continue up for two more 5.9 pitches to rubble-strewn ledge. Scramble right along the ledge for about 20m to near its end. Climb the first of two dihedral system split by many cracks, for two 5.10 pitches to a small belay stance. A short, unprotectable 5.9 pitch leads to easier ground and the top. Final three pitches are probably the same as *North Face–Ridge*.

174 North Face–Ridge   D+   5.6 A2   (12-16h)   9p   *246*

Yvon Chouinard, Jock Lang, Eric Rayson, Doug Tompkins, August 1965   *AAJ 15:39*

This route climbs to the col between the South and Central Towers before following cracks up the north side. It was first climbed as part of the North–South Traverse of all three Howser Towers.

Cross the bergshrund and ice-climb to the South–Central Col. Information is minimal but the first ascent party appears to have done five pitches of aid, followed by two or three pitches of mixed free and aid to the summit ridge. Final pitches are probably the same as *Thompson–Turk Right*.

Central Howser Tower — *East Side*

Climbs on the Central Howser Tower off the Upper Vowell Glacier.

175 South Ridge   AD   5.9 A3   (12-15h)   5p   *247*

Bruce Adams, Jim Cameron, David Goeddel, August 1972   *CAJ 56:73, AAJ 18:444*

This route climbs to the south col then follows the south ridge to the summit.

Cross the bergshrund and climb steep ice to the South–Central Col. Climb cracks for four pitches to the second prominent step on the ridge. The first ascent party rated these pitches 5.7 A3 but noted that they were done almost entirely on nuts. Traverse right onto the east face for a long, hard 5.9 pitch to the summit.

176 East Face   D-   5.7   (12-15h)   5p   *247*

Alan Spero, Alan Waterman, August 1974   *AAJ 20:150*

The *East Face* follows weaknesses up the centre of the face.

Cross the bergshrund and climb to the highest point of snow directly below the summit. Climb right up a short gully then back left to gain a vague depression. Follow the depression trending left halfway up the face to gain the top, 20m left of the actual summit.

177 North Ridge   D-   5.4   (12-14h)   5p   *247*

George Austin, David Bernays, James McCarthy, John Rupley, August 1955   *AAJ 10:105*

This route climbs snow and ice to the North–Central Col then follows the north ridge to the summit. It was the line of first ascent.

Cross the bergshrund and climb snow and ice to a short section of broken ground to the North–Central Col. Follow the ridge over fourth and low fifth-class terrain to a final short step that is passed by a chimney on the east side, to gain the summit.

CENTRAL AND NORTH HOWSERS — EAST SIDES

North Howser Tower — *East Side*

This section describes climbs on the North Howser Tower that start off the Upper Vowell Glacier.

178 **South Ridge**   AD   5.6   (12-16h)   200m   *247*

Conrad Kain, H.Frind, Albert MacCarthy, Bess MacCarthy, John Vincent, August 1916
CAJ 8:20

This route follows the snow and ice to the North–Central Col then up the south ridge to the summit. It was guided by Conrad Kain in 1916 for the first ascent of the mountain.

Cross the bergshrund below the left side of the east face and climb snow and ice, trending left into broken terrain that is followed to the North–Central Col. Follow the ridge proper, detouring right to bypass obstacles. Near the summit a photogenic window behind an exposed boulder is passed through, leading to a short scramble to the summit.

179 **East Face–North Ridge**   AD   5.4   (10-15h)   200m   *247*

C.Cranmer, Sterling Hendricks, Percy Olton, Polly Prescot, July 1938   CAJ 26:23, AAJ 3:295

This route climbs the far right side of the east face to gain the *North Ridge* which is then followed to the summit.

Cross the bergshrund at the far end of the east face and climb snow and ice into a gully that is followed over broken ground to the ridge crest. Follow it over fourth and low fifth-class climbing to the summit, generally bypassing difficulties on their east side.

180 **East Ridge–North Ridge**   AD   5.4   (10-15h)   250m   *247*

Fred Ayres, E.Little, D.Woods, J.Oberlin, July 1946   AAJ 6:447

Similar to the *East Face-North Ridge*, this route gains the upper east ridge which is followed to the *North Ridge*.

Cross the bergshrund at the far end of the east face and climb snow and ice to gain the east ridge. Follow the snow arête and broken rock to the *North Ridge*. Descend a gully southward to the notch in the *North Ridge* and follow the ridge crest over fourth and low fifth-class climbing to the summit generally bypassing difficulties on their east side.

181 **Preshaw Pillar**   D-   5.9   (12-15h)   8p

Nils Preshaw, Roy Preshaw, July 1990

Preshaw Pillar is described as "climbing the southeast face of the east pillar of North Howser Tower". The route is not marked on the photos.

Approach across the Upper Vowell Glacier towards the pillar. Try to locate a crescent-shaped crack with a detached block and a corner to its right, which is climbed to a belay at the top of the crescent crack. Face climb 5.7, moving left to easier ground followed by a 5.6 gully pitch. Traverse poor 5.7 rock to the ridge-line that is followed in four pitches around a 5.8 gendarme to the top of the pillar. Rappel down the south side.

APPROACH: 242
DESCENTS: 241

SOUTH HOWSER TOWER – EAST FACE

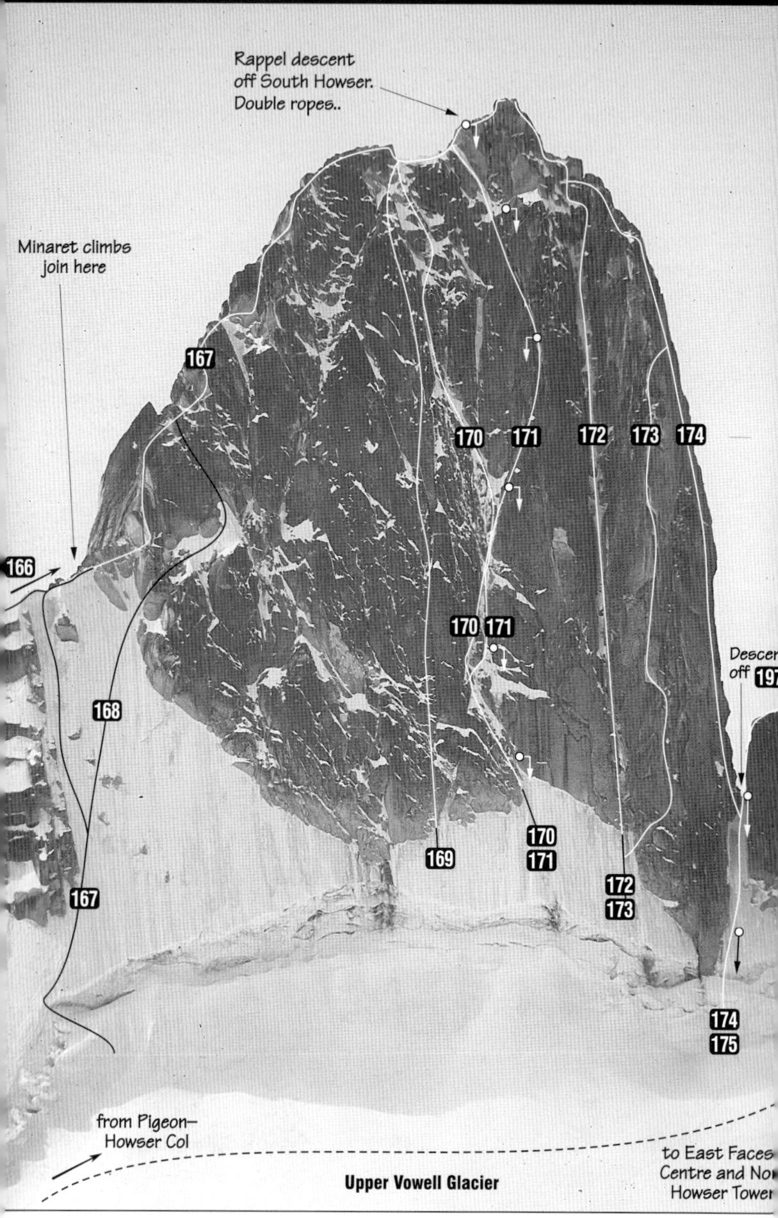
Rappel descent off South Howser. Double ropes..
Minaret climbs join here
167
166
170
171
172
173
174
170
171
Descen
off 197
168
169
170
171
172
173
167
174
175
from Pigeon–Howser Col
Upper Vowell Glacier
to East Faces Centre and No Howser Tower

ROUTES: **166–169** (242) **170–172** (243) **173–175** (244)

HOWSER TOWERS – EAST FACES FROM BUGABOO SPIRE

North Howser

Central Howser

South Howser

171
170
174
173

169 172 175

167

176 177 178 179
180

180

18

Upper Vowell Glacier

September 2002

182

NORTH HOWSER — NORTH SIDE

North Howser

Pigeon–Howser Col

South Howser

Central Howser

Howser North Shoulder approach to the Northwest and West faces of North Howser Tower

182 183

September 2002

view from the Vowells

from Bugaboo–Snowpatch Col

ROUTES: 167–169 (242) **170–172** (243) **173–177** (244) **178–172** (245) **182–183** (248)

North Howser Tower — *North Side*

This section describes climbs on the North Howser Tower that start in the vicinity of the North Shoulder Col. The north side of North Howser Tower, as described, includes the northeast, north and northwest face routes. They are approached over the Bugaboo–Snowpatch Col and then via a descending traverse north-westward beneath the icefall below the east faces of the Howsers (page 252).

Climbs: The climbs on the north side are very alpine in nature with much snow, ice and mixed climbing. They are also much longer than the east face routes and require a descent down the east face.

Times for the routes are given in hours for day climbs or in the number of bivys normally required for longer routes (biv) and are round-trip from the Kain Hut Basin. Slightly shorter times could be expected if camped at Bill's Pass in the Vowell Group.

Descents: The descent route from the North Tower follows the *East Face–North Ridge* route. See page 241 for the descent description.

182 **Northeast Face** *   AD+ 5.6 WI3 (12-16h)   12p   *247*
Rodger Debeyer, Kirt Sellers, September 1995

This classic alpine route climbs the hidden face between the east ridge and the *North Ridge* to gain the *North Ridge*, which is followed to the summit.

Approach from the Bugaboo–Snowpatch Col by descending northwest to the flats of the Vowell Glacier until able to gain the glaciated basin beneath the northeast face. Cross the bergshrund in the middle of the basin and climb steep ice to its highest point to gain mixed ground. Climb left around the first rock band then make a rightward ascending traverse to follow a straight line of alpine ice. Follow this to a final pitch that trends right to gain a minor notch in the *North Ridge*. Follow the *North Ridge* to the summit.

183 **North Ridge Integral** **   AD+ 5.4   (10-15h)   500m   *247*
Margeret Finlay, Ethne Gale, Rex Gibson, Tom Johnston, Alan Styles, Dave Wessel, July 1946
CAJ 30:159, AAJ 6:447

The *North Ridge* is a long, moderate and involved alpine ridge that deserves a much higher profile than it receives.

As with the *Northeast Face,* approach from the Bugaboo–Snowpatch Col. Gain a broad, shadowed snowslope that forms the bottom of the north side of the northeast face. Ascend the snowslope, bypassing the initial rock to the right. A short mixed pitch gains the snowcrest above. Climb the steepening ridge crest over broken ground to the first flat section of ridge, which is followed to where the *Northeast Face* joins. Continue up the ridge crest to the top of a gendarme-like feature, where the *East Ridge–North Ridge* joins in. Descend a 15m gully to the second flat section of the ridge where the *East Face–North Ridge* joins in and the east face rappel route descends. Follow the ridge crest over fourth and low fifth-class climbing to the summit generally bypassing difficulties to the east.

184 North–Northwest Face   TD- 5.8 A2   (1-2biv) 800m *250*

Gay Campbell, Bill Knowler, Peter Zvengrowski, August 1967   *CAJ 51:205, AAJ 16:174*

This route climbs the completely hidden face between the *North Ridge* and the huge west face of North Howser tower. At the time of the first ascent the face contained two circular snowfields but only the upper one remains, with the lower one being seasonal and melting out by late summer.

Approach as per the *North Ridge* (page 248). Once beneath the *North Ridge* continue along the bench glacier to the North Shoulder Col. Descend a steep, loose, boulder-filled gully to a small pocket glacier beneath the northwest face. Traverse in to the highest point of the small glacier and follow an often-wet gully feature in 3-5 pitches to gain a right-trending ramp system (5.6). Follow the low fifth-class ramp to scree or snow where the first snowfield once lay and continue up to slabby rock below the second snowfield where the *Northwest Buttress* joins in. Gain the second snowfield and climb to its highest point. Climb the upper wall in about seven pitches of fifth-class climbing. The first ascent party rated it 5.8 A2 but used little aid. The *North Ridge* is gained just below the summit.

185 Northwest Buttress   TD- 5.10 A1   (1-2biv) 1000m *251*

Fred Beckey, Brian Greenwood, August 1963   *AAJ 14:198*

This route follows a long deep gully on the left side of the true west face and joins the *North–Northwest Face* at the upper snowfield. It was originally rated 5.7 A2.

Approach as with the *North–Northwest Face* but continue down around the pocket glacier and talus slopes. Traverse south under the main wall and scramble up scree to reach the lefthand gully at the base of the imposing west face of North Howser Tower. Climb the gully up snow, ice, rock slabs and broken ground to its top and the intersection with the *North–Northwest Face* just below the second snowfield. Follow the *North–Northwest Face* to the summit of North Howser Tower or continue up rock right of the snowfield to gain the ridge leading to the summit. This variation (Ward Robinson, Mike Tschipper, August 1980) involves many mid-fifth class pitches with minor aid and some 5.10 free climbing.   Many options exist on the upper wall.

The First Ascent of the Hower Towers.

No doubt the divergence of opinion with regards to the
difficulties experienced on a particular mountain is greatly
due to the different climbing methods employed on its
various stretches; a little study of mechanical gymnastics
often turns a fearsome stretch into an amusing one.

A.H. MacCarthy, Canadian Alpine Journal, 1917.

HOWSER TOWERS – NORTHWEST AND WEST SIDES

Howser North Shoulder
approach from Upper
Vowell Glacier to
Northwest and West
sides of North Howser

185

184

ROUTES: 184 185 (248)

North Howser

Central Howser

South Howser

Minaret

West–East Pigeon Feather Col

184
185

See topos page 259–263

bivy boulder

difficult rappels possible

East Creek Basin

185

September 2001

ROUTES: 184 185 (248)

North Howser Tower — *West Face*

The magnificent west face of the Howser Towers presents the longest and most remote face in the Bugaboos, and is often compared with the Cirque of the Unclimbables and Patagonia.

Eight of the nine climbs on the west face are best approached via the North Shoulder Col, and one (the *Southwest Face*) is best approached from the East Creek Basin. This is due to the long spur below the South and Central Howser Towers which marks the northern extent of the Basin. The northwest side of the spur forms a major cliff, making an approach to the west face from East Creek problematic.

Climbing any of the routes on this face is a serious undertaking. The approach from the Kain Hut over the North Shoulder Col is long and gruelling, and the valley remote and wild. No human activity can be seen from the climbs and retreat, even from the base, is an epic. Lightning storms can brew up with alarming speed and retreat off the face is complex and time consuming; parties have been hit by lightning here, hence the route *Young Men on Fire.*

Approach. There are two ways to approach the foot of the west face climbs, either from the north or from the south.

(1) **North Shoulder approach**. Approach up the Bugaboo–Snowpatch Col then descend northwest to the flats of the Vowell Glacier and continue to traverse northwestward until beneath the *North Ridge.* Continue along the bench glacier to the North Shoulder Col of the Howser Towers. If leaving a base camp it is best sited here as the approach from this point is gruelling and this col can be re-gained from a descent of the *East Face–North Ridge* or the *North Ridge Integral.* Continue the approach by descending west from the Col down a steep, loose, boulder-filled gully to a small pocket glacier beneath the *North–Northwest Face.* Skirt the right side of the pocket glacier and continue left down scree and talus slopes. Traverse south under the wall and scramble up scree and snow to reach the base of the imposing west face of North Howser Tower.

(2) **East Creek Basin Approach**. It is also possible to reach the base of the west face from the East Creek Basin by following the approach to the west face of Central Howser Tower (pages 264). From the bivouac boulder, scramble west down the ridge-line a hundred metres or so until it is possible to cut down and right along a ramp/gully system to a terrace. From there it is possible to make three or four double rope rappels to reach the snow and ice beneath

the west face of North Howser Tower. This is not a fixed or well-travelled rappel route, and is a serious endeavour. Retreat is only possible back up the northern approach.

Climbs: The climbs on the west face are by far the longest and most committing in the Bugaboos. Any one of the eight routes can be considered as ranking with the finest hard climbs in the world. *All Along the Watch Tower* is the only completely free route, although *Armageddon, Spicey Red Beans* and *The Seventh Rifle* are all so close to being completely free that they can be treated as such. The climbs at the left side of the face follow the narrow, upper ridge to the true summit, a long, convoluted fifth class endeavour, requiring several hours of climbing, and the occasional short rappel. After a long climb on the west face this can be very taxing.

Times for the climbs are given as the number of bivys normally required, round-trip from the Kain Hut Basin. They are based on first ascent times but could vary widely. Most parties make the approach and bivy low on the route the first day, climb the route in one long day, bivy high, and complete the upper ridge and descend the final day. Aid climbing, porta-ledges and wall gear can add substantial time to the climb and the approach.

Descents: The North Tower descent route follows the *East Face– North Ridge* route. From the summit downclimb the *North Ridge* to a col overlooking the north end of the east face. Make three double rope rappels down broken terrain to the snow. One or two double rope rappels will make it over the bergshrund. Existing rappel anchors may be hard to locate. Carry rock gear for the stations and a V-thread for above the bergshrund.

The First Ascent of North Howser Tower, August 1916.

Left valley	*5:00 am*
Summit	*4:00 pm*
Valley Camp	*1:05 am*
Total	*20 hours valley to valley*
	(about 12–14 hours from present-day hut location.)

From Conrad Kain's logbook.

186 All Along the Watchtower *** ED2 5.12- (1-2 biv) 30-34p *260*

Ward Robinson, Jim Walseth, August 1981
FFA Topher Donahue, Kennan Harvey, August 1996   CAJ 66:85(1983), 1997:10, AAJ 1997:203

All Along the Watchtower is a highly sought-after but rarely climbed gem that is a rite of passage to the big time. It climbs the lefthand side of the west face to gain a long left-facing corner system high on the face. The lower section offers sustained 5.9-5.10 climbing, while the upper section is sustained at 5.11. It receives the least amount of rockfall of any route on the face.

The route starts at the left edge of the west face at the first toe of rock, right of a long, narrow gully. The first nine pitches are shared with *Armageddon* and *Warrior*. **1-3:** Follow 5.8 and 5.9 cracks, paralleling the gully to a good bivy ledge. **4-5:** Continue up and then right to a steeper crack and corner system (5.10). **6-9:** Climb straight up to fair bivy ledges. Small amounts of snow and water can usually be found in this area (5.9). **10:** *Armageddon* and *Warrior* continue straight up while *The Watchtower* leads left over easier ledges. **11-13:** Continue up small corners to more bivy ledges. **14:** Climb to the base of the long left-facing dihedral system (5.8). **15-18:** Climb an initial 5.10 pitch followed by multiple 5.11+ pitches and belay below where the corner jogs left (5.11+). **19:** The crux. Strenuous underclings and laybacks lead left then up to a belay (5.12). **20:** Start up the initial moves of the very thin crack until able to reach out right to a bigger crack, which is followed to terraces (5.11). **21-23**: Climb easier ground to the ridge (5.8). A long, convoluted fifth class ridge, requiring several hours of climbing, leads to the summit. Small bivy ledges can be found about halfway along the ridge to the summit.

187 Armageddon ** ED2 5.11+ A2 (1-2 biv) 30-34p *261*

Jonathon Copp, Mike Pennings, August 1999   *AAJ 40:227(2000)*

Armageddon climbs the first nine pitches of *All Along the Watchtower* then continues straight up the first corner system right of that route to rejoin it near the ridge. There is only about 4m of aid climbing.

1-9: Climb the first 9 pitches of *All Along the Watchtower*. **10-11**: Climb straight up towards the large, left-most dihedral system. Good bivouac ledges and often snow or water can be found here. **12-14**: Climb the right-facing corner system to below the first roof (5.8, 5.9 ,5.11+). **15**: Continue up the corner and over the roof. A thin 4m section of aid climbing on Peckers and Knifeblades is encountered (5.11+, A2). **16**: Continue up the corner to below the second roof and traverse right, with little gear, and up to gain the next corner system (5.11). **17-18**: Follow the new corner system (5.11, 5.10). **19-20**: Continue up the corner as it curves back left and gain the terrace system near pitch 21 of *The Watchtower* (5.11). **21-23**: Climb easier ground to the ridge (5.8). A long, convoluted fifth class ridge, requiring several hours of climbing, leads to the summit. Small bivy ledges can be found about halfway along the ridge to the summit.

**188 Warrior ** **   ED2 5.9 A3 ♦   (2-3 biv) 30-34p   *261*

Hugh Burton, Steve Sutton, August 1973   *CAJ 57:8*

Warrior was the first route on the left side of the face. The exact position of the upper half of the route is uncertain but is thought to follow cracks and corners right of *Armageddon*. Only the original 1973 description exists and details are vague for the upper half of the route.

1-9: The first 9 pitches are the same as *All Along the Watchtower*. **10-11**: Climb straight up, as for *Armageddon*, but trend more rightward. Good bivouac ledges, and often snow or water, can be found here. **12-19**: The first ascent party described it as "For the next four and a half pitches we followed the single crack. Nailing at first, it slowly widens out to three inches. …Nailing higher and higher the crack slowly bottoms out giving a beautiful pitch that stays hard all the way. …some overhangs now that exit on steep face climbing. A dicey section of aid then corners lead to a big ledge system atop a pillar that juts out from the wall." **20-21**: Two steep pitches lead to the ridge, presumably near *All Along the Watchtower*.

**189 Spicey Red Beans & Rice ** ** ED2 5.12- A1 (1-3 biv) 30-32p *259*

Eric Greene, Cameron Tague, August 1997   *CAJ 81:103(1998), AAJ 1998:239*

Spicey Red Beans follows the deep chimney system on the lower wall between *All Along the Watchtower* and *The Seventh Rifle* and follows a similar line to *Warrior* on the upper wall.

1-2: Follow the first two shorter pitches of *The Seventh Rifle* to where it breaks out right (5.10). **3**: Follow the loose drainage up to a chimney on its left side (5.6). **4-5**: Climb the chimney (5.9). **6-8**: Continue up the chimney and exit left up a ramp to a wide crack that is followed to a bivy ledge (5.10). **9**: Climb over a roof on the left side of the ledge and take the righthand crack to a stance (5.10). **10-11**: Traverse right toward a huge left-facing dihedral and follow it to a belay ledge (5.11+). **12-15**: Continue up the crack trending left on small ledges to gain a right-facing dihedral (5.12). Climb through overlaps and over a small ledge to a small dihedral (5.11). Step left and climb a wide crack in a huge right-facing corner for 2 pitches (5.10). **16**: Climb easier terrain (5.7). **17**: Climb a lichen-encrusted right-facing dihedral that the first ascent party commented would probably go free if it was cleaned (5.11, A1). **18-19**: Continue up left trending cracks and follow a right-facing corner to the ridgrcrest. Follow the long, convoluted fifth class ridge, requiring several hours of climbing, to the summit. Small bivy ledges can be found about halfway to the summit.

190 Mescalito   ED2 5.9, A3 ♦   (2-3 biv) 30-34p *259*

Hugh Burton, Steve Sutton, August 1974   *AAJ 19:166(1974)*

Mescalito is believed to follow a line on the lower wall between *All Along the Watchtower* and *Spicey Red Beans* to gain the huge dihedral system between the lefthand routes and The *Seventh Rifle*. The first ascent party took three bivouacs and used aid on 40% of the climb.

191 The Seventh Rifle **   ED2 5.11 A1   (1-3 biv) 30-34p   *262*

Chris Jones, Galen Rowell, Tony Qamar, July 1971   *CAJ 56:73, AAJ 18:61*

The Seventh Rifle was the first route up the massive west face and to date has had less than a handful of ascents. The original ascent involved only two pitches of aid climbing, which have since been freed, although a first continuous ascent has not been recorded. The route starts near the lowest point on the face and follows the vague buttress that generally divides the west face from the southwest face. The lower half of the route was hit by a very large rockfall in 2001 so beware of loose rubble on the lower pitches.

Start up a crack left of the lowest righthand toe of rock. **1-2**: Climb 2 short pitches to a drainage gully (5.9, 5.10). **3-12**: Climb the right wall of the gully to gain a chimney and wide cracks (5.9). Trend right gaining the base of a black, lower-angled wall, with slightly easier climbing up its right side to bivouac ledges on the blunt buttress. **13-14**: Climb two pitches up the buttress past another bivy ledge to a gully leading up left (5.9). **15-26**: The next dozen or so pitches climb 5.9 and 5.10 terrain up the gully. It follows the initial gully then breaks out onto the lefthand wall to avoid ice and chockstones. The first ascent used aid on one pitch. Higher up it passes through a loose recess and climbs steep cracks on the righthand wall before gaining the ridge crest. Follow the long, convoluted, fifth class ridge to the summit.

192 Young Men on Fire *   ED2 5.11- A4   (3-4 biv) 30-34p   *262*

Jerry Gore, Warren Hollinger, September 1994   *AAJ 1995:178*

Young Men on Fire follows a line right of *The Seventh Rifle* and *Shooting Gallery* on the steep lower face, joins those routes in the middle, then climbs the buttress to the right of the *Seventh Rifle* gully for the upper half. The first ten pitches are predominantly aid climbing. The first ascent party endured quite an epic, encountering snow, climbing through storms and finally being hit by lightning near the summit.

The climb starts below the right side of the steep white wall right of *The Seventh Rifle* toe of rock. **1**: Climb up and left to gain a long white corner (5.6). **2-6**: Follow the corner on aid, with the middle crux pitches taking Knifeblades and 0-00 TCUs. **7-10**: Continue straight up cracks on predominantly aid but with some free climbing mixed in (5.10, A2+). **11**: One fourth class pitch leads to a bivy ledge and the top of the lower wall. **12-13**: Climb easier terrain past another bivy ledge to The *Seventh Rifle* gully (5.9). **14-17**: Climb straight up, avoiding gullies to the left and right to gain the buttress above (5.10). **18**: Climb a crack just right of the buttress (5.11-). **19-22**: Continue up cracks joined by ramps to a very exposed bivy ledge (5.9). **23-24**: Continue up cracks (5.8). **25-26**; Mixed fourth and fifth class climbing leads to the ridgecrest (5.7). **27-31**: Follow the convoluted fifth class ridge to the summit.

Bring a standard big wall aid rack and plan for extended approach and climbing times if carrying porta-ledges and wall gear. The first ascent party spent 4 days on the route and multiple days ferrying gear on the approach.

---

193 The Shooting Gallery *   ED2 5.10 A2+   (3-4 biv) 30-34p   *262*
Christian George, Mark Synnott, September 1994   *AAJ 1996:203*

The Shooting Gallery follows a line left of *Young Men on Fire* on the lower wall then joins *The Seventh Rifle* at pitch nine. The first ascent party continued up for 2 more pitches. Believing they were on new ground they then descended 10m to the right to join the *Southwest Face*. The lower pitches have substantially less aid climbing than *Young Men on Fire* and it is thought they will go free if cleaned up and worked, giving a logical free line if combined with the upper *Young Men on Fire*.

The climb starts about 15m left of *Young Men on Fire* at the left edge of the steep, white wall. **1-2**: Climb up and left to gain the huge right-facing corner (5.8, 5.10). **3-5**: Climb the corner, and cracks right of the corner, through a loose chimney to a ledge belay. A short section of aid is encountered on pitch 4 (5.10, A1). **6**: Start on the left side of an arête, crossing to the right side to gain a ledge belay (5.10, A2+). **7**: Climb a short pitch up the arête and left to a poor bivy ledge (A2+). **8-9**: A 5.10 offwidth leads to a short A2 section then low fifth class climbing to a belay. A ridge crest then leads to a good bivy ledge on *The Seventh Rifle*. From here it is possible to link up with *The Seventh Rifle*, *Young Men on Fire* or the *Southwest Face*.

---

194 Southwest Face *   TD+ 5.10 A1   (1-2 biv)   16-20p   *262*
approached via East Creek Basin, see pages 264-267
route description page 268

"i skied the snowpatch in '90 with Reid Crooks. fun turns! we had a semi-belay, in which one end of 400' of rope was anchored at the top of the snowpatch and the other end to the skier. the rope would stop you if you fell, but not until you were at the edge of the snowpatch. i remember thinking it was steeper than i expected, but it was totally perfect conditions. Hope all's well in the great white north... Mike."

Mike Pennings, in an email to Marc Piché.

HOWSER TOWERS — WEST FACES

North Tower · Central Tower · South Tower · Pigeon–Howser Col · Pigeon Spire · Howser Bivy Boulder · East Creek Bivy Boulder

This massive spire [Howser Towers] and its many worthy companions show up very prominently from Sir Donald and other high peaks, and offer an excellent field for a two weeks expedition. Even though their altitudes may be somewhat in question, there is no possible doubt concerning the many difficult climbs they afford.

A.H. MacCarthy, Canadian Alpine Journal, 1917.

NORTH HOWSER – WEST FACE

North Howser

3412m

188 189

186 187

191 192 194

191

194

186 187 188 189 190

192
193

185   186
187   190 191
188   189
2510m

NORTH HOWSER TOWER – ALL ALONG THE WATCHTOWER

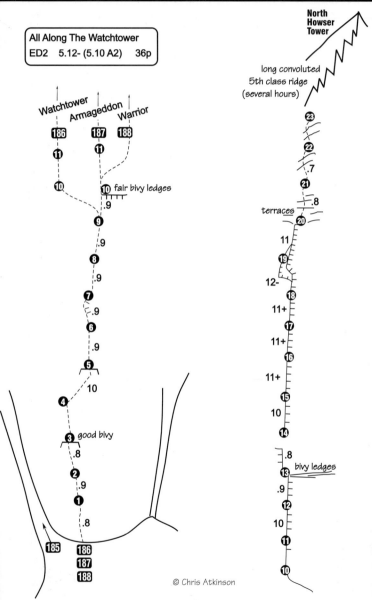

All Along The Watchtower
ED2   5.12- (5.10 A2)   36p

North Howser Tower

long convoluted
5th class ridge
(several hours)

Watchtower   Armageddon   Warrior
186   **187**   **188**

fair bivy ledges

terraces

good bivy

bivy ledges

© Chris Atkinson

NORTH HOWSER TOWER — ARMAGEDDON & WARRIOR

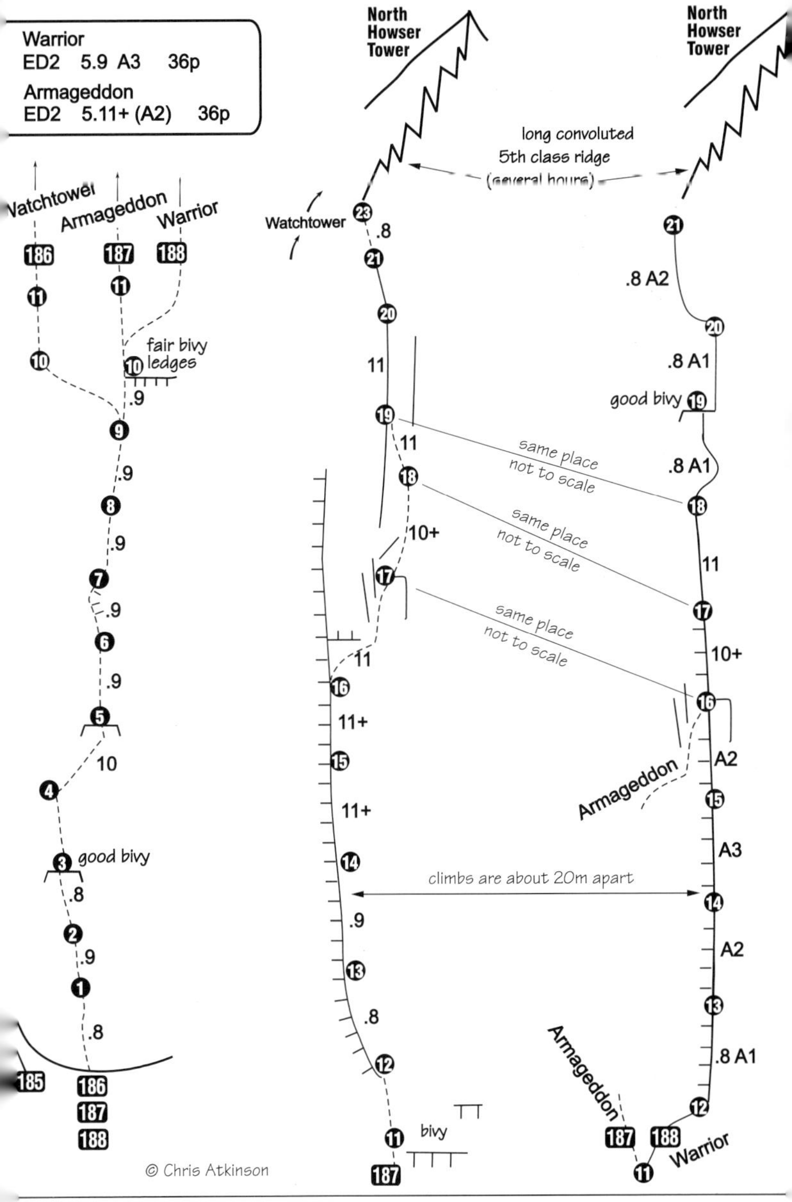

Warrior
ED2   5.9   A3   36p

Armageddon
ED2   5.11+ (A2)   36p

© Chris Atkinson

ROUTES: 185 (249) **186 187** (254) **188** (255)

NORTH HOWSER TOWER — LOWER WEST FACE

ROUTES: **186 187** (254) **188–190** (255) **191 192** (256) **193** (257)

NORTH HOWSER TOWER — UPPER WEST FACE

The East Creek Basin

The East Creek Basin, otherwise known as 'East Creek', lies to the west of the Pigeon Feathers and south of South Howser Tower and the Minaret. The East Creek Basin, as well as the west side of the Howsers are covered by small remnant glaciers and steep, loose moraines. It is bounded at the northern end by the Minaret and the long rock spur that extends far out from the foot of the *Beckey-Chouinard* route on South Howser Tower, at the east end by the steep walls of the Pigeon Feathers and at the south by Crossed Fish and Little Snowpatch Peaks. The basin is reached from the Kain Hut Basin over the Bugaboo–Snowpatch Col, up the Upper Vowell Glacier and through the Pigeon–Howser Col. The basin provides access to routes on the south and west sides of Central and South Howser Towers, including the Minaret, to the west walls of the Pigeon Feathers, and to the rarely climbed Crossed Fish and Little Snowpatch Peaks. The traditional East Creek Basin bivouac site, near the base of the Minaret, usually takes 3-5 hours from the Kain Hut Basin with heavy packs. Parties trying to climb the *Beckey-Chouinard* in a day from the Kain Hut Basin, should pass by here in under 3 hours.

The provincial park boundary originally followed the height of land from Flattop over the Pigeon Feathers and on over the Howser Towers, with the East Creek Basin being outside the park, but a 500 horizontal metre buffer zone has been added to include the area west of the height of land running from Flattop Peak to North Howser Tower. This is an important point as it means camping in and around the Pigeon–Howser Col is no longer allowed and climbers must now descend into the East Creek Basin past the base of the Minaret in order to camp outside the park.

Being outside the park, however, means that climbers may encounter some helicopter activity. It is essential that climbers manage their human waste effectively and responsibly in order to maintain the environmental integrity and access to this area.

Camping and Bivouacs. Traditionally climbers would camp on the rocky knoll on the Howser side of the Pigeon–Howser Col, bivy on their route and return to their camp. This was a prime spot to climb the *Beckey-Chouinard* in a day, as the descent ended close to the camp and big boots and crampons could often be left behind. Camping and bivouacs, however, are no longer permitted here.

Climbers must now descend into the East Creek Basin and camp outside the park (see approach below). The main issue with camping and bivouac sites has been the human waste and water contamination problem, which still exists in the Pigeon–Howser Col, despite no camping, due to the number of people climbing the *West Ridge* of Pigeon Spire. A group of concerned climbers (Friends of Bugaboo Park) are working on a solution to this problem, but climbers must help. Avoid high-use areas and areas near any water source, and if need be, pack your human waste down to the facilities at Applebe Camp or the Kain Hut. As for other camps and bivouacs, locate an area away from watersources and establish a single site so the area doesn't become completely littered, and pack out or burn all toilet paper.

A final thought; bivouacs on climbs are a traditional and anticipated part of longer routes, but planning a bivy in a no-stay area on the approach is a misguided choice of strategy. Climb fast and camp wisely.

Approach: Access to the East Creek Basin is via the Kain Hut Basin. Gain the Bugaboo–Snowpatch Col, continue up the Upper Vowell Glacier and on through the Pigeon–Howser Col. Follow steep scree trails southwest, down into the East Creek Basin to gain another glacier. Descend the glacier, trending right, but staying out from under the active and threatening Pigeon–Howser Icefall. Follow snow and ice down and right to beneath the Minaret on South Howser Tower. A bivy boulder and tent sites can be found here.

An alternative approach is via the Pigeon Fork of the Bugaboo Glacier, past the south face of Snowpatch and the east face of Pigeon Spire, to gain the East–West Pigeon Feather Col which gives access to a gully that drops into the East Creek Basin (pages 98, 109).

Climbs: Most of the climbs out of the East Creek Basin are challenging, quality wall routes. Most of the free climbs such as the *Beckey–Chouinard* on South Howser Tower, *Bad Hair Day* on the Minaret and *Fingerberry Jam* on the Pigeon Feathers, are also exceptional, high quality climbs.

Times given for the routes in East Creek Basin; the Pigeon Feathers and Howsers southwest sides, are given in either hours or the number of bivys normally required, and are round-trip from the East Creek Basin bivy. Hours, eg.(18-20h), denote that the route is generally climbed in a day and bivys, eg.(2-3 bivys), denote that most parties bivy on the route. These are approximations and many are based on only one ascent, usually by a strong party, plan accordingly.

EAST CREEK BASIN

THE WESTERN SPIRES AND EAST CREEK BASIN (AERIAL)

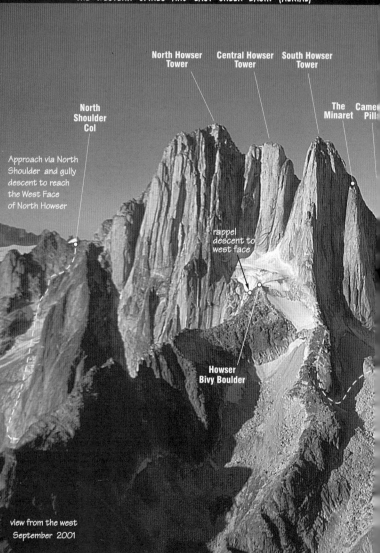

North Howser Tower

Central Howser Tower

South Howser Tower

North Shoulder Col

The Minaret

Came Pill

Approach via North Shoulder and gully descent to reach the West Face of North Howser

rappel descent to west face

Howser Bivy Boulder

view from the west
September 2001

EAST CREEK BASIN

HOWSERS INTRO: 239–240
WESTERN SPIRES MAP: 22

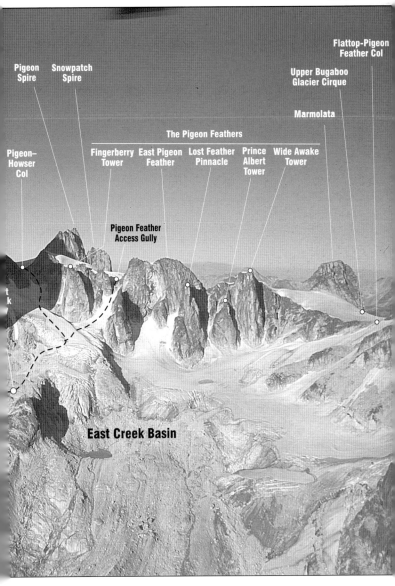

Flattop-Pigeon
Feather Col

Pigeon
Spire

Snowpatch
Spire

Upper Bugaboo
Glacier Cirque

Marmolata

The Pigeon Feathers

Pigeon–
Howser
Col

Fingerberry
Tower

East Pigeon
Feather

Lost Feather
Pinnacle

Prince
Albert
Tower

Wide Awake
Tower

Pigeon Feather
Access Gully

East Creek Basin

EAST CREEK BASIN

North Howser Tower — *Southwest Face*

Unlike the Big Eight which are approached over the North Shoulder Col, this, the most righthand and easiest climb on the North Howser Tower's west face is approached from the East Creek Basin. It lies immediately left of the Central Howser Tower and is accessed via a ramp from the glacier at the base of the east face of the Central Tower.

194 Southwest Face *   TD+   5.10 A1   (1-2 biv) 16-20p   262
Chris Jones, Archie Simpson, Oliver Woodcock, August 1970   CAJ 54:77, AAJ 17:389

The *Southwest Face* was the first foray onto the west face of North Howser Tower and although it sneaks onto the face at mid-height it still provides over a dozen long pitches of good climbing to the highest summit in the area.

From the East Creek Basin bivy follow scree down along the base of ridge descending from the *Beckey–Chouinard* to gain a shallow scree gully leading up to the ridge. Scramble up slabs and over boulders to gain the snow and ice below the west face of the Central Tower.

Traverse beneath the Central Tower and gain a gangway that leads out onto the southwest face. Follow the gangway to a short pitch that ends on a sharp arête. Make a short rappel to reach cracks that are followed up into the base of a large, imposing gully. The route follows this main gully system, climbing the left wall as the gully opens up. It is mostly 5.9 climbing with short sections of 5.10 and the occasional aid move. Just before the ridge the route crosses to the righthand side of the gully and exits right to gain the ridge one pitch from the summit. The upper gully contains snow and ice, and the middle section loose rock and running water.

Descent is down the *East Face–North Ridge*. See the West Face of North Howser Tower description (page 253) and topo (page 246, 259).

Love that granite.

Before reaching the base of this barrier [the Gendarme] we encountered several hard bits; in fact, on peaks of the Rockies, where the stone formation is rotten, such places would be termed difficult and dangerous; but when every hold is solid, difficulties are welcome and met with a smile.

Conrad Kain, American Alpine Journal, 1929-32.

Central Howser Tower — *Southwest Face*

This is the steep monolithic face which is set back from, and lies between the South Howser Tower and the North Tower.

195 Fear and Desire *   ED1   510   A3+   (1-2 biv)   9p   *270*

Nils Davis, Todd Offenbacher, July 1999   *CAJ 2000:30, AAJ 42:229(2000)*

Fear and Desire was the first route to be climbed on the west face of the Central Tower. It starts up cracks on the right side of the face directly below a step on the south ridge below the summit.

Approach as for the *Southwest Face* of North Howser and find a right-facing corner system left of the obvious *Spinstone Gully*. **1-3**: Climb three long aid pitches of mostly A1 with a section of A2 hooks on the second pitch to a ledge belay right of the start of a gully/chimney system. This is where *Chocolate Fudge Brownie* heads up and right. **4**: Lower left to skirt the gully where A2+ hooks lead to the right side of a flake past A3 copperheads to a belay. **5-6**: Follow the expanding A2+ crack above to a roof. Lower right and climb A1 to a belay ledge. **7**: Climb up and right on A3+ hooks to a loose flake and more hooking above to gain a crack leading to a belay below a small roof. **8-9**: A1 cracks lead up and left to gain the summit. The first ascent party stopped 10-20m short of the summit and rappelled the route.

196 Chocolate Fudge Brownie * ED1   5.9   A2   (1-2 biv)   10p   *270*

Sean Isaac, Brian Webster, August 1999   *AAJ 42:229(2000)*

Chocolate Fudge Brownie follows *Fear and Desire* for the first 3 pitches then climbs out right and up to gain the *South Ridge* at the top of the final tower.

The approach is the same as *Fear and Desire*. **1-3**: Climb the first 3 pitches of *Fear and Desire*. **4**: Continue up the corner as it trends right. **5**: Nail a right-trending crack to a bolt, and pendulum right to another crack. Follow the crack using copperheads and rivets to avoid a detached flake (A2). **6-7**: Follow the A1 corner to a flake belay where the corner arches right. **8**: Head up and left on A1 cracks. **9-10**: Climb a short corner to easy ground leading to the *South Ridge*, which can be followed to the summit in one pitch (5.8,A1). Bring a standard wall rack with heads, hooks and rivet hangers.

The first ascent party rappelled the route.

197 Spinstone Gully *   TD+   M7   (10-15h)   8p   *270*

Sean Isaac, Scott Semple, September 2002   *CAJ 86:137*

The route follows the gully on the west face between the South and Central Towers ending at the col. An enticing enchainment is to make one or two double rope rappels from the col, down the east face to gain the base of *The Big Hose,* which is then followed to the summit of the South Tower.

As with *Fear and Desire* gain the glacier below the west face. Climb the gully in eight pitches, over multiple chockstones to the col. Except for the first and last M4 pitches, all pitches were rated M6 or M7 by the first ascent party. Pitch 3 branches right out of the main gully with Pitch 4 regaining the main gully via a rappel. Descent is down the east face via two double rope rappels. A V-thread is required to clear the bergschrund.

Bring a rack of ice screws, cams to 3½ inches, nuts and a few pins.

CENTRAL HOWSER TOWER — WEST FACE

see topo on
page 246 for
descent
rappels

30m

45m A1

A1
A2+ hooks
loose flakes

A1

60m ×
A3+ ×× A1
hooks ×
×
A2+ back
expando clean A1
60m squeeze **195** **196**
A1

A2 A1
expando
55m
× heads +
××× rivets
A1 A2
× 50m
T-bone A2 30m
flake ×× ×
55m 30m M

A2 60m M6

60m A1/
10 65m M

× ice
chimney
60m A3 60m M
hooks
×
70m M4

55m A1 **197**
awkward

195 **196**

194

August 2002

ROUTES: **194** (268) **195 196 197** (269)

CENTRAL AND SOUTH HOWSER TOWERS — WEST FACE (AERIAL)

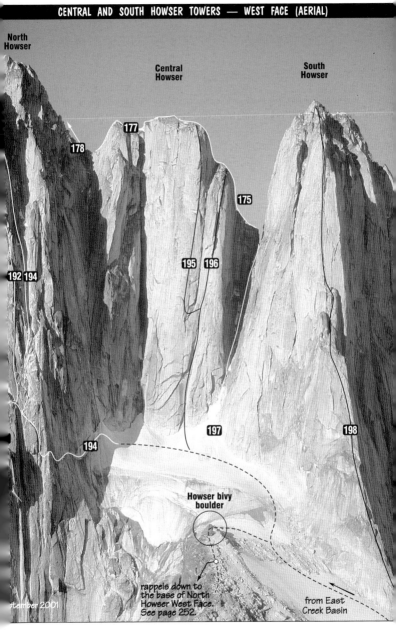

North Howser

Central Howser

South Howser

178
177
175
192 194
195 196
194
197
198

Howser bivy boulder

rappels down to the base of North Howser West Face. See page 252.

from East Creek Basin

tember 2001

ROUTES: 191 192 (256) **194** (268) **195–197** (269) **198** (272) **175–176** (244) **178** (245)

South Howser Tower — *Southwest Buttress*

198 **Beckey–Chouinard** *** TD+ 5.10   (14-20h)   20–22p *276*
Fred Beckey, Yvon Chouinard, August 1961   *FFS Ken Trout, June 1977*
FWA Phil Hein, Scott Flavelle, March 1981   *CAJ 45:127, 48:139, AAJ 13:241*

The *Beckey–Chouinard* is the Bugaboo classic and one of the most esteemed alpine routes in North America. It is a graceful line on a beautiful peak overlooking a wild and remote valley. The climbing is consistently in the 5.8 to 5.9 range with only the occasional short, cruxy sections and the route has numerous bivy ledges. The descent is down the opposite side of the tower and requires 6 double rope rappels from fixed stations.

From the East Creek Basin bivy follow scree down along the base of the ridge descending from the *Beckey–Chouinard* to gain a shallow scree gully leading up to the ridge. Scramble up third class slabs and over boulders to where the ridge narrows and a large split boulder blocks access. **1**: From a belay in small boulders step down right to gain an exposed slab on the right and climb cracks and flakes to a block belay on the ridge crest (5.5). **2**: Climb up the ridge crest (5.5). **3**: Where the crest steepens follow cracks and grooves left of the crest to a ledge belay behind a large block (5.7). **4**: Follow steep cracks just right of the crest to the left edge of a small overhanging bulge (fixed cam). Make an insecure move over the bulge and follow cracks past a horn to a steep, small ledge belay (5.10-, 50m). **5**: Climb cracks on the left side of the arête, stepping to the right side part way up and follow cracks to easy ground. Scramble over easy ground to gain a flake and a short chimney to the left, which leads to a slab belay, or belay on the crest (5.8, 60m). **6**: Handrail right over the arête and cross cracks to gain a big left-facing corner or climb directly up from the crest belay. Climb the corner to an alcove belay behind a jutting block (5.8, 60m). **7**: Continue up this stellar corner to a crack and belay at the start of some scree-covered ledges (5.8, 60m). **8**: Scramble over scree and belay at the upper bivy site. **9**: Climb up a chimney and cracks over blocks to a block belay where the wall steepens (5.6). **10**: Step left and climb a short strenuous crack to a ledge. Go right past a flake to reach two opposing corners and climb the righthand to the bivy ledges below the Great White Headwall (5.8). **11**: Walk left to the furthest bivy site and climb up to a wide crack in a right facing corner at the far left side of the headwall. (Lost in the Towers takes the crack on the right side of the headwall) Climb the wide crack to the top of the small tower and continue up a corner crack system. Follow the corner until able to break out left and up a short, steep wall to a small ledge belay (5,10-, 55m). **12**: Step up above the belay and make a hard balance move right back into the corner. Follow the corner past the guillotine blocks and a tough squeeze. Move to a belay at the start of a steep gully (5.9, 60m). Cracks on the left wall can be climbed at 5.10 to avoid the corner (5.10). **13**: Climb up the gully over chockstones to where it steepens into a capped corner. Climb the second crack on the left wall to a belay at the base of a long, shallow, right-facing corner (5.9, 60m). **14**: Follow the corner to a two-pin belay at a small notch (5.8, 30m).

15: Tension left (A0) into a gully (or free at 5.10+) and follow it to a belay at it's top (5.6). From the top of the gully, step down right to gain rappel slings and make a 20m rappel to ledges on the south side. Climb up and right around two indistinct buttresses to gain the ridge just right of the summit. This is steep and broken fourth-class terrain with numerous short, mid-fifth class steps. Bivouac sites are possible through here and near the summit. The rappels start about 20m south of the summit where most parties emerge from the broken terrain.

Bring a standard rack with extra 1½-2inch cams and one or two 4inch cams.

199 **Lost in the Towers Variation** TD+ 5.11 (16-20h)   20–22p   *276*
Wayne Kamara, Jim Walseth, August 1980
FFA Geoff Trump and partner, August 1999

Lost in the Towers is a minor variation of the *Beckey–Chouinard* that is usually climbed by people off route and lost in the towers.

Follow the *Beckey–Chouinard* to the ledge below the Great White Headwall. Climb the right-most crack, a very inviting right-curving and widening crack right of the standard route (5.10). Continue following the crack as it curves and exits the headwall through a flaring slot (5.10). Tension and aid right (C1) or free (5.11) up over very exposed terrain into a broad, slabby gully. Climb right and up for two pitches through a dihedral and a roof to gain the broken terrain on the *Beckey–Chouinard*.

200 **Catalonian Route**   ED1 5.10 A2   (1-2d)   20p   *275*
Joan Cabau, Edward Burgada, Antonio Masana, Joan Wenciesko, August 1983

The *Catalonian Route* climbs the large, imposing face between the *Beckey–Chouinard* and the Minaret and contains relatively little aid climbing.

From the East Creek Basin bivy site make a short and direct approach up snow to the base of the route just left of the lefthand Minaret gully. **1-3**: Climb an intial crack and continue up slabs to a belay at the base of a long crack (5.6, 120m). **4-6**: Follow cracks and corners to where it starts to steepen (5.9, 140m). **7**: Climb up and left out of the weakness (5.10, A1, 45m). **8-9**: Follow a crack to easier ground and a bivy site at the top of the first tower (5.10, 65m). **10-11**: Climb up towards the left side of the next tower (5.9, 75m). **12-13**: Climb a crack to the left side of the tower and on to its top (5.9, A2, 90m). **14-16**: Climb cracks and corners to easier ground (5.8, A1, 140m). Climb broken, fourth and fifth class terrain to the summit (5.5, 180m).

In August 1987, a trailer park in Edmonton Alberta was destroyed with loss of life by a violent tornado. It had passed over the Bugaboos earlier in the day, as Fabio Stedile was attempting to paraglide off the west face of Snowpatch. He was blown off the summit, landing on a ledge on the east face, climbed back up and beat a hasty retreat down the Kraus–McCarthy in the lightning and hail of the growing tornado.

CENTRAL AND SOUTH HOWSER TOWER — WEST AND SOUTH FACES (AERIAL)

ROUTES: 195–197 (269) **198** (272) **199 200** (273)

SOUTH HOWSER TOWER – CATALONIA ROUTE

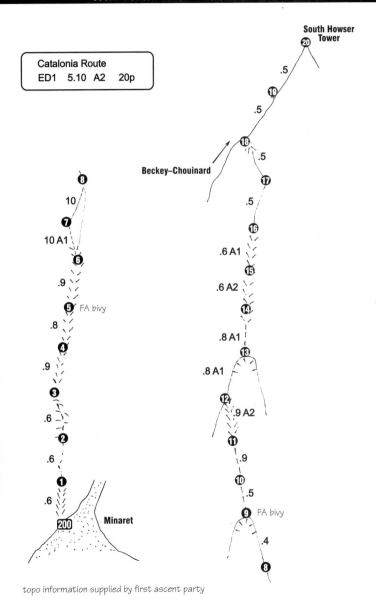

Catalonia Route
ED1   5.10   A2   20p

topo information supplied by first ascent party

SOUTH HOWSER TOWER — THE BECKEY CHOUINARD

summit beyond

Great White
Headwall

foreshortened view from
near start of the climbing

tension left to gully pitch

.8 gully

.9 squeeze
.8 hands

.9 balance move
into corner

.8 cracks

10- hand/fist

bivy sites

alcove belay

mid-5th

.8

10- bulge

mid-5th

mid-5th

mid-5th   right side of ridge crest

.8
hand
/fist

.8

ROUTES: 198 (272) **199 200** (273)

SOUTH HOWER TOWER — BECKEY–CHOUINARD

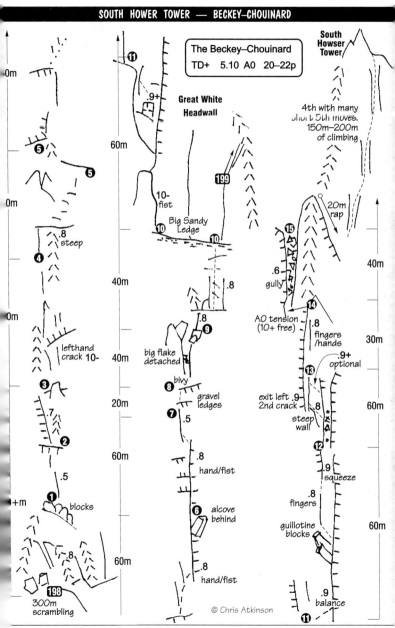

The Beckey–Chouinard
TD+   5.10 A0   20–22p

South Howser Tower

Great White Headwall

4th with many short 5th moves.
150m–200m of climbing

20m rap

.9+

10-fist

Big Sandy Ledge

.15 .6 gully

AO tension (10+ free)

.8 fingers/hands

.9+ optional

exit left .9 2nd crack

.8

steep wall

.9 squeeze

.8 fingers

guillotine blocks

.9 balance

big flake detached

bivy

gravel ledges

.5

.8 hand/fist

alcove behind

.8 hand/fist

300m scrambling

lefthand crack 10-

.8 steep

.7

.5

blocks

.8

© Chris Atkinson

South Howser Tower — *Minaret*

201 **West Face**

The incomplete *West Face* route was the scene of attempts to make it the second route up the Minaret between the *Italian Pillar* and *Bad Hair Day,* and then to make it the first free route. Information is vague but the potential *West Face* line is no longer the attraction it once was.

202 **Bad Hair Day** *   ED1 5.12-   (1-2 biv) 18-24p *280*

Lizzy Sculy, Heidi Wirtz, August 2002   *CAJ 86:88, Alpinist 2:60*

This was the first, and to date, only free route up the Minaret. The route links up sections of many of the routes on the face, starting at the *West Face* and finishing up the *Southwest Pillar.*

Follow a very short approach from the East Creek Basin bivy site up snow to gain the left side of the Minaret at the beginning of the gully. **1**: Climb a short 5.5 crack to gain a grassy ledge that is followed right to a belay next to a chimney/gully system. **2-3**: Cross the gully to a crack, which is followed up and back to the base of a left-facing corner (5.8, 90m). **4**: Start up cracks left of the corner then climb down right through the corner to a horn on the arête and continue right into a corner. Follow this for a short distance until able to climb down to the base of a pillar (5.10R+). **5**: Climb the left side of the pillar (5.9). **6**: Climb a short distance down the right side of the pillar and over to the base of an intimidating chimney (5.6). **7**: Follow a hand-crack to the first roof, cross under it and climb over it through an offwidth to a small stance (5.11). **8**: Climb an offwidth to a big chimney (5.10). **9**: Climb a short pitch up the right side of a V-crack to a big ledge (5.8). **10**: Cross the ledge to the right and downclimb 15m to a right-facing corner then climb to a belay stance (5.4). **11**: Follow the dihedral for a long pitch to a small belay ledge (5.11). **12**: Climb another long pitch up a groove and through a roof to a belay ledge (5.11+/12-). **13**: Traverse up and right to a good belay ledge at belay 7 on the *Southwest Pillar* (5.9 35m). **14-18**: Follow the *Southwest Pillar* for four or five pitches to the top of the Minaret.

The climb from the top of the Minaret to the summit of the South Tower is long, with broken low-mid fifth class terrain and short steps up to 5.10. Follow the line of least resistance. It is possible to rappel *Doubting the Millennium*

203 **Italian Pillar** *   ED1 5.10+ A4 (2-3 biv) 14-20p *280*

Fabio Stedile, Fabrizio DeFrancesco, July 1987   *AAJ 1988:148*

This route takes a direct and independent line up continuous crack systems on the left side of the Minaret.

Locate a left-facing corner system capped by a large roof on the left side of the Minaret. **1-2**: Climb the corner over the first small roof and continue over the second big roof (5.9, A4). **3-5**: Continue up face cracks and small corners to the top of a small pillar where the first ascent party had a hanging bivouac: mostly sustained 5.10 free climbing with a small amount of A2 aid climbing. **6-7**: Climb cracks and corners to gain the ledge on pitch 6 of *Bad Hair Day* (5.10, A2). **8**: Scramble right along the ledge and back up

into a left-facing corner. **9-14**: Climb the corner and continue up face cracks and over small roofs to gain the top of the Minaret (5.9, A2).

As with *Bad Hair Day* the climb from the top of the Minaret to the summit of the South Tower is long with broken low-mid fifth class terrain and short steps up to 5.10. It is possible to rappel *Doubting the Millennium*

204 **Retinal Circus**   ED1   5.11 A2   (2-3 biv) 12-18p   *280*

Zak Smith, Aaron Martin, August 2000

This line climbs face cracks between the *Italian Pillar* and *Doubting the Millennium*. Details are limited but the first ascent party climbed the route in a single day and freed the majority of the route with the main aid being around pitches four and five where the the the crack sytems become less continuous.

205 **Doubting the Millennium** ** ED1 5.10, A3   (2-3 biv) 12-18p   *281*

Bobby Schultz, Jay Sell, July 1999   AAJ 42:229(2000)

This route follows the attractive crack system left of the *Southwest Pillar* joining that route near the top.

Locate a crack left of the *Southwest Pillar* that splits an offset roof. **1**: Start right of the crack and face climb to join the crack at the first left-hand roof. Follow the crack through the next right-hand roof and continue to a belay (5.8, 60m). **2**: Continue up the crack on aid and over the long roof until forced to pendulum left to another crack, which is followed to a belay (A2, 60m). **3**: Continue up the crack until able to lower right to the base of a left-facing corner system (60m). **4-7**: Climb the corner in four pitches to gain the ledge where *Bad Hair Day* enters from the left (5.10, A3). **8-12**: Follow the *Southwest Pillar* to the top.

The first ascent party rappelled the route from the top of the Minaret.

206 **Southwest Pillar** *   ED1 5.10+ A3   (2-3 biv) 12-18p   *281*

Jon Jones, Gerry Rogan, August 1972   CAJ 56:22

This was the original route up the Minaret and takes a direct line up the righthand side of the pillar. The first few pitches are often wet.

Start in the farthest righthand crack system that passes the right side of the lower roofs. **1**: Climb the crack past the first roof and belay at the second (A1, 60m). **2**: Start up the crack until forced to pendulum left into another crack which is followed to a belay (A3, 60m). **3-5**: Follow this crack system for three pitches to a good bivy ledge (5.8, A1, 180m). **6**: Climb a crack at the left end of the ledge to a slab (5.8, A1). **7**: Continue up the slab to a ledge belay where *Bad Hair Day* and *Doubting the Millennium* enter from the left (5.8). **8**: Climb a groove to a good stance (5.10, 45m). **9**: Head right, up, and right again to the base of a small roof (5.8, 60m). **10**: Climb a short pitch over the small roof and up a ramp to the base of an offwidth (5.9). **11**: Climb up the offwidth to a ledge (5.10+). **12**: Climb left up flakes to a crack and a left-facing corner to the top (5.9).

The climb from the top of the Minaret to the summit of the South Tower is long with broken low-mid fifth class terrain and short steps up to 5.10. Follow the line of least resistance. It is possible to rappel *Doubting the Millennium*

SOUTH HOWSER TOWER — THE MINARET

Minaret

Pigeon

Pigeon–Howser Col

Pigeon–Howser Icefall

203 202

202

203

204

206
205

ROUTES: 202 203 (278) **204–206** (279)

SOUTH HOWSER TOWER – THE MINARET

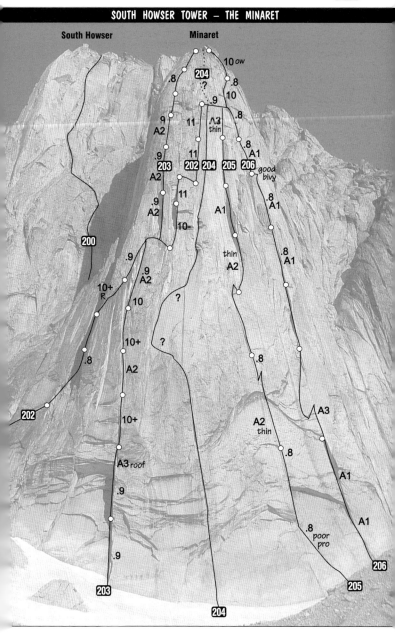

South Howser   Minaret

ROUTES: 200 (273)   **202 203** (278)   **204–206** (279)

South Howser Tower – *Camerons Pillar*

207 **South Face**   TD   5.8   A2 ♦   (12-14h)   9p   *283*

Robin Mounsey, B.Beattie, July 1974

The exact position of this line is uncertain but it is believed to climb the left side of the face between the Minaret and the Pigeon–Howser Icefall to join *Cameron's Pillar* at the top of the vague pillar.

1-2: Gain the far right side of the Minaret and climb up and right for 2 pitches. **3-5**: Climb crack systems to a chimney. **6-9**: Climb left and up a chimney past a roof to a sling belay. Continue up cracks and a chimney to the top of the pillar and the top of pitch 8 on *Cameron's Pillar*.

Rappel as for *Cameron's Route* or continue up more broken terrain to gain the *East Ridge*.

208 **Cameron's Pillar** *   TD+   5.11+   (10-12h)   8p   *283*

Topher Donahue, Patience Gribble, August 2000   *AAJ 43:249 (2001)*

Cameron's Pillar climbs a vague pillar in the middle of the face between the Pigeon–Howser Icefall and the Minaret. The ledge systems are loose but the climbing in between is very good.

From the East Creek Basin bivouac site gain the base of the wall right of the Minaret. Follow the wall right towards the Pigeon–Howser Icefall passing red-varnished rock to gain the first of a series of red-coloured ledges. **1**: Climb a right curving crack (5.10-). **2**: Start up a dihedral switching to a crack on the face of the dihedral and belay on a ledge (5.10-). **3**: Climb past a teetering pillar, over a ledge, into a chimney and belay behind another pillar (5.8). **4**: Follow a black, right-facing corner (5.10-). **5**: Continue up a left-facing corner onto a ledge and scramble left to its end (5.10). **6-8**: Climb three 5.11 pitches up cracks up the steep wall of the orange pillar, switching right to another crack on the last pitch (5.11+).

The first ascent party rappelled the upper three pitches to the ledge, descended fourth-class terrain to the low point in the ledge and made another four double rope rappels to the ground. It would also be possible to continue from the top of the pillar up more broken ground to gain the *East Ridge*.

In August 1987, Fabio Stedile and Frabrisio Defransesco climbed Surf's Up on Snowpatch in under three hours from the valley car park.

SOUTH HOWSER TOWER — CAMERON'S PILLAR

Minaret Summit

Cameron's Pillar

167

Pigeon–
Howser
Icefall

208

207

205 206

East Creek
Basin

Photo: Marc Piché

ROUTES: **167** (242)   **205 206** (279)   **207 208** (282)

Pigeon Feathers	2930m—2990m

The Pigeon Feathers divide the Pigeon Fork of the Bugaboo Glacier from the East Creek Basin. Their eastern side is relatively gentle and glacier-covered but the west side is a complex array of rock walls, towers and pinnacles. Development of the western walls has only recently began but has produced some fine free and aid climbs.

West Peak: (Fingerberry Tower)	2930m
East Peak Main	2990m
East Peak (Lost Feather Pinnacle)	2900m
Southeast Peak (Wide Awake Tower)	2950m

Approach: The main approach to the Pigeon Feathers is through the Bugaboo–Snowpatch Col and the Pigeon–Howser Col and down into the East Creek Basin, which then gives access to the climbs. Two alternative approaches are up the Pigeon Fork of the Bugaboo Glacier with one gaining the access couloir at the col between the West and East Pigeon Feathers and the other going through the Marmolata–Pigeon Feather Col and on through the Pigeon Feather–Flattop Col into the East Creek Basin. The Pigeon–Howser Col approach is generally the easiest with the other two approaches sometimes being used as a descent route back to the Kain Hut Basin. All approaches entail extensive glacier travel and loose terrain.

Descent: Descent from the Pigeon Feathers is generally down the Bugaboo Glacier side. For the West Peak (Fingerberry Tower) downclimb the ridge, which leads towards Pigeon Spire. This entails traversing fourth and low fifth class terrain to gain the Bugaboo Glacier, followed by a descent of the gully between the West and East Peaks to regain the base of the routes. For the main East Peak, steep snow leads down to the East–West Peak gully. For the Southeast Peak, a descent down broken rock and steep snow leads to the Marmolata–Pigeon Feather Col followed by easy glacier travel through the Pigeon Feather–Flattop Col on down into the East Creek Basin. See the route descriptions for descents of Lost Feather Pinnacle (page 286) and Wide Awake Tower (page 287).

West Peak — *Fingerberry Tower*

209 Gar Wall   D+ 5.10 A2   (9-12h)   7p   *292*
Rodger Debeyer, Kirt Sellers, August 2001

Gar Wall climbs around the left side of the huge roof between the west and south faces and continues straight to the summit.

From the lowest point of the face, where a tarn sometimes forms, traverse up across rubble strewn ice to a point directly below the left side of the huge roof. **1-2**: Climb broken cracks and a corner to below the roof (5.10, A2). **3**: Tension left at a bolt and climb left around the roof to a bolt belay (5.10, A2). **4**: Climb up and right and follow the crack to Gar Ledge and a bolt belay (5.8). **5-7**: Continue straight up cracks to the top of the tower (5.10, A2)

The first ascent party fixed the belay stations with bolts and rappelled the route.

210 Fingerberry Jam ***   D+ 5.12-   (7-10h)   5p   *293*
Topher Donahue, Patience Gribble, August 2000   *AAJ 43:249(2001)*

Fingerberry Jam climbs a series of thin, clean cracks on the south side of the West Peak (Fingerberry Tower). This is a very attractive and sustained climb.

The base of the tower can be approached from the Pigeon–Howser Col or the West–East Pigeon Feathers Col or directly from the East Creek Basin bivy. From the lowest point on the face, where sometimes a tarn forms, hike up snow to the righthand edge of the south face. **1**: Scramble up from the right to a small ledge with large blocks on it. Step out left onto the face and follow a crack up and slightly left to a belay below a small roof/alcove (5.11-). **2**: Follow the crack above and climb the left crack at the first intersection, which leads up into a overhanging slot and a belay ledge above (5.11+). **3**: Follow joining cracks above until the climbing becomes very difficult then face climb left (5.12-) to gain another crack leading to a ledge, which is followed right to a belay at the base of a corner (5.12-). **4-6**: Climb corners and cracks, trending right to gain the summit (5.10).

To descend, rappel *Gar Wall* or downclimb the *Northeast Ridge* over fourth and low fifth class terrain to either the gully that descends south to the base of the route or onto the ice near the *West Ridge* of Pigeon Spire.

If I had a place to sleep at night and wasn't hungry, then the world was in order as far as I was concerned.   Hans Gmoser.

East Peak — *Main Peak*

211 Crack of Noon *   D   5.9+   (5-7h)   6p   *291*

Mark Austin, Dave Scott, August 1990

Crack of Noon climbs the right side of the north wall of the East Peak of the Pigeon Feathers. This wall makes up the south side of the west-facing gully separating the West and East Peaks.

Gain the west-facing gully between the West and East Pigeon Feathers and traverse into a notch between the main peak and a small, lower pinnacle on the west side. **1**: From the notch climb a corner to a semi-hanging belay (5.9+, 35m). **2**: Move right out of the main corner into a finger crack that leads to a ledge. Continue up and step right across a chimney on to a face and a ledge belay above (5.8, 30m). **3**: Step right around an exposed edge and climb up and back left to a ledge belay on top of a block (5.6, 25m). **4**: Step left and climb a steep face to a zig-zag crack that is followed to a right-trending corner and a belay (5.9, 30m). **5**: Climb up and right to a chimney that is followed until it is possible to step right to a crack leading to a ledge belay (5.8, 25m). **6**: Climb a slab to the summit blocks (5.7).

To descend, downclimb a steep snow arête to the top of the East–West Pigeon Feather Col.

East Peak — *Lost Feather Pinnacle*

212 Lost Feather *   TD-   5.10 A3   (12-16h)   9p   *294*

Gene Kistler, Todd Offenbacher, July 1995   *AAJ 1996:203*

When viewed from the East Creek Basin, the west side of the East Peak of the Pigeon Feathers appears as a large armchair with two lower pinnacles as the arms. *Lost Feather* climbs the southern pinnacle.

The face can be gained from the East Creek Basin by skirting the base of the west face of the East Peak, involving a short, steep, crevassed section of ice, or from the Bugaboo Glacier via the Pigeon Feather–Marmolata Col and the Pigeon Feather–Flattop Col. **1**: Locate a corner system left of the toe of the face, just where the snow begins to curve uphill. Climb the corner switching to a crack on the left wall halfway up (5.10, 45m). **2**: Continue up the corner as it curves left to a ledge belay (5.10, 35m). **3**: Follow a crack up and left and over a small roof to a ledge belay (5.10, A2, 35m). **4**: Climb up and right to a belay on a blunt arête (5.8 A3, 45m). **5**: Continue up to an excellent bivouac ledge (5.8 A3, 45m). **6**: From the right edge of the ledge squeeze out right to gain the start of a long crack system leading to the top of the pinnacle. Climb the crack to a pedestal belay (5.10, A2, 45m). **7**: Continue up the 4-5inch crack and use a crack on the left wall to gain a belay inside the base of a chimney (5.10+, 50m). **8**: Follow the chimneys to a belay on the prow (5.10, 45m). **9**: Continue up the chimney and cracks to the top of the pinnacle (5.8, 40m).

From the top of the pinnacle traverse for two pitches along the sharp ridge crest to where it abuts the main wall, from here make three double rope rappels down the right side of the ridge towards the Southeast Peak. These rappels lead into a gully that is descended to the base of the route.

Southeast Peak — *Prince Albert Tower*

213 Dingleberry Spam ***   D   5.10+   (6-8h)   5p   *289*

Sean Isaac, Guy Edwards, August 2002   *CAJ 86:137*

Between Lost Feather Pinnacle and Wide Awake Tower stands a shorter wall split by clean vertical cracks. *Dingleberry Spam* climbs a line between the vertical cracks and the snow gully to the right.

1: Climb a right-angling face crack/flake up the yellow wall between the face cracks to the left and the snow gully to the right. Continue up a stemmimg chimney to face moves leading right to a belay (5.10-, 60m). **2**: Scramble up blocky fourth-class terrain to a ledge belay out left (60m). **3**: Climb a hand-offwidth crack for a short section and move right on a flake/handrail (5.10, 30m). **4**: Climb a hand-crack to a flake leading right then continue up another crack to a ledge belay (5.10-, 30m). **5**: Move to the left end of the ledge and climb a corner to a steep chimney with chockstones (5.10-, 50m).

The first ascent party rappelled the route. Make two double rope rappels from slung blocks to the top of pitch 2 then scramble down beside the snow gully to a final rappel station near the first belay.

Southeast Peak — *Wide Awake Tower*

214 Wide Awake ***   TD- 5.10+ A2   (12-16h)   8p   *295*

Nils Davis, Todd Offenbacher, August 1999   *AAJ 2000:229*

Wide Awake climbs the right side of the prow on the East Creek Basin face of the Southeast Peak (Wide Awake Tower) of the Pigeon Feathers.

The face can be gained from the East Creek Basin by skirting the base of the west face of the East Peak, which involves a short, steep, crevassed section of ice, or from the Bugaboo Glacier via the Pigeon Feather–Marmolata Col and the Pigeon Feather–Flattop Col. **1**: Climb an open book dihedral on the right side of the prow to a ledge belay (5.9, 60m). **2**: Continue up a chimney and cracks to a ledge belay below a roof (5.8, 35m). **3**: Climb up and right around the roof and follow the 4 inch crack past a loose flake to a belay (5.10+, 60m). **4**: Continue up the crack to a belay below another roof (5.10 A1, 55m). **5**: Climb right around the roofs and continue to a belay (A2). **6**: Follow the crack to the ridge (A2). Freed by second at 5.12. **7**: Make a 15m rappel down the opposite side and scramble small ledges to a belay. **8**: Follow a chimney and cracks to the top of the tower (5.10, 55m). Bring 60m ropes and extra 4 inch cams.

To descend from the summit, scramble down rock and snow to the Bugaboo Glacier and the Pigeon Feather–Marmolata Col and continue west to the Pigeon Feather–Flattop Col and the base of the route or down the Bugaboo Glacier to the Kain Hut Basin.

APPROACH / DESCENTS: 284

PIGEON FEATHERS — SOUTHWEST FACES IN EAST CREEK BASIN

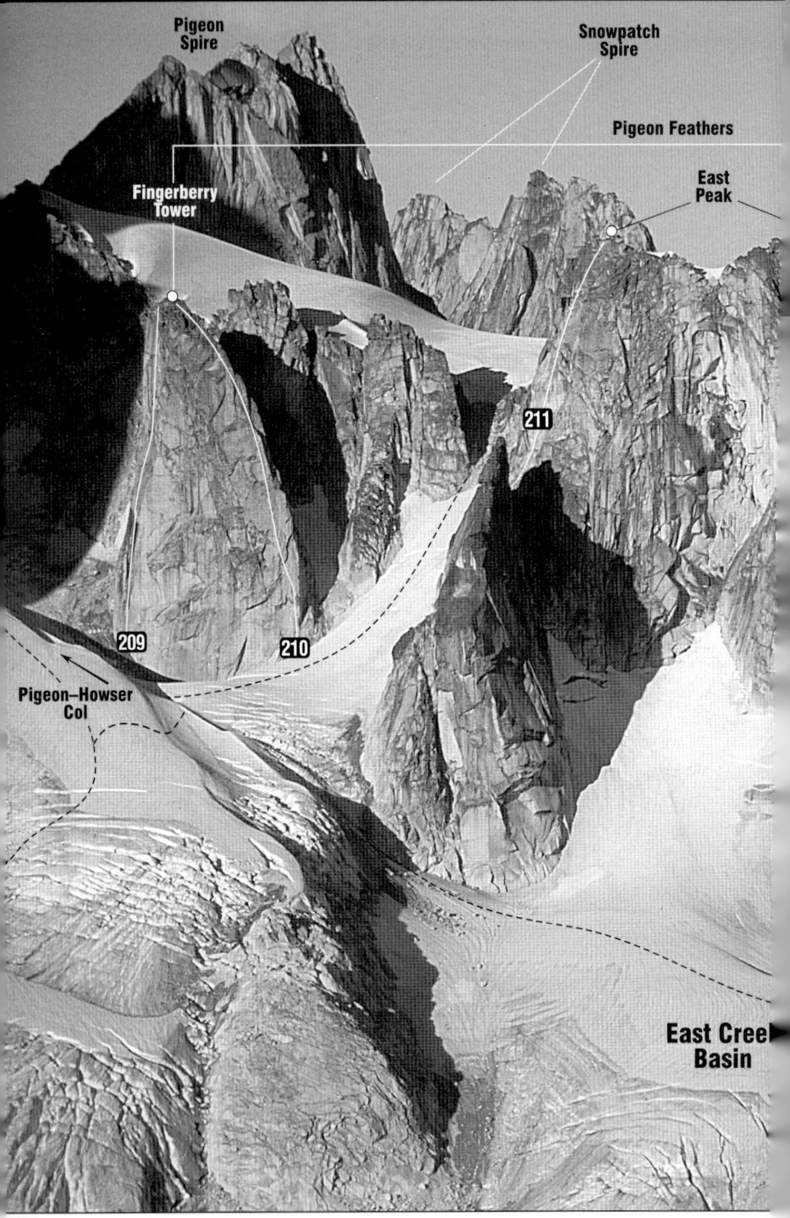

Pigeon Spire
Snowpatch Spire
Pigeon Feathers
Fingerberry Tower
East Peak
211
209
210
Pigeon–Howser Col
East Cree
Basin

ROUTES: 209 210 (285) **211** (286)

Pigeon Feathers

Lost Feather Pinnacle

Prince Albert Tower

Wide Awake Tower

213

214

Pigeon Feathers –Flattop Col

2

SOUTH HOWSER TOWER AND PIGEON FEATHERS WEST PEAK

South Howser

Pigeon–Howser Col

Pigeon Feathers Fingerberry Tower

Pigeon Spire

208

bivy boulder

East Creek Basin

210

ultra-wide angle lens view

August 2002

Bugaboo Spire, and the first recorded use of a sloper.

We returned to the gendarme and after a short rest I tackled the perpendicular fifteen-foot wall. Several diagonal cracks offered firm handholds, but were not large enough for the toes; the old proverb "Half a loaf is better than none" comes often to a climbers mind. Near the top I was stuck for a few minutes, the edge being smooth and without holds of any kind. I applied the vacuum grip and pulled myself up and over.

Conrad Kain American Alpine Journal 1929-32

ROUTES: 208 (283) **210** (285)

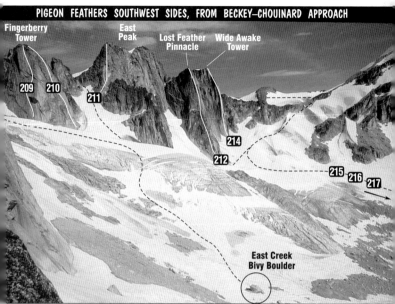

PIGEON FEATHERS SOUTHWEST SIDES, FROM BECKEY–CHOUINARD APPROACH

After the first ascent of Bugaboo Spire.

The rest of the descent was made without any difficulties, and so ended the most interesting climb I had in my seven seasons of Canadian mountaineering. Without hesitation I say that the ascent of Bugaboo Spire offers as many thrills and difficulties as any of the aiguilles in the Alps which I have climbed. I also feel confident that mountaineers who make a trip to this group of the Purcells will not be disappointed.

Conrad Kain, American Alpine Journal, 1929-32

PIGEON FEATHERS WEST PEAK — FINGERBERRY TOWER

West
Face

South
Face

7

6

.8
A1

5

10
A2

4

.8

3

10
A2

2

1

Pigeon–Howser
Col

August 2OC

209

ROUTES: 209 (285)

PIGEON FEATHERS WEST PEAK — FINGERBERRY TOWER

descent down
northeast ridge

possible
finish

face climb
to left

Pigeon–Howser
Col

August 2002

ROUTES: 209 210 (285)

PIGEON FEATHERS — LOST FEATHER PINNACLE WEST FACE

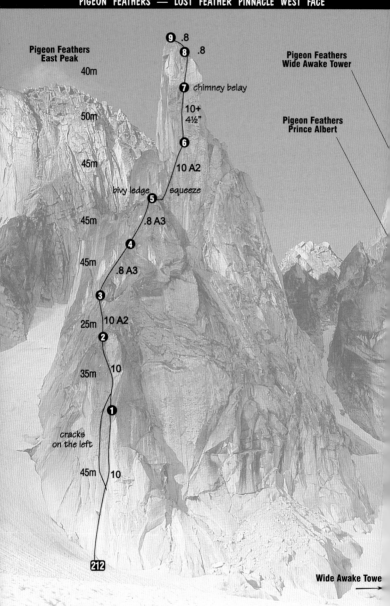

Pigeon Feathers
East Peak

40m

Pigeon Feathers
Wide Awake Tower

Pigeon Feathers
Prince Albert

9 .8
8 .8

7 chimney belay

50m

10+
4½"

45m

6

10 A2

bivy ledge **5** squeeze

.8 A3

45m

4

45m

.8 A3

3

25m 10 A2
2

35m 10

1

cracks
on the left

45m 10

212

Wide Awake Towe →

PIGEON FEATHERS, SOUTHEAST PEAK — WIDE AWAKE TOWER

rappel 15m
off backside

hidden

7

6

A2 / 12

5

A2

4

A1 or 10

3

10+

2

.8

1

.9

60m

60m

60m

60m

60m

60m

7

55m

10

15m rappel

6

Lost Feather Pinnacle

214

ROUTES: 214 (287)

Crossed Fish Peak	2836m

Crossed Fish Peak stands between Flattop Peak to the east and Little Snowpatch to the west. It is attached to Flattop by a 2700m col and to Little Snowpatch by a 2753m col. This fourth class summit is rarely visited but gives outstanding views of the Pigeon Feathers and the south side of South Howser Tower.

Approach: Crossed Fish is reached from the East Creek Basin, which is gained via either the Upper Vowell Glacier and the Pigeon–Howser Col, or the Bugaboo Glacier and the Marmolata–Pigeon Feather Col. The latter is quicker and avoids a very short icefall and steep rock slabs below the west face of the Pigeon Feathers.

Descent: Descent from Crossed Fish is back down the *East Ridge* to the Flattop–Crossed Fish Col and down the snow couloir into the East Creek Basin.

215 **East Ridge** AD 4th (8-10h) 250m *298*

Edith Aston, William Buckingham, Pierre Garneau, Peter Geiser, Sue Redpath August 1961
AAJ 13:242

From the southeastern side of the East Creek Basin, cross the glacier beneath the northwest face of Flattop Peak (beware of rockfall) and climb the snow couloir to the Flattop–Crossed Fish Col. Continue to the Crossed Fish summit over broken fourth class terrain. This route is often climbed on the way to Little Snowpatch.

FLATTOP PEAK AND CROSSED FISH — SOUTHWEST FACES IN EAST CREEK BASIN

Flattop Peak · Crossed Fish · Little Snowpatch · East Creek Valley · 12 · 215 · 216 · 217 · East Creek Bivy Boulder 50m · Beckey-Chouinard approach · Beckey-Chouinard approach

Little Snowpatch   2915m

Little Snowpatch is the westernmost of the two peaks extending west from Flattop Peak. It makes up the southwestern end of the East Creek Basin and is attached to Crossed Fish Peak by a 2753m col. To date the peak has had only two recorded ascents, an astonishing fact given the amount of activity that occurs on nearby Pigeon Spire.

Approach: Approach to Little Snowpatch is from the East Creek Basin via either the Upper Vowell Glacier and the Pigeon–Howser Col, or the Bugaboo Glacier and the Marmolata–Pigeon Feather Col. The latter is quicker and avoids a very short icefall or steep rock slabs below the west face of the Pigeon Feathers.

Descent: The first ascent party descended the *East Ridge* route to Crossed Fish–Little Snowpatch Col then a rotten gully to the south. The Upper Bugaboo Glacier cirque was then gained via the Thimble–Flattop Col. From there an East Creek Basin camp can be regained, or the Kain Hut Basin via the Marmolata–Pigeon Feather Col and descent down the Pigeon Fork of the Bugaboo Glacier.

216 **East Ridge**   AD   4th   (10-12h)   400m   *299*

William Buckingham, Pierre Garneau, Peter Geiser, August 1961   CAJ 45:126, AAJ 13:242

This route is climbed in conjunction with a traverse of Crossed Fish Peak.

From the southeastern side of the East Creek Basin, cross the glacier beneath the northwest face of Flattop Peak (beware of rockfall) and climb the snow couloir to the Flattop–Crossed Fish Col. Continue to the Crossed Fish summit via the *East Ridge*. Descend to the west over increasingly precarious terrain until forced to rappel the final 50m to the Crossed Fish–Little Snowpatch Col. Climb a series of third and fourth-class slabs and cracks to the summit. "An excellent vantage point for viewing the south and west faces of the Howser Spire massif" concluded the first ascent party.

217 **Northwest Face**   TD   5.10 A2   (1 biv)   17p   *299*

Steve Sheriff, Gray Thompson, Jon Turk, July 1994   AAJ 1995:177

This route ascends the right side of the northwest face, easily viewed from the normal East Creek Basin camp. The first ascent party commented, "The rock is excellent Bugaboo granite, solid except for a few pitches with loose debris in the lower third of the route."

Descend the glacier beneath the northwest sides of Flattop and Crossed Fish Peaks to reach scree slopes leading to the base of the northwest face of Little Snowpatch. Cross the base of the face to the far end where the scree falls steeply away from the slabs.

Climb weaknesses up the steep, broken slabs left of the west buttress until able to trend left to gain a prominent dihedral system. Climb the dihedral to its top and exit left, level with the steep, white wall of the southwest face. Trend left to broken ground (first ascent party bivouac). Continue trending left up the steeper wall to gain easier terrain leading to the summit. The route may be done in one long day from an East Creek Basin camp.

CROSSED FISH — NORTHWEST SIDE

Flattop
Peak

Crossed
Fish

Little
Snowpatch

215

216

view from East Creek Basin

ROUTES: **215** (296) **216** (297)

LITTLE SNOWPATCH — NORTHWEST FACE

ossed
Fish   216

217

view from East Creek Basin

ROUTES: 216 217 (297)

The *Beckey–Chouinard*, South Howser
Tower, pitch 10 above Big Sandy Ledge.
climber: John Forrest.
photo: Mark Klassen.

The *East Face* of Pigeon Spire pitch 10
approaching the headwall.
climber: Pat Sheehan.

Lydia Marmont, Marc Piché, Brian Webster at East Glacier Camp. Snafflehound Spire beyond.

Approaching Bugaboo Spire,
Kain Hut Basin.

Lydia Marmont on Wallace Peak.
Bugaboo Spire North Face beyond.

East Creek Basin bivouac, below the
South Howser Tower and the Minaret.

The *Beckey–Chouinard*, South Howser
Tower, on pitch 12.
climber: Tim Haggarty

Guy Edwards attempting the incomplete West Face on the Minaret. South Howser Tower. photo: Sean Isaac.

The *Big Hose*, South Howser Tower.
climber: Joe Josephson.
photo: Grant Statham.

Chris Atkinson on the approach trail to the Kain Hut.
Bugaboo Glacier and the Hounds Tooth beyond.
photo: Kevin McLane.

pitch 1 of *McTech Arete,* Crescent Spire.
climber: Chuck McCafferty.

The upper pitches on the south
face of Snowpatch Spire.
climber: Paul McSorley
photo: John Walsh photography.

pitch 3 of *Spinstone Gully*, first ascent.
Central Howser Tower.
climber: Scott Semple
photo: Sean Isaac.

Dingleberry Spam, Pigeon Feathers, first ascent.
climber: Guy Edwards.
photo: Sean Isaac.

Chocolate Fudge Brownie, first ascent.
Central Howser Tower.
climber: Brian Webster.
photo: Sean Isaac.

pitch 1 of *Krause–McCarthy*,
Snowpatch Spire, first winter ascent.
climber: Kirk Mauthner
photo: Brad Shilling

pitch 3 of *Perma Grin*, South Howser Tower,
first ascent, climber: Scott Semple
photo: Sean Isaac.

East Glacier Camp,
East Peak behind.
climber: Brian Webster

On the Archduke Trio traverse
climber: Peter MacPherson
photo: Marc Piché

Corto Zonal, first ascent, pitch 1.
Snafflehound Spire.
climber: Marc Piché.

Vowell stone:
Snafflehound Sp

THE VOWELL GROUP

The little known and visited Vowell group is one of the remote granite treasures of the Purcell mountain range. Located north of the Bugaboos, they can be seen from many of the classic routes in the Spires. There has been relatively little climbing activity due to the length of the approaches and the amount of effort and commitment necessary for a successful trip.

The granite is of the same geological formation as the Bugaboos, but there are many differences in its character. Although quality varies from excellent to unpleasant, it is generally good on steeper weathered formations and ridges. The rock is more fractured than that of the Bugaboos, the cracks are sharp and deep but there are fewer face features to depend on. The ridges tend to be solid and blocky but areas where glaciers and permanent snow have recently melted should be avoided, as they are loose and difficult to negotiate.

Travel within the Vowells is more complex than in the Bugaboos. The glaciers are more broken and many of the regular approach and descent routes require multiple rappels, which can be difficult to find and rarely established, therefore it is important to bring sufficient webbing and pitons to fix all rappel anchors. This is a remote area, bring a map a compass and know how to use them.

Most Peaks in the Vowell group lie within the boundaries of the Bugaboo Glacier Provincial Park. This means that all the rules and issues described on pages 26-27 apply here as well. The slow increase in human traffic over the years has had little impact as of yet, but the integrity of this beautiful and remote area must be maintained. Human waste management will be the first major issue to surface and special consideration should be given to water supplies and camping areas. Toilet paper should be burnt and all garbage must be carried out.

In the route descriptions, times given try to approximate that spent on the route and descent, and unlike the main Bugaboo Spires, do not include approaches due the the variable means of access to most of the Vowells routes. The lengths are given in pitches where appropriate, and in metres of vertcal elevation gain otherwise. Note that the latter will entail 25%–50% more actual climbing than the figure indicates.

The climb lengths do not include the glacier approaches, which can be substantial undertakings, but with one exception, all climbs can be considered as one-day enterprises.

Peak Ordering

Archduke Trio	2680m	Thunderstorm Tower	2917m
Robert the Bruce	2865m	Split Rock spire	2822m
Howard the Duck	2790m	East Peak	3077m
Wallace Peak	2947m	Centre Peak	3058m
Little Wallace	2797m	West Peak	3127m
Mount Kelvin	2955m	North Peak	2866m
Snafflehound Spire	2985m	Osprey Peak	2907m
Spear Spire	2992m	Vowell Peak	2990m
East Peak Sub One	2900m		

Vowell History

Formerly a part of the Bobbie Burns group then renamed the Vowells. This range has hosted several Alpine Club of Canada and Kootenay Mountaineering Club camps. These camps have accounted for the majority of first ascent activity to date. Although there had been some climbing activity in the previous years, the Georgia Engelhard party, led by Swiss guide Ernst Feuz made successful first ascents on many of the major peaks in 1939. In 1958, the Bill Buckingham Party was successful in making the first traverse of the main group from Spear Spire to Wallace Peak. After a couple of trips to the range including the first ascent of the classic *Archduke Trio*, Robert Kruszyna, accompanied by Charles Fay and Jim Herbert traversed the technical, complex ridge from Sub-One to East Peak over one and a half days exploring much new ground along the way. More recently, Hamish Mutch and Steven Horvath along with a few other members of the Kootenay Mountaineering club have made several trips to the Vowells, which have resulted in many classic firsts. The 1980s and 90s saw a handful of serious yet mildly successful attempts on many of the remaining unclimbed faces. The most notable of these being the first ascent of the stunning *West Face* of West Peak in 1981 by Scott Flavelle, Keith Flavelle and Mike Down.

The first big wall climbed in the alpine in North America was the 1959 ascent of the East Face of Snowpatch Spire by the legendary Fred Beckey and Canadian Hank Mather, complete with wooden wedges and prussic cords. Mather also made the first 5th-class route on the Squamish Chief.

Approaches

Due to the complexity of the terrain in the Vowells, the climbing is best described in four distinct areas. There are many ways to approach the area but, in recent years the route taken from the Bugaboos has become the most reliable. Travel from one area to another is difficult, and involves real climbing and many rappels, which with huge packs becomes difficult. For this reason, most parties take on a base-camp style approach to the range, and tend to focus on one area (map, page 23).

The most common approach to the Vowell group is via the Kain Hut Basin and the Bugaboo–Snowpatch Col, then toward Bill's Pass to reach the **East Glacier Cirque** and the **West Glacier Cirque**. Some parties will make the trip in one very long day, but most will overnight at the Kain hut. (page 25) Be warned that this approach has a steep and heavily crevassed stretch of glacier near Bugaboo Spire that is often icy.

Follow the directions for the approach to the Bugaboo-Snowpatch Col (pages 161, 172). Navigate through many crevasses down the Vowell Glacier heading northwest while staying close to Bugaboo Spire until the glacier becomes flat. Cross this area known as the Vowell Lagoons in the direction of Bill's Pass [GR 121231]. The large glacial ponds that appear in the late summer can be difficult to negotiate and may add some time to the approach.

To East Glacier Cirque. Parties enroute to the East Glacier Cirque will be turning north around the Lagoon then up a wide talus filled gully, which leads to the small glacier below Wallace Peak and Howard the Duck (unnamed) to the southeast. From the Wallace Col [GR 134237], where there is a striking view of the Archduke Trio, head down and left. Contour below Wallace, Kelvin and pass very close to the east Face of Snafflehound to avoid the Wallace Glacier Icefall. This glacier is very broken and can be challenging in low snow years. A short distance ahead is a slabby rock island protruding from the ice. This is the East Glacier Camp [GR 136250] where good campsites are abundant though slightly off level. Beware of the icefall above the slabs, it is not very large, but it is active! Keep a safe distance between it and your tent. There are many water sources and a resourceful packrat of legendary reputation.

To West Glacier. Parties heading to the West Glacier area follow the route described for the East Glacier Cirque to where the talus gully meets the small glacier below the south face of Mount

Wallace. Turn left aiming for a point slightly left of the lowest section of the ridge running between Wallace and Little Wallace [GR 128235]. There is a good campsite just off the glacier and below Little Wallace [GR127232]. From the crest of the ridge make several rappels down very blocky terrain to the relatively flat West Glacier below. Take sufficient tat for these rappels, as the anchors may be difficult to find. The best camping is at the Centre Peak–East Peak Col [GR 257131], where good campsites and water can usually be found.

To Bill's Pass. Continue northwest from the Vowells Lagoons to [GR 121231], where rocky campsites lie just outside of the park boundary.

To the Malloy Igloo. Parties interested in climbing in the Malloy Igloo area of the Vowells will descend from Bill's Pass in a northwest direction which leads to the head of the north fork of East Creek and a basin surrounded by very active seracs. From here it is necessary to ascend out of the basin negotiating many crevasses while maintaining a northwest heading. From the flats of the Malloy Glacier it is a short distance to the Malloy Igloo [GR 108262]. There are also many good camping spots in the area depending on the objective. The Igloo itself is run by BC Parks and is comfortable for up to 4 people. At this point, no permits are necessary.

Via the Cobalt Lake Trail. (page 24) Another albeit less popular approach avoids the Kain Hut Basin entirely by hiking up over the ridge just north of North Post Spire, near Cobalt Lake then down the west side of North Post on goat trails to the toe of the Vowell Glacier. This approach can be difficult to find, very loose in places and quite a bit longer than the others.

The trail starts at a small sign approximately 2km before reaching the climbers parking area (there are some small pullouts nearby but be careful not to block the road). Follow this bushy trail to the ridge then side-hill along the south side within view of Cobalt Lake and down into the saddle below North Post. From this point the trail is difficult to follow although there may still be some cairns visible from when the trail was used as the approach to the GMC camp at the toe of the Vowell Glacier. Head slightly downhill and left toward a flat bench on the ridge, bordering *North Post Couloir*. Follow the faint goat trails, which lead down steep scree and into the couloir proper. Cross the bench at mid-height in the couloir to talus under the slabby northwest face of North Post then work down carefully to the gravel flats below. Walk up and onto the glacier on its left (east) side and stay left through both icefalls; at this point the Vowell Lagoons (described above) will be 2km to the west.

Via Vowell Creek. Traditionally, the area was also approached from Vowell creek. Starting from the small town of Parson on Highway 95, follow the south fork of the Spillimasheen forest service road for about 60km to either Malloy Creek and access to the Malloy Igloo, or further south to the park boundary and access to the Vowell Glacier. Both of these approaches have lost popularity over recent years due to many of the roads and bridges falling into disrepair or being de-activated by the Ministry of Forests. The route up Malloy creek consists of several kilometres of bushwhacking and creek crossings eventually becoming easier on the east side. Pass Iceberg Lake, then climb third class slabs under the west face of Osprey Peak to the Malloy Igloo.

Descents

While many of the descents in the Vowells are simple or specific to a particular route, there are two which serve as common descents for many routes and are best described here for simplicity.

Kelvin Northeast Gully. This descent reverses the *Northeast Gully* route on Mount Kelvin and is used to return to the East Glacier Cirque from the Classic Traverse and Mount Kelvin (page 347). From the col, make one 30m rappel to loose sandy ledges then work down and slightly right, staying out of the main part of gully (unless it is still snow-filled) and being careful of rockfall, with short steps of down climbing to the bergshrund. Cross the bergshrund to the Wallace Glacier.

Spear–East Peak Col Rappels. Used to return to the East Glacier Cirque from routes on East Peak, Spear Spire and Snafflehound, this descent is often wet and quite involved (page 331, 351). At this point, the anchors are pitons and fixed gear, which are in the path of running water. With more traffic, they may be moved to the left (south), which would greatly improve this descent.

From the East Peak side of the Spear–East Peak Col, follow broken terrain down to a flat area and the first anchor. Make 5 single rope rappels to the East Glacier below.

Crescent Spire

Bugaboo Crescent Col

Bugaboo Spire North

Bugaboo Spire South

Bugaboo-Snowpatch Col

Snowpatch Spire North

Snowpatch Spire South

Anniversary Peak

Snowpatch-Pigeon Col

Vowell Group East Glacier Camp Approach

The Lagoons

VOWELL PANORAMA

South Howser Tower

Central Howser Tower

North Howser Tower

North Howser West Face, approa North Shoulder Co

Pigeon Spire

Pigeon–Howser Col

Upper Vowell Glacier

Bills Pass
Malloy Igloo
Conrad Group
Approach

view from Little Wallace Camp, Vowell Group
Sept 2002

VOWELL PANORAMA

THE VOWELLS GROUP

Mount Wallace
Robert the Bruce
Mount Kelvin
West Glacier
West Peak
Archduke Trio
Snafflehound
Centre Peak
Spear Spire
North Peak

Classic Traverse

Bills Pass

Archduke Col

Archduke Glacier

view from Bugaboo Spire

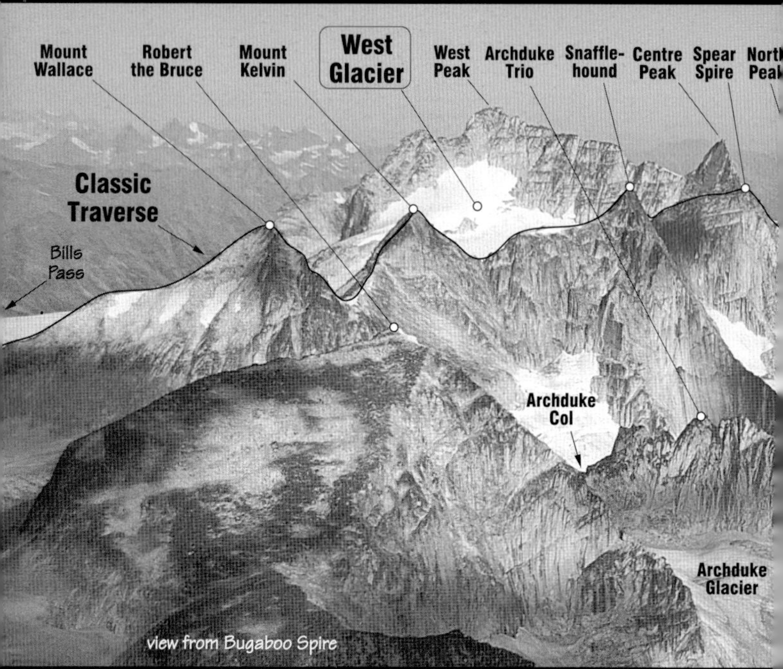

THE BUGABOOS – NORTHWEST SIDES

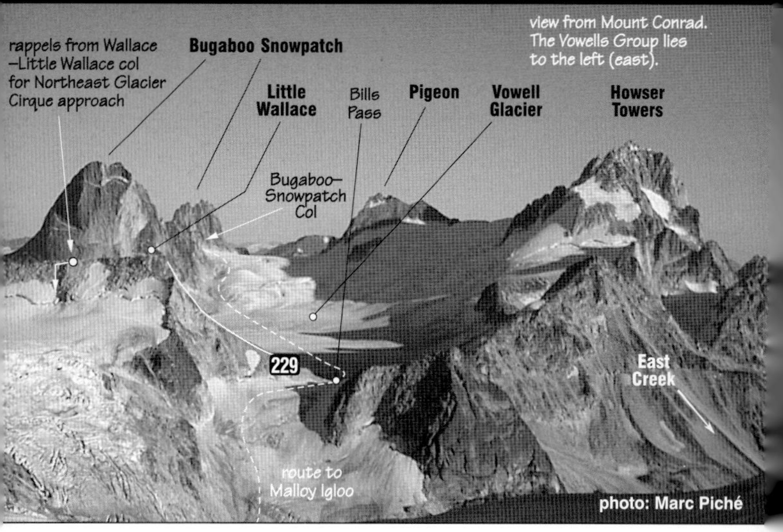

view from Mount Conrad.
The Vowells Group lies
to the left (east).

rappels from Wallace
–Little Wallace col
for Northeast Glacier
Cirque approach

Bugaboo Snowpatch

Little Wallace

Bills Pass

Pigeon

Vowell Glacier

Howser Towers

Bugaboo–
Snowpatch
Col

229

East Creek

route to
Malloy Igloo

photo: Marc Piché

VOWELL PANORAMAS

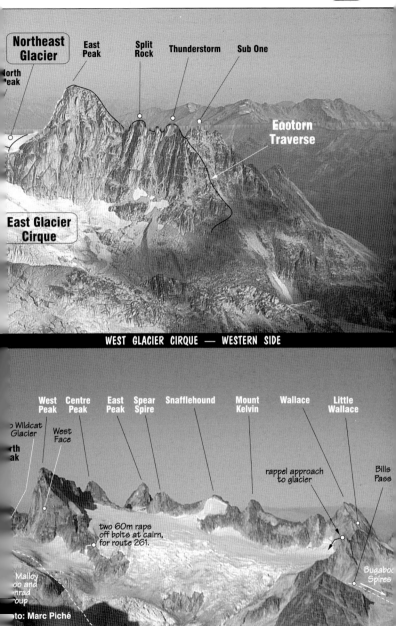

Northeast Glacier

orth eak

East Peak

Split Rock

Thunderstorm

Sub One

Enotorn Traverse

East Glacier Cirque

WEST GLACIER CIRQUE — WESTERN SIDE

> Wildcat Glacier

rth ak

West Peak

West Face

Centre Peak

East Peak

Spear Spire

Snafflehound

Mount Kelvin

Wallace

Little Wallace

rappel approach to glacier

Bills Pass

two 60m raps off bolts at cairn, for route 261.

Malloy oo and nrad oup

Bugaboo Spires

to: Marc Piché

VOWELL PANORAMAS

EAST GLACIER CIRQUE

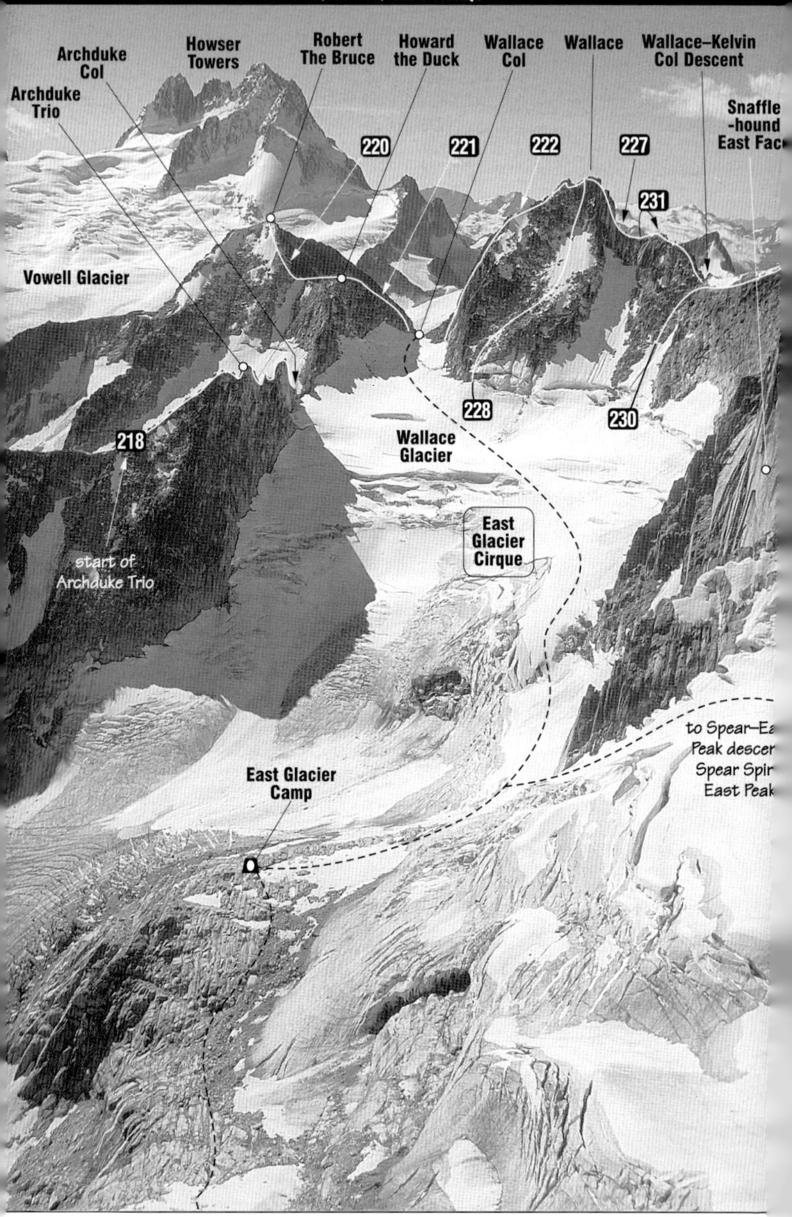
Archduke Col
Howser Towers
Robert The Bruce
Howard the Duck
Wallace Col
Wallace
Wallace–Kelvin Col Descent
Archduke Trio
Snaffle -hound East Fac
220
221
222
227
231
Vowell Glacier
228
230
218
Wallace Glacier
East Glacier Cirque
start of Archduke Trio
to Spear–Ea
Peak descer
Spear Spir
East Peak
East Glacier Camp

ROUTES: 218 (334) **220–222** (336) **227 228** (337) **230 231** (338)

EAST GLACIER CIRQUE PANORAMA

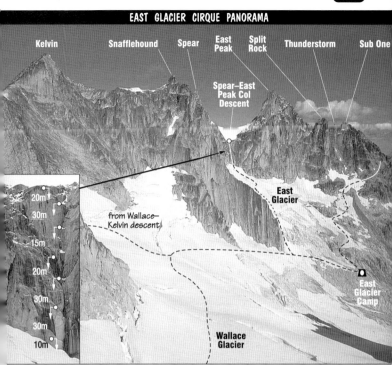

Kelvin — Snafflehound — Spear — East Peak — Split Rock — Thunderstorm — Sub One

Spear–East Peak Col Descent

East Glacier

20m
30m
15m
20m
30m
30m
10m

from Wallace–Kelvin descent

East Glacier Camp

Wallace Glacier

LITTLE WALLACE RAPPELS TO WEST GLACIER

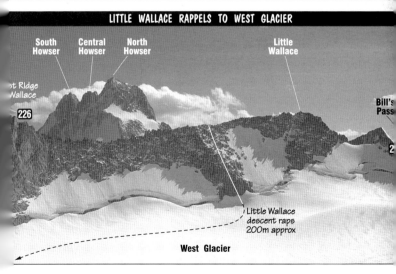

South Howser — Central Howser — North Howser — Little Wallace

st Ridge
Wallace

226

Bill's Pass

Little Wallace descent raps 200m approx

West Glacier

ROUTES: 226 (337) **229** (338)

VOWELL GROUP – EASTERN AND CLASSIC TRAVERSES

Mount Wallace · Mount Kelvin · West Peak · Snafflehound · Centre Peak · Spear Spire · West Glacier · Archduke Trio

Classic Traverse   AD 5.5   (8-12h)   *332*

William Buckingham, Arnold Guess, Robert Page, August 1958   *CAJ 42:53, AAJ 11:312*

Several of the relatively small peaks in the Vowells are conveniently linked together by blocky granite ridges which, when combined with their low-angled nature create this fine, long traverse. It was originally climbed in a south-to-north direction from Wallace, but has since been done starting from the north end of Spear. Most of the climbing is in the 4th class range with only short sections of low-5th. The crux lies in getting around a 100m high bump on the ridge near the Wallace–Kelvin Col, usually climbed on the west side and requiring a couple of short rappels.

Climbs encountered

Wallace	*West Ridge*	226	page 337
Wallace	*Northeast Ridge*	227	page 337
Kelvin	*South Ridge*	230	page 338
Kelvin	*North Ridge*	232	page 338
Snafflehound	*South Ridge*	237	page 340
Snafflehound	*North Ridge*	234	page 339
Spear	*South Ridge*	239	page 341
Spear	*North Ridge*	240	page 341

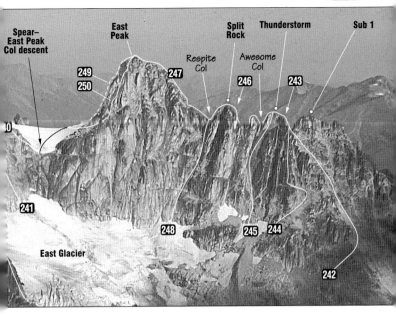

Eastern Traverse   TD   5.8   (1 biv)   *333*

Charles Fay, Jim Herbert, Robert Kruszyna, July 1964   *CAJ 48:99*

A long, technical and committing traverse. Several shorter variations have been done over the years but the original complete traverse sees very little traffic. The traverse is from Sub One to East Peak climbing Thunderstorm Tower and Split Rock Spire along the way. Dry conditions are an asset as much of the climbing beyond the summit of Thunderstorm Tower is on the shady north side, which, at this elevation is often snow covered for several days after storms. The climbing is mostly low-5th class but there are some sustained sections of mid 5th up to 5.8. The first ascent party bivouacked at the Respite Col below the *East Ridge* of East Peak. Escape can be made down the *South Spur* descent route but may be easiest down the north side to the Northeast Glacier once past Thunderstorm Tower.

Climbs encountered

Sub One	*Awesome Col*	242	page 342
Thunderstorm Tower	*North Ridge*	243	page 342
Split Rock Spire	*North Chimney*	246	page 343
East Peak	*East Ridge*	247	page 343

Archduke Trio   2680m

The most notable of all formations in the Vowell group, the Archduke Trio is a sharp ridge extending northeast from Robert the Bruce, which separates the Vowell and Wallace drainages. It has been described as a series of Ritz crackers on edge over 1000m long, 200m high and often no more than 1m wide at its crest. To date, this is the only route on this incredible feature and it is a must-do.

218 Archduke Trio   AD+   5.7   (8–10h)   200m   *335*

Leigh Andrews, Robert Kruszyna, August 1963   CAJ 48:93

This is the classic line of the Vowell Group. It follows the spectacular tall and narrow knife-edge ridge that descends northeast from Wallace Peak and parallels the Vowell glacier to Tamarack Glen. The route is usually climbed from north to south, started from the basin below the northeast face of Robert the Bruce. The technical and traversing nature of this line is similar in character to the climbing between the north and south summits of Bugaboo spire. This route is not often climbed and the anchors may need new slings and pitons.

From the East Glacier Camp, walk up the glacier to the Archduke Col [GR 136239]. Head through the col and down the Archduke Glacier then up a large talus slope to the crest of the ridge.

Start up the blocky ridge to just below the first summit, which is traversed on the left to a notch. A short section of knife-edge leads to a sharp pinnacle with slings round its top. Lower off these to a notch then continue on the ridge proper until it is necessary to do a series of rappels and short traverses. The last of these rappels should finish in a horizontal crack system 10m below the ridge crest on the southeast side. Gradually follow this crack under the next summit and back to the crest. More traversing, rappelling and down-climbing will lead to a ledge system on the northwest side which is followed for 80m to a variety of possible exits back to the ridge, the last chimney being the easiest. 100m of 3rd class leads to the final three rappels and the Wallace Glacier.

In 1988, two climbers on the Beckey–Chouinard were hit by lightning and sustained multiple burns, melting their polypro underwear to their legs. They rappelled the route and returned to the Kain Hut where they spent another week climbing before seeking medical attention.

Allegro Andante Presto

Archduke Col

218

Allegro Andante Presto Archduke Col

Archduke Trio

Wallace Glacier

climber: Peter MacPherson
photo: Marc Piché

ARCHDUKE TRIO

Robert the Bruce   2865m

This mountain stands tall above the Vowell Glacier and is the first peak encountered when approaching the Vowells from the Bugaboos. There is little technical climbing as most features are low angle with the exception of the sheer east face, which has yet to receive an ascent. The summit views of the Vowells, Bugaboos and specifically the *Archduke Trio* are great.

219 South Slopes   F   3rd   (2-4h)   380m *347*

D.P. Richards, I.A. Richards August 1938   *AAJ 3:292-369*

This route is mostly hiking but can be slightly more challenging depending on route finding. From the Vowell Lagoons, head north around and over several moraines until it is possible to gain the long talus covered *South Slope*. Follow this to the summit.

Descend route or Northwest Ridge to the Wallace Col.

220 Northwest Ridge   PD 4th   (1-2h)   180m *347*

F.A. Unknown

From the Wallace Col, scramble over loose blocks and the summit of Howard the Duck. A nice way to get a good view of the area.

Howard the Duck   2790m

The small peak on the northwest ridge of Robert the Bruce, which forms the Wallace Col with the southeast ridge of Wallace Peak.

221 West Ridge   PD 4th   (1-2h)   80m *347*

F.A. Unknown

From the Wallace Col, scramble over loose blocks to the summit of Howard the Duck.

Wallace Peak   2947m

This peak forms a cornerstone separating the Vowell, Wallace and West Glaciers and is probably the most often-climbed peak in the Vowells. Wallace offers a handful of great south-facing routes and is also the start or finish of the *Classic Traverse*. Easily climbed from all three camping areas and sometimes done as a big day from the Kain hut, this is the perfect summit to get a good sense of the lay of the land.

222 Southeast Ridge   AD 5.8   (6-8h)   250m *347*

Jim Alt, Stephen Arseneault, Volker Vogt, June 1967   *CAJ 56:73, AAJ 16:176*

This is the ridge rising northwest out of the Wallace Col. It is steep at first, and then eases off to 4th class scrambling to the summit.

Start at steep right facing corner directly above col. Climb a few short pitches up to 5.8 to gain ridge, scramble over blocky terrain and some short sections of low-5th to summit. Descend by down climbing the *West Ridge*.

223 **Living The Dream**   AD   5.8   (6-8h)   250m   *347*
Chris Atkinson, Lydia Marmont, September 2002

This sunny route is on the right side of the southeast face and starts from the bottom of a large snow scoop. It climbs the right hand of the 2 obvious crack systems then follows the *Southeast Ridge* to the summit.

1: Climb a broken crack to small ledge then into a left-facing corner. When this crack widens, step right onto a face crack and up to belay ledge. (5.8, 50m). **2:** Step right and climb parallel cracks back left to belay ledge. (5.8, 30m). Scramble over blocky terrain and some short sections of easy 5th to summit. Descend by downclimbing the *West Ridge.*

224 **Envy!**   AD   5.10   (6-8h)   250m   *347*
Marc Piché, Brian Webster, September 2002

Another great, sunny route 5m left of *Living The Dream.* It climbs the left hand of the two obvious crack systems then follows the *Southeast Ridge* to the summit. **1:** Climb a hand- fist- face-crack to a belay ledge. (5.8, 45m). **2:** Climb a steep finger-crack on the left to a belay ledge. (5.10, 30m). Scramble over blocky terrain and some short sections of low-5th to summit. Descend by downclimbing the *West Ridge.*

225 **South Face Horvath–Mutch**   AD   5.7   (6-8h)   7p   *332*
Steven Horvath, Hamish Mutch, July 1998   CAJ 1999:116

This is a sustained climb on good rock in the middle of the southeast face. Start directly below the summit in a recessed alcove. Climb 7 pitches of 5th class and one of 4th class to the summit.

Descend by downclimbing the *West Ridge.*

226 **West Ridge**   PD+   low 5th   (4-6h)   250m   *347*
J. Briggs, W. Briggs, R. Collins, Peter Robinson, August 1952   CAJ 36:97

A nice ridge which, is most often used as a descent route and also the start or finish of the *Classic Traverse* (page 332). Gain the Wallace–Little Wallace Col then follow the ridge to the summit making slight detours to the right (south) when faced with difficulties. Descend route.

227 **North Ridge**   PD+   low 5th   (6-8h)   300m   *347*
William Buckingham, Arnold Guess, Robert Page, August 1958   CAJ 42:53, AAJ 11:312

Most often climbed as part of the *Classic Traverse*, it also sees some ascents from the Wallace Glacier via the *Northeast Gully* route on Mount Kelvin.

From the Wallace–Kelvin Col, climb the ridge proper until it becomes steep. Traverse left onto the *Northeast Face* and climb this over snow and loose rock, to avoid two gendarmes on route to summit.
Descend by rappelling route or by *West Ridge.*

228 **Northeast Face**   PD+   4th   (6-8h)   300m   *347*
Hamish Mutch, Peter Tchir, August 1984

An aesthetic snow and ice covered face that guards the entrance to the East Glacier Cirque. Cross the bergshrund then climb steep snow and ice around loose rock bands directly to the summit. Descend route or *West Ridge.*

Little Wallace   2797m

Rising above Bill's Pass, this peak is far more impressive from this
perspective than from any other. Often overlooked, there is some
rock climbing here, which makes for a nice stop on the way to the
West Glacier area if camping at Bill's Pass.

229 Viagra Ridge   AD+ 5.8   (6-8h)   8p *328*
Steven Horvath, Hamish Mutch, July 1998   *CAJ 1999:116*
When viewed in profile from just east of Bill's Pass, the gendarme at mid
height reveals the rationale behind the name. From Bill's Pass, wander up
steep scree for to the base of the broad ridge. Climb 5 pitches of good rock
up to 5.8, over the gendarme proper (which is a little run-out) then exit in a
small saddle. From this point, there are three easier pitches of loose and
sandy rock to the summit. Descend by walking off the south side.

Mt Kelvin   2955m

Due north of Wallace Peak, Mt Kelvin is one of the least climbed
peaks in the Vowells. From the east it is part of the skyline above
the East Glacier Cirque and is somewhat dwarfed by the east face
of Snafflehound. Usually climbed as part of the *Classic Traverse.*

230 Northeast Gully–South Ridge   PD+ 4th   (3-6h)   300m *347*
J. Cooke, J. Cooke, Peter Robinson, H. Walton, L. Worth, September 1953   CAJ 37:104
This grungy route is most commonly used as a descent when returning to
East Glacier Camp. Cross the bergshrunds of the upper Wallace Glacier to
a slightly elevated mixed snow and rock rib on the left of the gully. If there
is sufficient snow, climb the gully to the rock band directly below the lowest
point in the ridge, the col between Mount Kelvin and the small bump at the
base of the *North Ridge* of Wallace. Otherwise, climb the rib to this same
point being careful of loose blocks along the way. From the col, scramble
to the summit past an old mining claim stake very high on the ridge.

231 Hummingbird Ledges–South Ridge PD+ 5.4 (4-6h) 280m *332*
Howard Bussey, Gerry Caron, Kevin O'Connel, Martin Taylor, August 1982   CAJ 1984:87
This somewhat contrived route gains the *South Ridge* from the west side of
the mountain. From the West Glacier, cross the bergshrund then climb a
gully to the south side of the prominent bump in the Kelvin–Wallace col.
Descend the east side of the col 50m then climb up and right (5.4) to gain
the ridge just beyond the top of the bump. Descend on the east side until
it is necessary to make a rappel into the col and the start of the *South Ridge.*
Scramble to the summit past an old mining claim stake very high on the ridge.

232 North Ridge   PD 4th   (1-2h)   300m *332*
William Buckingham, Arnold Guess, Robert Page, August 1958   CAJ 42:53, AAJ 11:312
Frequently climbed or descended as part of the *Classic Traverse* (page 332),
this ridge consists of good fractured rock with little technical difficulty.

Snafflehound Spire   2985m

North of Mt Kelvin and south of Spear Spire on the *Classic Traverse,* Snafflehound is the Monarch of the East Glacier Cirque. Its incredibly smooth east face can be seen from many places in the Bugaboos and has drawn much attention. The rock on the steep faces is often excellent, but otherwise quite broken.

These routes are best accessed from the East Glacier Camp.

233 East Ridge   TD 5.9   (10-14h)   500m *332*

Dave Anderson, Steve Barnett, Bruce Carson, Mark Wiegelt, August 1972
CAJ 56:73, AAJ 18:445

This elegant-looking route rises above the east face starting just above East Glacier Camp. From the camp, climb the glacier to gain the ridge approximately 50m above its start. Follow the crest of the ridge for nearly 19 pitches, up to 5.9, to the summit. Descend by climbing down the *South Ridge* of Snafflehound then over Mt Kelvin then down the *Northeast Gully* (page 347) or rappel the East Peak–Spear col (page 331) (2–4h).

234 Southeast Ridge   TD 5.10+   (12–18h)   480m *332*

James Blench, Rob Orvig, August 2001

This is the complex stepped ridge, which forms the slightly curving border along the left side of the East face.

From the East Glacier Camp, ascend the glacier to the east face of Snafflehound then across to the base of the climb. There are several options for starting this route from both sides of the ridge: the condition of the bergshrund will likely be the deciding factor. Once the ridge proper is gained follow the crest in several short steps traversing on ledges when necessary (5.10+ with lots of low-5th), to where it joins the top of the east face, then scramble to the summit. Descend by climbing down the *South Ridge* of Snafflehound then over Mt Kelvin then down the *Northeast Gully* (page 347) or rappel the East Peak– Spear col (page 331) (2–4h).

235 Cuento Corto   5.10   (2–4h)   2p *348*

Chris Atkinson, Lydia Marmont, Marc Piché, September 2002

This short, excellent route on the right side of the east face catches the midday sun and offers a great alpine cragging experience.

From East Glacier Camp, ascend the glacier to the major corner that forms the right side of the east face. Approximately 50m left is a shallow left-facing corner where a huge flake meets this otherwise blank section of the east face. Cross the bergshrund to ledges directly below a left facing corner.

1: Climb the corner to a ledge below the start of the flake. (5.8, 25m).
2: Climb the shallow corner to the ledge at the top. Belay at a two-bolt anchor. (5.10, 35m). Descend to the glacier in 2 rappels, the first of which is from bolts, the second from a horn.

236 **Corto Zonal**   5.11-   (2–4h)   2p   *348*

Chris Atkinson, Lydia Marmont, Marc Piché, September 2002

This interesting and sustained route starts 5m right of *Cuento Corto*. When combined, these two routes make for a great half day of climbing. The second pitch has 2 fixed pitons but is still a bit run out. Approach as for *Cuento Corto* to the ledge, which marks the start of that route.

1. Climb the first corner until it is possible to exit right onto a ledge. Traverse the ledge and climb the short steep corner above to another ledge and comfortable belay. (5.9+, 35m). **2.** Palm, smear and stem up the flaring corner through 2 small overlaps to the loose ledge and 2 bolt anchor.(5.11-, 25m).

Descend to glacier in 2 rappels, the first of which is from bolts, the second from a horn.

Accordian Wall. This is the south-facing wall that forms the ridge, which descends from the right side of the east face to very near the East Glacier Camp. The many corners along this face resemble the folds of an accordion. Although there is little information, evidence of climbing activity is visible. Most routes are 2–3 pitches long and many were climbed using aid. There is a lot of potential here for more crag-style climbing close to camp.

The following three routes are best accessed from the West Glacier Camp.

237 **South Ridge**   PD+ 5.4   (1–2h)   230m   *348*

William Buckingham, Arnold Guess, Robert Page, August 1958   *CAJ 42:53, AAJ 11:312*

Most often climbed or down climbed as part of the *Classic Traverse* (page 332) and also enroute to the *Northeast Gully* descent. This route offers nice climbing and great views. The climbing is on low angle slabs except for one short steep section near the top.

238 **North Ridge**   PD 4th   (1–2h)   160m   *348*

William Buckingham, Arnold Guess, Robert Page, August 1958   *CAJ 42:53, AAJ 11:312*

Also part of the *Classic Traverse* (page 332) this route is for the most part a low angle scramble.

Descent. Descent from the summit is made by walking and downclimbing to the north on steep snow and ice then over the bergshrund to the West Glacier Cirque. To return to the East Glacier Cirque, walk north to reach the Spear–East Peak Col then follow description on (page 331) to the East Glacier below, or follow directions for the northeast gully descent (page 347).

Spear Spire   2992m

The starting point of the original *Classic Traverse*, Spear Spire is at the north end of the obvious chain of peaks which form the western skyline as seen from the East Glacier Cirque. Both the east and west flanks are steep, compact granite with few continuous weaknesses. Spear Spire is sometimes climbed to get to the Spear–East Peak Col as a descent from Snafflehound Spire. The summit block fell to the East Glacier in the early 1980s.

239 **South Ridge**   PD 4th   (1-2h)   150m   *349*

William Buckingham, Arnold Guess, Robert Page, August 1958   *CAJ 42:53, AAJ 11:312*

This route is part of the *Classic Traverse* and can also be accessed by climbing the snow slopes on the west face of Snafflehound to the Snafflehound–Spear col. From the col, climb the narrow ridge around several towers to the base of an overhanging gendarme. Descend to a ledge on the east, which is followed across the face to a chimney northeast of the summit tower. Climb the chimney and a series of small ledges on the south side to the summit. Descent can be made by downclimbing the chimney to the ledge, then down the *South Ridge* or *North Ridge*.

240 **North Ridge**   PD 4th   (1-2h)   120m   *349*

William Buckingham, Arnold Guess, Robert Page, August 1958   *CAJ 42:53, AAJ 11:312*

This route marks either the beginning or the end of the *Classic traverse*. From the glaciated Spear–East Peak Col, scramble the ridge to the large ledge which crosses the face on its east side. Follow this to a chimney on the northeast side of the summit tower. Climb the chimney and a series of small ledges on the south side to the summit. Descent can be made by downclimbing the chimney to the ledge, then down the south or north ridges.

241 **Northeast Face**   AD 5.6   (4-6h)   360m   *349*

Charles Fay, Jim Herbert, Robert Kruszyna, July 1964   *CAJ 48:96*

Little is known about this loose and exposed route that starts just right of a prominent couloir on the right side of the east face. Head up and left from the East Glacier Camp and climb the east glacier next to Snafflehound to the flats above and the start of the route. Much of what was permanent snow in this gully has now melted away creating a serious rockfall hazard. From high on the East Glacier, cross the bergshrund and climb the right side of the couloir on lower 5th class rock to where it becomes steep. Enter couloir and follow it until forced back right by overhangs. Climb several rope lengths of cracks, thin slabs and chimneys to the *North Ridge,* which is then followed to the summit. Descent can be made by downclimbing the chimney to the ledge, then down the *South Ridge* or *North Ridge*.

East Peak Sub One   2900m

The starting point for the *Eastern Traverse*, East Peak Sub One is somewhat scrappy compared to the rest of the Vowell group with broken and friable rock on all sides.

242 Awesome Col Route   PD+ 4th   (4-6h) 300m *333*

Lawrence Coveney, Sterling Hendricks, Percy Olton, Polly Prescott, Marguerite Schnellbacher,
July 1938   CAJ 26:24, 48:98, AAJ 3:296

The start of the *Eastern Traverse* and a nice easy day on its own. From East Glacier Camp, descend loose talus then cross under East Glacier being careful of icefall above. Cross the basin and ascend snowslopes below Thunderstorm Tower then contour around the sandy shoulder to the large gully. Climb the gully if snow filled or its flank if not to the Awesome Col then scramble north to the Summit. Descend route.

Thunderstorm Tower   2917m

An indistinct peak east of Split–Rock Spire, with a huge rockfall scar on its southeast face, Thunderstorm Tower is one of the rarely climbed *Eastern Traverse* peaks. It is granite and does have more than one route to its summit, but the rock is of lesser quality.

243 North Ridge   AD- 5.5   (2-4h) 320m *333*

Charles Fay, Jim Herbert, Robert Kruszyna, July 1964   CAJ 48:99

Part of the *Eastern Traverse,* follow the description for the *Awesome Col* route on East Peak Sub One to the Awesome Col. Climb the blocky north side of the ridge in 4 pitches to the crest, then on to the summit.

244 South Spur   D   5.9   (8-12h) 320m *333*

Chris Atkinson, Lydia Marmont, Marc Piché, Brian Webster, September 2002

This route climbs the mossy south face and is an alternate start to the *Eastern Traverse* with a lot of scrambling and short cruxes. From East Glacier Camp, descend loose talus, then cross under East Glacier, being careful of icefall above. Cross the basin and ascend snow slopes to sandy shoulder. Traverse west on the highest ledge that runs halfway across the face. Climb several pitches up a gully then move left to the crest of a faint rib that leads to a deep notch in the ridge. Climb two pitches (5.9) on the north side of the notch to gain the ridge, which is followed to the summit over several short pitches. Descent can be made by reversing the route or by doing a series of rappels from horns and blocks down the south face from a point on the ridge approximately 200m northwest of where the route joins it. There will likely not be any anchors on either descent so bring lots of extra webbing.

245 South Face   D+   5.9   (8-12h) 320m *333*

James Blench, Rob Orvig, August 2001

This route climbs the big right facing corner directly below the Summit. From East Glacier Camp, descend loose talus then cross under East Glacier being careful of icefall above. Scramble up and left for several hundred metres to the base. Climb the corner past the huge rockfall scar to the Summit! Descend route or *South Spur*.

EAST PEAK SUB ONE // THUNDERSTORM // SPLIT-ROCK // EAST PEAK

Split–Rock Spire   2822m

Directly east of East Peak, Split–Rock Spire is rarely climbed. To date, it has no direct route to its summit and has only been climbed as part of *Eastern Traverse.*

246 **North Chimney**   D+ 5.8   (2-4h) 340m *333*
Charles Fay, Jim Herbert, Robert Kruszyna, July 1964   *CAJ 48:99*
Part of the *Eastern Traverse.* Rappel west from the summit of Thunderstorm Tower to the ridge then do a descending traverse on the north side of the spire. Climb a difficult corner to the ridge on the west side of the gendarme then do one rappel to the base of the chimney formed by the huge detached flake. Climb the awkward flake to a chimney that is followed to the summit. Rappel on south side and traverse west to where it is possible to rappel into a gully, which is then climbed back up to the Respite Col.

East Peak   3077m

The second tallest peak in the Vowell group, East Peak was the focus of many of the early expeditions to the area. Standing alone just north of the Spear–East Peak Col, it is also the termination point for the other grand link up in the area, the *Eastern Traverse.*

247 **East Ridge**   D+ 5.7   (4-8h) 480m *351*
Charles Fay, Jim Herbert, Robert Kruszyna, July 1964   *CAJ 48:99*
The last leg of the *Eastern Traverse*, this route follows the mixed snow and rock up to 5.7 on and near the ridge proper to where it meets the *North Ridge* at a small peak. A short rappel leads to a chimney system, which is then followed to the summit. Descend via the *North Ridge.*

248 **South Face Right**   D   5.8   (8-12h) 480m *351*
Gregory Markov, Thom Nephew, September 1972   *CAJ 56:73, AAJ 18:445*
To date, the only route on the impressive south face of East Peak. Head up and left from the East Glacier Camp and climb the east glacier next to Snafflehound to the flats above. Traverse the flats to the base of the route directly below the Respite Col. Scramble up slabs to the chimney system, which is then followed to the *East Ridge*. Follow *East Ridge* to summit. Descend via the *North Ridge.*

249 **North Ridge**   PD+ 5.4   (3-6h) 480m *350*
Georgia Engelhard, Francis North, Ernest Feuz, August 1939   *CAJ 27:29, AAJ 4:84*
A nice route to a major peak in the Vowell Group. From the Northeast Glacier, climb scree and ledges on the northwest face until it is possible to gain the ridge; follow it over slabs to a small peak. A short rappel leads to a chimney system, which is followed to the summit. Descend the route.

250 **Upper South Face**   D+ 5.10+   (6-10h) 220m *351*
Nick Rapaich, Carl Trescher, August 2000
An impressive line on the steep south face. From the West Glacier, traverse right on ledges to the start of an major crack system. Follow this with increasing difficulty through a wide section to the summit in 5 pitches. Descend via the *North Ridge.*

Centre Peak   3058m

At the north end of the West Glacier Cirque, the triangular south face of Centre Peak is easily recognized. Being in the physical centre of the group, the rock here is excellent on all sides. For this reason, there are many routes of all grades established primarily on its south face, all of which lead directly to its billiard-table size summit.

The following five routes on Centre Peak were established by guides working at the Canadian Mountain Holidays Bobbie Burns Lodge. They are clean, well protected and all of excellent quality.

251 Southeast Ridge   AD   5.6   (3-6h)   190m   *352*
From the Centre–East Peak Col. Climb the ridge directly to the Summit.

The next four routes are accessed by crossing the bergshrund directly below the Centre–West Peak col, then traversing onto the large ledge that runs across the base of the face.

252 Buffy V.S   AD   5.6   (3-6h)   8p   *352*
Buffy climbs the prominent inside corner on the right side of the face and finishes on the *Southeast Ridge*.

253 Count Chocula   AD   5.7   (3-6h)   7p   *352*
Climb on and near the arête just left of *Buffy* to join the *Southeast Ridge* near its top.

254 Love at First Bite   AD+ 5.9   (3-6h)   6p   *352*
A slightly more sustained route just right of centre that follows a straight line to join the *Southeast Ridge* 40m short of the summit.

255 Reflections   AD+ 5.10b   (3-6h)   4p   *352*
The most difficult route on the face. Slightly more committing and runout as it follows some slabby sections to good cracks that lead to the top of the *West Ridge*.

256 West Ridge   AD   5.6   (3-6h)   4p   *352*
From West Glacier, climb past bergshrund to Centre–West Peak col proper. Gain ridge and climb 3 pitches in corner. Finish on a slab to the summit.

257 North Ridge   AD   low 5th   (3-6h)   180m
Georgia Engelhard, Francis North, Ernest Feuz, August 1939   *CAJ 27:29, AAJ 4:84*
The line of the first ascent, this route starts from the rarely visited Northeast Glacier. From the West Glacier, gain the Northeast Glacier via the Centre–East Peak Col. Contour to the north and across the *North Ridge* to a pocket glacier which lies between the northwest face of Centre Peak and the north face of West Peak. Follow the ridge over good rock to the summit.

Descent. For all routes, via four 60m rappels directly below the summit (page 352). Alternately, the *West Ridge* can be descended with only one rope by leaving a few slings behind.

West Peak   3127m

The highest peak in the Vowells, West Peak is located at the northwest end of the West Glacier Cirque. The rock is good all around and although there are some routes established on the southeast side, the true gem is the rarely visited west face.

258 Rapaich–Trescher   AD 5.8   (3-6h)   4p *352*
Nick Rapaich, Carl Trescher, August 2000
A nice moderate route just west of the Centre–West Peak Col. Climb the big right facing corner to the ridge crest. Descend via the next corner to the west in three rappels.

259 High Anxiety   AD+ 5.10-   (4-6h)   4p *352*
Nick Rapaich, Carl Trescher, August 2000
This climbs the steep face just west of the previous route. The first pitch climbs broken terrain trending slightly right. Follow a left leaning, right facing corner (5.10-) to a ledge. Climb one more rope length to a ledge, which is then traversed rightward to the ridge crest. Descend via the next corner to the east. (Same descent as previous route)

260 Southwest Ridge   PD 4th   (2-4h)   150m *352*
Georgia Engelhard, Francis North, Ernest Feuz, August 1939   *CAJ 27:29, AAJ 4:85*
This is the line of the first ascent of the mountain. Gain the ridge from the West Glacier and follow this over many blocks to the summit. Descend via same route.

261 West Face   TD+ 5.8 A2   (2 days)   13p *353*
Mike Down, Keith Flavelle, Scott Flavelle, July 1981
The most involved route in the Vowells to date, this route climbs the seldom seen and striking west face of West Peak. Best approached from the Malloy Igloo, reach the base of the route from near the top of the Wildcat (North) Glacier. Climb the obvious left facing dihedral in several steps directly to the summit. Aid was used on nearly half of the climbing and the first ascent party bivied on the summit. Descend via rappels (page 329).

North Peak   2866m

Northeast of both West and Centre Peaks, North Peak stand alone above the Wildcat Glacier. The broken northwest face has some nice climbing but the rock is of a lesser quality than its neighbours.

262 South Ridge   PD low 5th   (4-8h)   260m
Georgia Engelhard, Francis North, Ernest Feuz, August 1939   *CAJ 27:29, AAJ 4:85*
From the Wildcat (north) Glacier, climb steep loose ledges to the col south of the peak. Follow ridge to summit. (Two shoulder stands and one short rappel were required on the first ascent!) Descend by scrambling down southeast face to the col then downclimbing to glacier.

263 South Ridge Variant   PD+   5.7   (4-8h)   260m
Skip King and ACC party, August 1971   *CAJ 55:28*
From the Wildcat (north) Glacier, climb steep loose ledges then two pitches slightly left of previous route to join it about halfway up. Descend by scrambling down southeast face to the col then downclimbing to glacier.

264 Wildcat   AD   5.8   (4-8h)   280m
Roko Koell and party, summer 1997
Slightly left again of the *South Ridge Variant*, this route is more sustained and joins the ridge closer to the summit. It is also possible to step left onto clean slabs (5.9) to avoid the chimney/gully feature. Descend by scrambling down southeast face to the col then downclimbing to glacier.

Osprey Peak   2907m

Situated at the far northwest boundary of the Vowell Group, Osprey Peak's east face is seen as a large scree and talus covered slope. The unclimbed west face, overlooking the Malloy Glacier icefall is quite steep and the granite is of reasonable quality.

265 East Face   PD   3rd–4th   (2-4h)   150m
W. Briggs, R. Morden, Peter Robinson July 1954   *AAJ 9:111*
From the Malloy Igloo, wander up the glacier in a semi-circle to Pernicular Pass (col southeast of east face) then up the face to summit. This can be done any number of ways on a variety of terrain, ranging from scree and talus to easy slabs. Descend same route.

266 South Ridge   PD+   5.5   (2-4h)   350m   *354*
John Burcombe, Skip King, August 1971
Climb the south end of the imposing west face on the left side of the obvious chockstone filled chimney to the south ridge. Follow it easily to the summit. Descend *East Face*.

Vowell Peak   2990m

Directly north of Osprey Peak, it is ironic that the peak which is the namesake of the entire group is of least interest to modern climbers. Entirely outside of the granite formation, the rock is a combination of shale, slate and a broken and friable quartzite.

267 South Ridge   PD   4th   (6-8h)   260m
J. Turner, M. Ward, July 1959
From the Malloy Igloo, contour down and around the west face of Osprey Peak until it is possible to ascend to gain the col at the base of the *South Ridge* of Vowell Peak. Follow this ridge to the summit. Descend via the same route.

WALLACE — NORTHEAST SIDE

Mount Wallace

Descent

227

Wallace Col

222

Wallace Glacier

228

230

Kelvin Northeast Gully

shadow of Arch Duke Trio

WALLACE — SOUTHWEST SIDE

Wallace

Howard the Duck

Robert the Bruce

226

225 224 223

221

220

219

to Little Wallace raps

to Vowell Glacier Lagoons

ROUTES: 219–222 (336) **223–228** (337) **230** (338)

SNAFFLEHOUND SPIRE — EAST FACE

ROUTES: 233–235 (339) **236–238** (340)

SPEAR SPIRE — SOUTHEAST SIDE

Spear
Spire

Spear–East
Peak Col

239

240

Desce

241

East Glacier

ROUTES: 239 240 (341)

view from Spear–East Peak Col

same place

249

250

25

ROUTES: 249 250 (343)

ROUTES: 246–250 (343)

WEST PEAK — SOUTHEAST SIDE

West Peak

Centre Pea

260

259 258

West Glacier

same place

Centre Peak

256   255   254   253   252   251

West Glacier

ROUTES: 251–256 (344)

WEST PEAK – WEST FACE

261

to Malloy Igloo

to Northwest Face
of North Peak

262 263 264

Wildcat Glacier

ROUTES: **261 262** (345) **263 264** (346)

OSPREY PEAK — WEST FACE

chockstone-filled
chimney

266

Malloy
Igloo

ROUTES: 266 (346)

THE CONRAD GROUP

A short distance northwest of the Vowells is the Conrad Icefield, the largest glacial mass in the Purcell Mountains and which encompasses several large peaks. These peaks are much more sprawling and more heavily glaciated than those of the Vowells and Bugaboos, and the climbs are mostly characterized by very long glacial approaches and technically easier mountaineering objectives; they provide an almost mini-expedition experience. Probably the most common traffic in the area are ski touring groups on the famous Bugaboos to Rogers Pass traverse. Commonly reached via the Malloy Igloo or Vowell Creek approaches (pages 324-325).

Information on these peaks and their routes has been kept to a minamum to provide objectives for those climbers searching for unknown adventures.

Mount Conrad   3279m

FA D.P Richards, I.A Richards, Conrad Kain, August 1933

Easily identified as the tallest peak in the group, Mount Conrad is heavily glaciated on all sides and only has a few routes to its summit. This was Conrad Kain's last mountain and was climbed from the location of the Bugaboo Lodge to the summit in an astonishing twelve hours!

Mount Malloy   3023m

FA D. Anderson, W. Bailey, B. Bishop, G. Cole, C. Murley, S. Rodman, 1957

Slightly northeast of Mount Conrad and directly across the Malloy glacier from the Malloy Igloo, this peak is heavily glaciated on all sides with two major icefalls cascading into Malloy creek on its flanks.

Mount Thorington   3036m

FA V. Day, R. Morden, P. Robinson, July 1954

Several kilometres northwest of Mount Conrad, Thorington is the furthest away from the Bugaboo parking area. Steep on all sides, there are a handful of ice routes for adventurous explorers.

CONRAD GROUP PANORAMAS

Conrad

Thorington
(hidden)

Malloy

view from Vowells
West Glacier

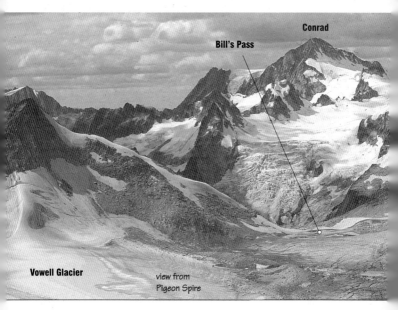

Conrad

Bill's Pass

Vowell Glacier

view from
Pigeon Spire

CONRAD GROUP

	topo	text
ANNIVERSARY PEAK ------		92
Anniversary Glacier ------------	106	92
Anniversary Chute --------------	106	92
Southwest Ridge ---------------	108	93
Northwest Ridge ---------------	110	93
North Face ----------------------	110	93
HOWSER PEAK ---------------		94
East Ridge ---------------------	108	95
Northwest Ridge ---------------	108	95
North Face Right ---------------	108	95
North Face Centre -------------	108	95
THIMBLE PEAK ---------------		96
North Ridge ---------------------	109	96
Southeast Ridge ----------------	109	96
FLATTOP PEAK ---------------		97
Northeast Ridge–Face --------	109	97
Southeast Ridge ----------------	109	97
HOUNDS TOOTH -------------		100
Northwest Face -----------------	110	100
North Face Variation -----------	110	100
Gilcrest Raabe Route ----------	110	100
MARMOLATA --------------------		101
East Ridge ---------------------	111	101
North Face ---------------------	111	101
West Ridge–North Face ------	111	101
South Face–West End --------		102
South Face ---------------------		102
Southeast Buttress -------------		102
EASTPOST SPIRE -------------		114
Northeast Ridge ----------------		115
Northwest Ridge ---------------		115
West Face ----------------------	144	115
Shelton Route ------------------	144	116
Flaming Hack Arête -----------	144	116
South Face Left ----------------	145	116
South Face ---------------------	145	116
Classic Grit --------------------	145	116
Southeast Ridge ----------------	145	117
East Face ----------------------		117
CRESCENT SPIRE -----------		118
West Ridge ---------------------	146	119
WIMTA -------------------------	146	120
Clean and Dirty ----------------	146	120
Paddle Flake Direct -----------	147	120
Paddle Flake -------------------	147	121
Left Dihedral -------------------	147	121
Westside Story -----------------	147	122
Roof McTech -------------------	147	122
Energy Crisis ------------------	147	122
McTech Arête -------------------	147	123
McTech Direct ------------------	147	123
Woza Moya ---------------------	147	124
Dunlop's Dangle ----------------	147	124
Surprisingly Subsevere -------	147	124
SW Gully—South Ridge ------	146	125
Southeast Slopes --------------		125
Northeast Ridge ----------------	150	125
CRESCENT TOWERS --------		126
North Ridge ---------------------	148	127
Northwest Side -----------------	148	127
Northwest Gully -----------------	148	127
Lion's Way ---------------------	148	127
Lions and Tigers ---------------	148	127
Tiger's Trail --------------------	148	128
Lost in Space ------------------	148	128
Thatcher Cracker --------------	149	128
Edwards–Neufeld ---------------	149	128
Ears Between -------------------	149	129
Eyore -------------------------	149	129
COBALT LAKE SPIRE -------		130
Southwest Face ----------------	152	131
West Ridge ---------------------	152	131
North Ridge ---------------------	152	131
BRENTA SPIRE ----------------		132
South Ridge ---------------------	153	133
Southeast Face -----------------	154	134
Southern Comfort --------------	154	134
Southeast Spur -----------------	154	134
Another Fine Day --------------	154	134
North Ridge ---------------------	154	135
Vockeroth Route ----------------		135
NORTHPOST SPIRE ---------		136
Southwest Ridge ---------------	142	137
Fast Eddie Lives ---------------	157	137
Free Heeling -------------------	157	138
East Ridge ---------------------	156	138
Northpost Couloir ---------------		138
N Ridge–NE Rocks -------------		138
In Search of NW Passage ---		139
North by Northwest -----------	155	139
Northwest Face -----------------	155	139
NWt Face, West Side ----------	155	139
BUGABOO SPIRE -------------		161
Kain Route ---------------------	170	163
Herr2 Route --------------------	173	163
Japanese Pillar -----------------	173	164
Cooper—Gran -------------------	173	164
Symposium ---------------------	173	164
Midnight Route ------------------	173	164
Thanks for the Handout ------	173	165
Harvey–Roach -------------------	173	165
Pretty Vacant -------------------	175	165
Vacant and Obscure -----------	175	166
Where's Issac? -----------------	175	166

	topo	text
Northeast Ridge	175	166
North Face Direct	176	167
North Face	176	167
West Face	177	168
West Face Direct	177	168
SNOWPATCH SPIRE		179
Snowpatch Route	189	182
Beckey–Mather Route	190	183
Vertical Party	190	183
East Face Diagonal	190	184
In Harm's Way	190	184
Deus ex Machina	190	184
Deus ex Machina Var.	190	184
Les Bruixes Es Pentinen	190	184
Parker–Brashaw	192	185
Sunshine Wall	192	185
Warrior's Way	193	185
Hockey Night in Jersey	193	186
Sweet Silvia	193	186
Tom Egan Memorial	193	186
White Ducks in Space	192	187
The Power of Lard	193	187
Hobo's Haven	193	188
Bugaboo Corner	194	197
Banshee	194	197
Sunshine Crack	194	198
Dark Side of the Sun		198
Buckingham Route	210	200
Gran–Hudson	211	200
Quasimodo		201
Flamingo Fling	210	201
North Summit Direct	211	201
Tower Arête	211	202
Super Direct	212	202
Beckey–Greenwood	212	202
Tam-Tam Boom	212	203
Beckey–Rowell Route	212	203
Wildflowers	212	204
Kraus–McCarthy Route	213	204
Mark Stewart Variation	213	204
Furry Pink Arête	213	205
Which Way	213	205
Degringolade	213	205
Rock the Casbah	213	206
Attack of the Chipmunk	213	206
Surfs Up Direct	213	206
Surfs Up	213	207
The Beach	213	207
South Face Left		215
ASTA	217	215
South Face Direct	217	215
Edwards—Jessup	217	216
South Face Upper	217	216
Lightning Bolt Crack		216
PIGEON SPIRE		221
West Ridge	229	223
Tail–Feather Pinnacle R	233	224
Tail–Feather Pinnacle L	233	224
Feather Fallout	233	224
Northwest Face	232	225
Wingtip Arête	232	225
North Face	232	225
Millar–Shepard	232	226
Pigeon Toe	232	226
Cooper–Kor	235	226
Cleopatra's Alley	235	227
Southeast Buttress	235	227
Southeast Slabs	237	227
South Face	236	228
Parboosing Route	237	228
Lambrice Tour	237	228
Turk–Seashore	237	228
HOWSER TOWERS		240
SOUTH HOWSER		240
East Ridge Integral	246	242
East Face–Ridge	246	242
East Face Variation	246	242
Thompson–Turk	246	242
Perma Grin	246	243
Northeast Face	246	243
The Big Hose	246	243
Thompson-Turk Right	246	244
North Face–Ridge	246	244
Beckey–Chouinard	276	272
Lost in the Towers	276	273
Catalonian Route	275	273
CENTRAL HOWSER		240
South Ridge	247	244
East Face	247	244
North Ridge	247	244
Fear and Desire	270	269
Chocolate Fudge	270	269
Spinstone Gully	270	269
NORTH HOWSER		240
South Ridge	247	245
East Face–North Ridge	247	245
East Ridge–North Ridge	247	245
Preshaw Pillar		245
Northeast Face	247	248
North Ridge Integral	247	248
North–Northwest Face	250	249
Northwest Buttress	251	249
All Along the Watchtower	260	254
Armageddon	261	254

	topo	text		topo	text
Warrior	261	255	**SNAFFLEHOUND SPIRE**		339
Spicey Red Beans	259	255	East Ridge	332	339
Mescalito	259	255	Southeast Ridge	332	339
The Seventh Rifle	262	256	Cuento Corto	348	339
Young Men on Fire	262	256	Corto Zonal	348	340
The Shooting Gallery	262	257	South Ridge	348	340
Southwest Face	262	268	North Ridge	348	340
MINARET		278	**SPEAR SPIRE**		341
West Face		278	South Ridge	349	341
Bad Hair Day	280	278	North Ridge	349	341
Italian Pillar	280	278	Northeast Face	349	341
Retinal Circus	280	279	East Peak Sub One		342
Doubting the Millennium	281	279	Awesome Col Route	333	342
Southwest Pillar	281	279	**THUNDERSTORM**		342
South Face	283	282	North Ridge	333	342
Cameron's Pillar	283	282	South Spur	333	342
PIGEON FEATHERS		284	South Face	333	342
Pigeon Feathers Traverse	109	99	**SPLIT–ROCK SPIRE**		343
Northeast Ridge		99	North Chimney	333	343
Gar Wall	292	285	**EAST PEAK**		343
Fingerberry Jam	293	285	East Ridge	351	343
Crack of Noon	291	286	South Face Right	351	343
Lost Feather	294	286	North Ridge	350	343
Dingleberry Spam	289	287	Upper South Face	351	343
Wide Awake	295	287	**CENTRE PEAK**		344
CROSSED FISH PEAK		296	Southeast Ridge	352	344
East Ridge	298	296	Buffy V.S	352	344
LITTLE SNOWPATCH		297	Count Chocula	352	344
East Ridge	299	297	Love at First Bite	352	344
Northwest Face	299	297	Reflections	352	344
Vowells Classic Traverse	332	332	West Ridge	352	344
Vowells Eastern Traverse	333	333	North Ridge		344
ARCHDUKE TRIO	335	334	**WEST PEAK**		345
ROBERT THE BRUCE		336	Rapaich–Trescher	352	345
South Slopes	347	336	High Anxiety	352	345
Northwest Ridge	347	336	Southwest Ridge	352	345
HOWARD THE DUCK		336	West Face	353	345
West Ridge	347	336	**NORTH PEAK**		345
WALLACE PEAK		336	South Ridge		345
Southeast Ridge	347	336	South Ridge Variant		346
Living The Dream	347	337	Wildcat		346
Envy!	347	337	**OSPREY PEAK**		346
South Face	332	337	East Face		346
West Ridge	347	337	South Ridge	354	346
North Ridge	347	337	**VOWELL PEAK**		346
Northeast Face	347	337	South Ridge		346
LITTLE WALLACE		338	**MOUNT CONRAD**		355
Viagra Ridge	328	338	**MOUNT MALLOY**		355
MOUNT KELVIN		338	**MOUNT THORINGTON**		355
NE Gully–South Ridge	347	338			
Hummingbird Ledges	332	338			
North Ridge	332	338			

Elaho Publishing Corp.

Box 370, Squamish, BC. V0N 3G0. Canada.

Guidebooks for Climbers.

By Climbers.

Contacting the Authors or the Publisher

It would be much appreciated if you are able take a moment to forward any comments or observations you may have on this guide, either to the authors or to the publisher. The authors also welcome any correspondence on omissions, errors, new routes and new topos.

For general commentary on developments and new route activity in the Bugaboos and in other areas covered by Elaho guidebooks, please follow the links at **www.elaho.ca**

Chris Atkinson and Marc Piché   thebugaboos@yahoo.com
Elaho Publishing   stone@elaho.ca